Elizabeth Newman

Drawings

Contents

Interview with Elizabeth Newman

Francis Plagne and Helen Hughes

January 17, 2023

EN These early ones are not really figurative drawings. They are copies of other images.

FP What about these landscape pictures, though?

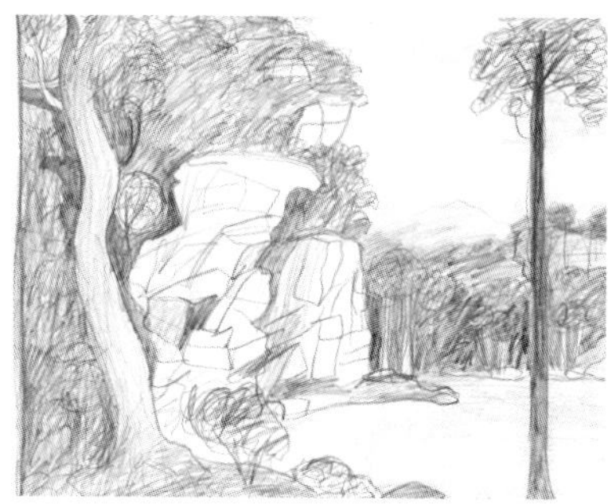

1

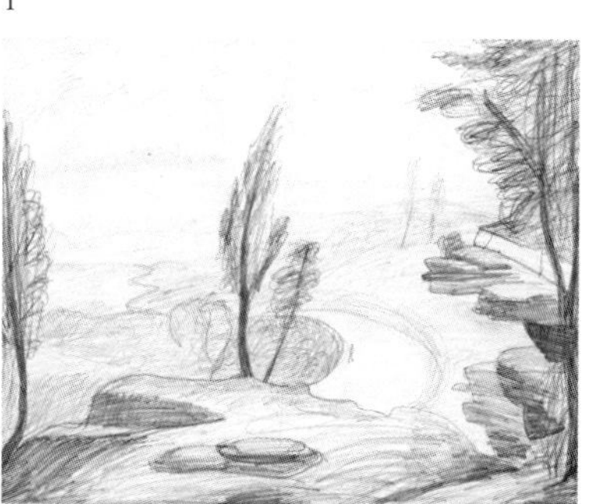

2

1 *Untitled*, 1985, pencil on paper, 35.5 × 47 cm.

2 *Untitled*, 1985, pencil on paper, 35.5 × 47 cm.

3 *Untitled*, 1985, conte crayon on paper, 29 × 41.5 cm.

4 *Untitled*, 1987, pencil on paper, 78 × 48 cm.

EN They're copies of other pictures.

FP Do you remember making them?

EN Yeah, I do, absolutely. I used to draw a lot. This is why the work is so old-fashioned, in a way, because we used to think drawing was the key to everything or the beginning of everything. You had to be able to draw. I used to practice drawing. To what end I didn't know but I believed it would lead to something useful. I remember looking at, choosing an image and then I would do a copy of it. To find out what? I don't know, you find out something by doing it. Perhaps space and composition. But there was also something about doing it in that scribbly way where I wanted to capture something.

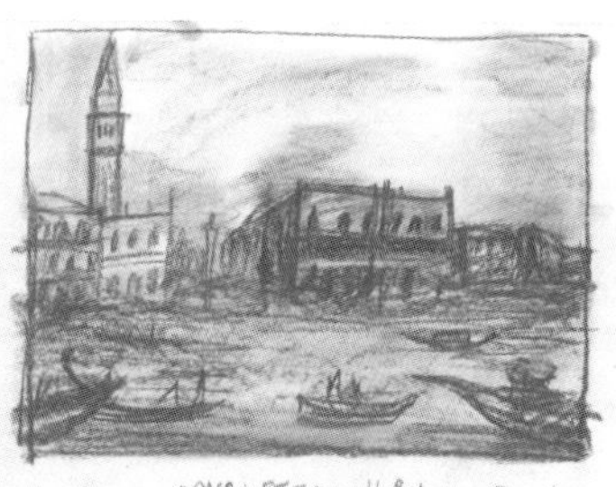

3

HH Were you sitting in a museum drawing this?

EN No, it would have been out of a book.

FP There's a Canaletto copy that's titled at the bottom.

EN Yes, yes. I was looking at the greats. I suppose I was trying to learn something. I didn't know what, but I'd been taught that you copy from the model or the still life or ... I thought I had to learn something, but I wasn't really sure what it was when I was doing it.

HH Is this around the time you made those drawings of the insides of museums? Like this one?

EN They're two pictures from a *Life* magazine. They were both in a magazine article about the new wing of the Met or something.

HH "Living artists."

FP There's all this '80s stuff. There's what looks like a Baselitz sculpture or something like that.

EN Yeah, it was totally contemporary! In a funny way I was aware of the irony but also earnest at the same time, sort of split between the two. I could tell they were kind of funny. When they've got figures in them, they're funny, aren't they? I don't know why. A little human being in the space.

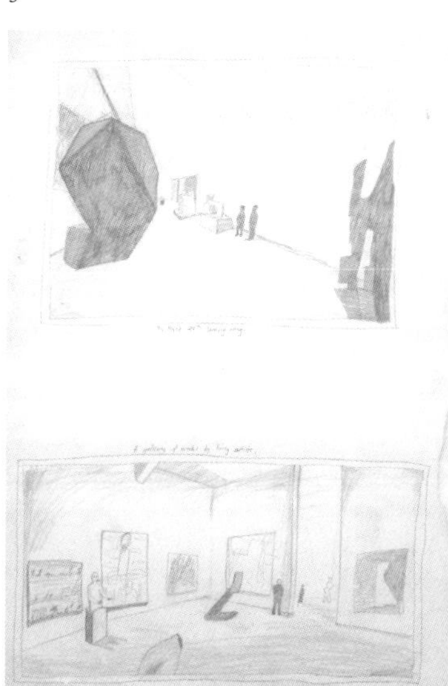

4

FP They're also kind of funny because they're drawings of these perfect geometric objects, made from stainless steel or whatever, but they've been done in pencil.

EN Yes. There's a kind of undermining, isn't there? An irony or making fun of.

FP To go back to what you said about this very traditional idea of copying from old masters, learning from the greats, and so on: are those ideas that had currency when you went to art school?

EN Oh, absolutely, that's where I got it from. I went in 1981 and it was just on the cusp of struggling into postmodernism. I mean, it was all very much modernism. The people who taught there, you know, these guys in their middle age, big painters: Paul Partos, Gary Sansom. Mainly men, except Elizabeth Gower. It was an expressionist mode, you know. You were looking for something unique in yourself, something original, your style, and that would come from drawing, knowing how to use your tools: touch and line and composition. We did life drawing. It was essentially a humanist expressionist model. That was what art really was. And then at the same time we would have been taught by Janine Burke about the new age, which wasn't really postmodernism yet. There was the *Popism* show at the gallery, and Elizabeth Gower, and John Nixon, Howard [Arkley], Peter Tyndall. It was really hard to put the two together. I was kind of split between these two modes. Norbert [Loeffler] would be teaching us about "the new painting" in Germany. I was innocent, open to learning everything, trying to understand where I was in all of that. There was still the idea that you had to be good to be allowed to do it.

HH Was drawing always taught as something that you do in preparation for the actual work, not a finished product?

EN Pretty much. And that's why I have so many, because I would do them when I didn't know what to do with a big painting or I didn't know how to do the painting. And because I had the work ethic model where you had to go to the studio all the time, I'd think, I don't know what to do, I'll just do some drawing. And I guess that produced ideas. But it's very hard to translate the ideas in a drawing to a painting. They're quite different.

HH And how does drawing sit alongside your painting practice now?

EN Well, every now and then I feel like doing it. I see them more as works in their own right because they do something unique that the painting doesn't. But it's still that idea of using an expressionist mode to discover something that you don't know, that you will find something in there that you can't think of but will come in the process, which is so different to how many people make art now.

HH Do you think artists now are very research-oriented and figure it all out in advance?

EN Yes, it's very conscious, it's the ego deciding, "I'm interested in this, I'm going to make a project about that, and it will be like this." Like advertising or the creative industries. I don't think many people work in this kind of mode anymore.

HH The drawings of images in magazines have quite a lot in common with the *Pictures* generation kind of stuff and, weirdly, with *Popism*, don't they?

EN Yes, but I didn't really know what I was doing. It was, "Oh, something in this picture is attracting me and I'll draw it." And then once it's finished, I can see it's quite funny. It's not knowing ... Because I never understood what they were doing. "Okay, that's Pop Art." I didn't have that sensibility at all. I mean, I was still pulled in the authentic direction or split between the contemporary and the past. It's a sort of unknowing thing and then coming to know. It's both unknowing and then I go, "Oh, no, that's kind of interesting." There's a consciousness of how it fits into art, that I can make it art. But when I make it, I go into the unknowing thing, not judging, and that seems to work. Because when you think with the ego, you can only think one thing, so it's pretty dull.

HH What do you mean?

EN You're conscious of what you're thinking and it's pretty limited. And then when you stop thinking, if you ever can, there's just so much more stuff that you're not in control of but that comes through you. Does that make sense?

FP And it is you but in a different way.

EN Yeah, it's you and it's not you and it's...

***

FP Are your paintings done without preparation, these days, except maybe those Imi Knoebel four-sided ones?

EN Yeah, the diagrams. Exactly. Looking for colours, just notes to myself.

HH I like those drawings, with four or five on the page, just figuring out colour combinations.

EN Exactly. And then I look at them and go, "Oh, that's a nice drawing."

FP I remember you saying once that sometimes the colour schemes for those paintings come from other places, from other paintings.

EN Yes, I take them from fashion or an ad I might see in a fancy magazine. I see the four—five, you need five colours.

FP Oh, because of the centre.

EN Yeah, it's hard to get five. Four is sort of okay. Sometimes I will use a source like that and then maybe one idea produces another one. In the last show at Neon Parc there's a little one that's all white, different kinds of white. That idea comes from doing them, I suppose, not from looking.

FP Otherwise, you would never make a drawing to prepare for a painting anymore. But would you have done that when you were younger?

EN Well, I thought I was, but then I came across the difficulty of the fact that you couldn't leap from one medium to another.

HH Because of the colour?

EN No, the material. Painting is awkward and indirect, whereas drawing with a crayon is really direct. Using a brush, you're one step removed. And the paint doesn't... You know, there's many things you can do with paint. I still find painting completely novel and difficult. Where am I going to end this mark? You just don't know what you're doing. Well, in the geometric ones I do know because I know the consistency of the paint and the opacity or whatever. And the line. That's very clear to me. And when I don't know what to do, I will do that. Or when I feel inspired by the colours.

FP It seems that you couldn't make the free, expressive paintings all the time.

EN Yeah, they're really hard and scary. You're going to waste a lot of material, if it doesn't work out.

FP Do you ruin a lot of them?

EN Just a few. No, see, I'm good at knowing when I'm ready. And I don't make that many. The more you work on them, the crappier they get. They have to be really light and fresh.

FP The look of your work really depends on that feeling that it's only the bare minimum of what needed to be there to make something happen. Otherwise, it becomes something else, sort of decorative.

EN Totally, totally. Yes, to keep them new and not in the "mode of" or the "genre of." I always want to see something that I haven't seen before. So, the more kind of weird they are, the better.

FP When you look through a lot of images of your work, on the screen or in a book, you notice things that repeat a lot, like these top-heavy compositions.

EN Yeah, they're always the same, in a way, aren't they?

FP Do you think that comes out of the desire for them not to resemble things you've seen in other people's art?

EN No, I think that comes out of who I am! And it's a very limited range, really. There's always a familiarity. It's really hard to tell what year these are from. Even some more recent ones look like the thirty-year-old ones.

***

EN It's cute.

HH It's like writing in a notepad or something.

EN I was working with the rectangle. And I'm aware that it's kind of like a text. It's a sign of a text, isn't it? It's a cartoon version of writing, of a page. And pink, you know ... I think I read in a book, a *How to Paint* book, that you shouldn't use pink. So, I thought, "Okay, I'm going to use pink."

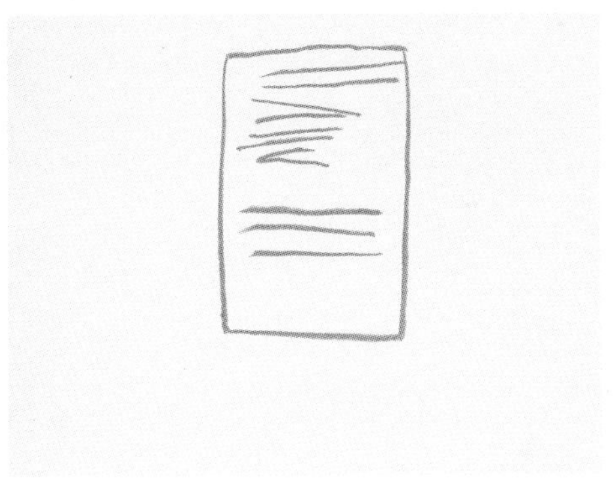

5

FP With the slanting lines, it's a sign of a text, but it's also like a reflection. It could be a mirror or something like that. Because there's so little detail.

EN Yeah. I think they're so minimal and so barely there because I'm interested in that moment where, it's hard to say, but ... It's the moment of the subject being present, without all the bells and whistles of the ego, if you know what I mean, just the bare minimum of "here I am." Like the child, you know. My daughter Rachel did this thing, it was so bizarre. She'd have a piece of paper and she'd do a funny oval shape in each corner and then she would cut it with scissors in each corner. It seemed to me like the most basic articulation of a human being. And it's interesting that it had a cut in it. They're all like that in a way.

HH Yes, I was flipping through the yellow book [*Elizabeth Newman: More than what there is* (Melbourne: 3-ply, 2013)] this morning and in the introduction to it you talk about drawing, writing, and cutting being the same thing.

EN Oh, yes, because they are. Drawing, writing, and cutting. I can see the link between cutting and drawing.

HH Because it's about incision and imprinting.

EN Yeah, I think making a mark and making a cut are pretty similar. And you can think of writing in two ways: as a material practice but also as a practice of representation or signification, an abstract thing. It's both material and abstract. And even at the abstract level it is a cutting and a cutting that creates something. A cutting or a drawing or ... I see them as all linked in a signifying way. They're all the same practice.

HH I love these ones, where you're scribbling and it's kind of like filling in a mass, like you are colouring in something but then also perhaps erasing something underneath it.

EN I think there is a link with the child, obviously, with how children are trying to articulate something. I've never been interested in narrative art or allegory. So, it's not trying to express *something*. It's a bit before that, I think. More basic.

HH But it's not automatic in the surrealist sense.

EN Ah, well, I think it is a bit similar. But maybe they were trying too hard. I mean, I use the same process.

HH Of disassociation?

EN Yeah.

FP In terms of the process of making, do you find that making a drawing is less loaded? Could you just sit down with a piece of paper and do one? Whereas going into the studio to make a painting. . .

EN Yeah, it's the money and the materials. With a piece of paper, if you hate

5 *Untitled*, 1990, pastel on paper, 28 × 39 cm.

6 *Untitled*, 1986, pencil on paper, 15 × 20 cm.

6

it, you just chuck it out. Yes, they were all practice runs.

HH Some of the drawings seem like they might not even have begun life as drawings. Perhaps you're making a shopping list or a note to yourself or notes in a lecture and then you've ripped the page out. Like the one with notes from a Badiou lecture.

EN Exactly, they're notes to myself. With that one in particular, they're two different kinds of notes and then I was aware that there was this big gap in the middle. I just thought it was a really nice composition. And it's telling you something. For the viewer, it's directing them towards a certain thought? Badiou or this thing about sublimation. So, there's a sort of educational push in some of it. Or it's a homage to these ideas and these people, very much linking my practice to the greats who have come before me.

HH I like that about the Met drawing too because it's like a continuum between the modernist gallery and the living artist.

EN Yeah, I mean, it's got a lot in it because it's got the Black guards or invigilators. It tells you a lot.

FP And it's also interesting because you were looking at that magazine here, away from the "centre" of the artworld.

EN Yeah, exactly. I mean there was the canon or the tradition and we were formed in relation to it. You had to honour it. Yes, that's very different now.

HH You've been writing and painting this Goya phrase, *Las Pinturas Negras*, for the last couple of years.

EN I just think it's an interesting phrase, you know. It refers to the Goya paintings, to something particular. But it also refers to the content that he's talking about, the darkness. It refers to art and representation in relation to this real thing, these real lives and real life. I just find it very full of gravitas.

FP There's a series done around the same time with really heavy phrases, like the one that says "All Against All" or one that says "Root of All Evil" in Latin. It's kind of funny because it's like a description. It's like, "Here they are, the dark paintings."

EN It's showing that there's the mass of the real world and all the horrible things that are happening in it and then there's painting. It's a representation as opposed to something much bigger.

FP Also dark in the sense of obscurity, perhaps? The obscurity of the practice.

HH I think of other black paintings, like Ramsden.

EN Yes, and there's the light paintings, with the lights on them.

HH And you've got the lights on/lights off coupling.

EN Yeah, which is a reference to the work by Martin Creed but it has bigger resonance. So, yes, that refers to Goya, but it goes beyond that. The representation is both small and big. It does a tiny little thing, but it's also kind of pointing you outwards.

FP Would you say that's how those phrases come to take their place in your work, because they can do both things at once?

EN Oh, absolutely. To me they always have to be equivocal, ambiguous, multivalent, you know.

FP What about the one that says, "The permanent green of experience?" What is that?

EN That's a quote from Freud, actually.

FP What does it mean? What's the green?

EN It's bizarre, isn't it? He's talking about the difference between theory and practice. It's a spring metaphor, isn't it? Real life is green and theory is... I can't really remember.

FP Grey?

EN Yeah, or something like that. I'm saying the same thing, I suppose, just there, trying to articulate something as a framework. It's a thin framework in response to the big mass of reality. That's a human being's job, in a way, to name and articulate what is happening because it's always so big.

Maybe it also implies that you can't ever fully capture it.

FP It's too much.

EN And it's permanent, it's permanently green.

HH As in young?

EN Yes, I guess so, and verdant and growing. And then it refers to colour, to experience as opposed to representation. But even when you make an expressionist painting, it's still, as we know, caught within the whole discourse of history, current affairs, it's never pure.

HH I love the green Coca-Cola works.

EN Yeah, they're cool, aren't they? I did a green one because it's not green, it's red, you know, and the black ...

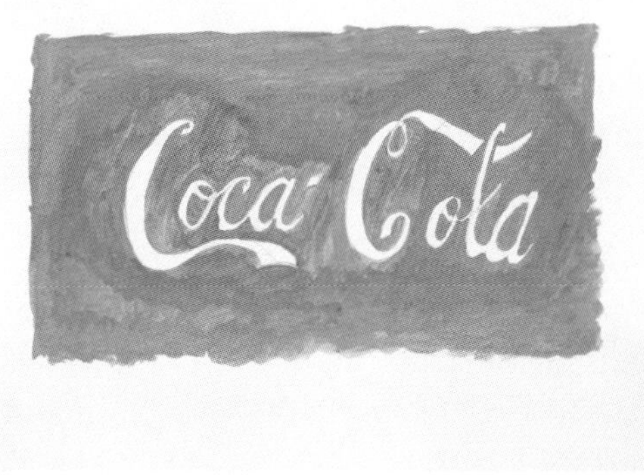

7

7 *Untitled*, 2019, gouache on paper, 38 × 57 cm.

8 *Untitled*, 1991, oil pastel on paper, 42 × 30.5 cm.

FP Though, there is a green Coca-Cola, isn't there?

EN Is there?

HH The environmentally friendly one?

FP Yeah, one that has stevia in it ...

EN They copied me! To take something so well-known and then do something to it ... I think I got the idea listening to Jimi Hendrix playing the *Star-Spangled* thingy. And I was like, "Oh, that is so cool." It's the same kind of aesthetic to take something like that and then do something rock and roll with it. So, yeah, the fact that it was hand drawn and badly and then it's a different colour.

FP It kind of looks pathetic or sort of sad, in a nice way.

EN Yeah, totally. That's my thing.

FP There's something about the way you treat the Coca-Cola logo, as if it's been emptied. That's part of that mistreatment: it's been turned into a blank surface to go next to your other pieces.

EN Yeah, so there's something quite aggressive or undermining, rebellious, I suppose. That's often a bit of a push. I think that even when I was trying to be in submission to and honour these greats that came before me, there was also the alternative emotion of making fun of them or something. I think that my strength is in my weakness. My strength is in all the mistakes or the failures or what didn't work. I was aware of that early on.

***

FP What about this drawing called *Family*? I thought of it before when you were talking about children's drawings.

EN It's got the four elements. I would have done that and then gone, "Oh, there's four different things: family." So, the red-black, scribbly thing is obviously like the mother.

HH Obviously.

EN And then the rectangle is paternal. It's the contrast between something raw and unsymbolised and then something that becomes coherent.

HH Even though that's how you would express yourself in a sense on the page.

EN Yes. Well, in fact, I do both. And then, "Oh, what's the little black thing?" Something really abject, you know.

HH Or a full stop.

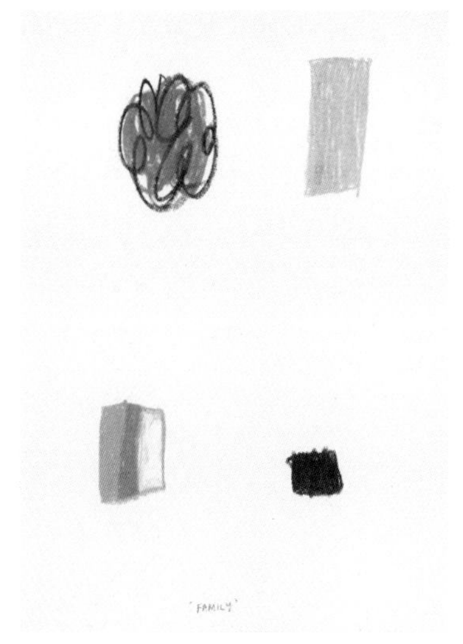

8

EN Yeah. I mean, I don't know. It's just a random ...

FP And the child is split in two, in three.

EN Yes, or are they both children? Is that a dog? I don't know what. But, yeah, they're very minimal expressions of deep subjectivity, I guess. And without the title, it could just be abstract, but then writing "family," you know, is a conscious kind of intervention. How is that a family?

FP But at the same time, is it also suggesting that there's an aspect of looking at this image, even without the text that is always going to be ...

HH Forming associations?

FP Yeah. Or do you see those associations as invented in putting the text there?

EN Yes, I wasn't intending it when I was doing it at all.

HH Is that always how you come up with your titles for works? Post-facto?

EN Yes.

FP And there aren't that many titles.

HH Although there were more than I expected when I was going through the book today. *Mother Love*, for example, which is really nice.

EN Yes, they're very precise when I do have them. Precise and enigmatic. The title is always enigmatic. I don't understand other people's titles, really. What is a title? It adds something to the work. It doesn't describe the work. It's another conscious sort of attribution, layer. It's this sort of combination of being naive and innocent and then being really knowing about what makes something art. Being unthinking or whatever, and then being aware of the whole discourse of art and how that works, I suppose.

FP And kind of looking for this moment of art in that failure and naivety.

EN Yes, yes, and that would explain the found objects. But isn't it bizarre that you see things and you don't know whether you're the only one seeing it that way or if others see it that way? They don't, you know. The clothing rack that I found on the street and Naomi Evans put it in the show in Brisbane...

HH It was in David [Homewood]'s show as well, right? At Utopian Slumps.

EN Yes, David put it in the show and Naomi was interested in all the holes, all the absences, the signification of the nothing, you know. So, when I see that in the street, I see it as a framing of a hole, of nothing, but there was someone who wrote about the show, and he quite liked it except for that. "Why would you put a clothes rack in?" You know, sort of seeing it as a narrative. "It's just a clothes rack!" But I don't see it as a clothes rack. Well, I know it's a clothes rack, of course, but I'm looking at things in a visual way, I suppose, and you just never know what other people see. Have I told you that people come here and they think that's [pointing to Lucina Lane painting, which is an empty frame with some fabric in the middle] a mirror? What are they looking at?

***

FP Are these done with crayons?

EN Oil pastels. It's just sort of seeing what I will come up with. I mean, they always articulate something that figures, to come back to your earlier

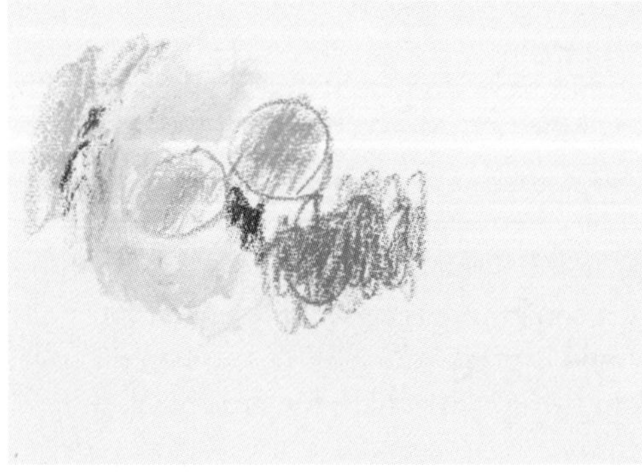

9

9 *Untitled*, 2011, oil pastel on paper, 29.7 × 21 cm.

question, don't they? You know, they're two elements or three objects in relation to each other. At a very primitive level, the purple in relation to the orange, they're in a kind of dialogue in some way. They're primitive ways of articulating some experience that's not narrative, you can't recognise it, it's funny, it's not to be shared, it's very private in a way. I don't know what it is. So, does it have meaning or not? It doesn't really have meaning.

FP But it has some kind of resonance for others.

EN Well, I imagine. Yes.

FP Because that experience is, on some other level, shared. . .

EN I guess so. I mean, is it? This is what I don't know.

HH Have you had people have intense reactions to your work before? Or who read it in kind of an uncanny way?

EN Juan [Davila] has said interesting things to me. About that show I had at Monash with the big coloured things on the wall and then the pipe in the middle. He's really switched on. He said there's something abject about the pipe, obviously, and anal and gross and whatever. And then the joyous, more Apollonian big paintings. That contrast between something symbolic and then something abject and non-symbolic. I thought, "Oh, wow, that's a really interesting observation." And then when I did these pink and green and yellow paintings, he said they were paintings of the nursery as opposed to the dark ones, which are more mature. He reads it in that kind of psychoanalytic way. And see, I have trouble, some people, they're suffering and they use their suffering to make art. I can't do that at all. I have to feel upbeat and safe and happy, you know. It's a really primitive thing, just colour, to be able to play, I suppose. And that's very early.

HH Were you taught to use colour in your drawings at art school?

EN No.

HH I was thinking that at art school it would be lead pencil.

EN For drawing? Charcoal. And then Geoff Lowe introduced me to the red, the Sienna red, the Renaissance kind of colour. I'm trying to look at what the raw materials are that go into making the picture. It's the mark, it's the material, it's the smudgy bit, it's the frame. It's deconstructive in that way.

FP Something like charcoal or pastel, they're very sensuous kinds of materials that you smudge around. But would you ever do a drawing with biro? Or does it not work because of the material?

EN There's a few in there with a felt-tip pen. Texta.

FP They also feel nice to use.

EN Yeah, they're great, they're fantastic. Yes, it's very libidinal in that way.

Even the Scribble Feels like Talking: The Drawings of Elizabeth Newman

Erik Jensen

If there is a difference between Elizabeth Newman's drawings and her paintings, it is that the drawings are funnier. This is Newman's distinction: she doesn't know why, but the drawings make her laugh. They share with humour its fleetingness and its promise of failure. They are self-conscious and that is funny. They are ironic without intending to be so. Newman's work is often like this, although it is deadpan and easily reads as serious. Jokes stop working when you explain them and painting has a tendency to explain.

***

It is hard to say which are the first drawings, because they happened all at once. Time does not run in one direction for Newman. There's not one phase and then another but several phases at the same time. She stops to ask if this makes sense.

Initially, Newman thought of drawings as practices. They were a kind of fitness. She was trained to believe that drawing was the basis of everything. Sometimes she would draw to learn. She would make sense of an artwork by copying it. She would draw a Canaletto or the side of a Judd sculpture with an Agnes Martin behind it. She would never enter the work she was reproducing, however. There was never anything more. She says this is like with a tree log: when you cut the log, you think you'll see into the tree, but all you see is another surface.

Early on, if she didn't know what to do, or was too scared to make a painting, she would draw. The opposite is true now. The drawings terrify her. She avoids them. To make one she has to feel very safe and secure—very sane, she says. She calls it difficult and vulnerable. If she doesn't know what to do, she will make a painting instead. The monochromes feel like a skin between her and the world and making them is a form of protection.

She says the drawings are better than the paintings. They are briskly made and a surprise. She vacillates: the drawings are inconsequential or they are the most important.

***

The shocking part of these drawings is their sincerity. Newman means every one of them. When she draws four shapes and writes "family" it is exactly what she says it is. When she takes a line and bends it twelve times, the wonky, jug-like tridecagon is perfect.

Newman calls the act of drawing libidinal. She says there's a sort of sensual, visceral enjoyment in making the image. For a short period, she drew with makeup. She did this after Geoff Lowe gave her a book on paint technique. The book instructed her on which colours could be used together and what had to be applied first and so on. She ignored this and used hand cream. The book said never to use pink and so she did. She was making fun of brown paintings. She was ridiculing the obsession with structure and form.

In these makeup drawings, she applies lipstick as a child might on a cousin. There is pleasure and rage in the way the pigment eats up the paper. The shapes that are left recall a mouth or a cheek, described without restraint, with no edges to them, just more and more of the excitement of colour. The outcome is guileless and determined. The works are spiky but not only spiky.

Sometimes she draws with tape. When she cuts a flap into carpet or fabric, the incision is also drawing. Newman works from a place of great attention. Her drawings feel as if they have been cared for, their small achievements noticed and celebrated. She is both child and parent. Her drawings are stubborn and deliberate and curious and patient.

***

Unlike with her paintings, Newman often signs her drawings. It is as if she is insisting: this is a work, this is finished. She does so a long time after the drawing is made.

Her initials resemble the broken palindrome that has fascinated her work: the levidrome of "on" and "no" that clicks from one meaning to its opposite, like a coin rolled over knuckles. The other word for this is semordnilap.

The first no was a no to everything: capitalism, humanism, anything bad. She made it after reading Yvonne Rainer's "No Manifesto," its rejection of virtuosity and spectacle and magic. She had also read Freud's argument that negation was really affirmation.

For Newman the no contains an inevitable, fundamental yes. She says a no is an attempt to say what is not there, to find a signifier of negation. She says that if you identify what you don't like you are also identifying what you do like. If you say what is in you, you are also saying what is outside you.

With her initials, it gets close to working. She is trapped by what she was given at birth. One way it is almost "end" and the other way it is not quite "new."

In 1992, Newman wrote her initials on a piece of paper. She then wrote her first name, all in capitals: "Elizabeth." She drew the letter "E" twice, and then her initials again, as if practicing, as if it were homework. She scribbled over this until what she had left was a storm cloud. This was also her. Underneath, she wrote "Mistake."

***

When Newman draws, she draws the frame first. She sets out the four sides of a rectangle and then she starts. Her drawings are sometimes concerned with filling space, filling up a page, colouring in. She works in short lines, bundled together like sticks. There is darkness in the overlap and pause of texta ink. The works are often unconscious or automatic.

She keeps the drawings in a plan cabinet in the piano room near the back of her house. They are not filed in any special way. Many are on scraps of paper, torn or showing through marks from the drawings made on top of them.

Except for the copies of other works, she says, she never thinks of another artist when she draws. She says this is proof that the drawing is primary, that it exists in a place almost before art. She cannot think of an artist whose drawings she admires. She says drawings often seem ugly to her.

Newman tries again. She likes Seurat's drawings better than his paintings. When she was younger, she loved Twombly, whose paintings are really drawings. Other than that, she is skeptical. Her own drawings are often bright. It would be wrong to call them ugly. They know the temperature of sunlight in a room. They know how to be joyful and silly.

***

Newman's pictures are full of language. Even the scribble feels like talking. Sometimes they feel like the problems of analytic philosophy. They have in them the elements of reason and logic. Something is always standing in for something else: a line, a mark, a smudge of colour.

When Newman first made text drawings, she was shocked at how radical they were. She was so angry and their banality felt provocative. She often talks about her work as if it is confronting, as if the simplicity is outrageous.

The text is always transcription. When she finds a phrase, she will use it over and over, the works like placards at a rally. The repetition is not frustration. She feels heard: that was never the problem. Still, she feels she has to say it again. She has to get it through to you. The process contains the slippages between what is said, what is expressed, and what is heard or understood.

If she finds a statement she likes, she wants to see it several different ways. Each has a value of difference and similarity. This is especially true of the phrase she borrowed from an essay by Geoff Lowe and Jacqueline Riva, a sentiment that proves itself again with the fact of each new iteration: "The true collector looks for the work that is unfinished."

The talking in Newman's work is often political. She is worried about the brevity of the future. She is troubled by consumption. She feels for the oceans. She celebrates small acts of resistance: "Please remove me from your mailing list."

Her darkest drawings are about light. She keeps practicing the text for Goya's black paintings. She copies out Martin Creed's instructions for a light switch. She is circling a pun on light and enlightenment. She clips a phrase from Lacan: "some little lights in a perfectly dark field."

Newman likes the way the words describe human ignorance, the smallness of knowledge, the not knowing of experience, and the sense of wonder in a dark universe. The full quote is: "The first step to be made in the philosophy of the *Lumières* is to know that day has not dawned and that the day in question is only that of some little lights in a perfectly dark field."

***

The drawings always precede the paintings. That is not to say they are preparatory. They function almost as a reminder that two things can exist at once. Her drawings all seem to ask the same question: which work is the work and why not also this one?

Frequently, she is making at the limit state. The threat of failure in her work is not from what is there but what is not. Nothing is at risk of collapsing under the weight of anything else.

Newman is interested in the slightest interventions. She is edging towards the point at which something is an artwork and something is not. It is a game of subtraction, like pick-up sticks.

The confidence in her drawings is in the eloquence of emotion. Her work knows what it is to be confused and to say so. It knows what it is to feel anger and to describe it. Newman says so much of her work is about lack, about articulating what is lacking. The cohering force is her insistence that the work is completed. If there were a term for this, it might be expressionist minimalism.

***

Newman's drawings exist before trauma. They come from before a lonely childhood. Their engine is innocence. To make them, Newman returns to a child state. She empties herself of experience. She calls this going to the nothing. "Going to the nothing is like trying to get to what is the most me," she says. "It is the most authentic, which is the way we think about it: the most primitive, the most infantile, or whatever."

She calls the drawings the first articulation. She says they have no content at all. There is no narrative. She is reducing herself to get there. "This is the thing about my work: it's blank, isn't it?" she says. "There's no reference. I mean, occasionally when I draw something you can recognise a reference, but generally they're just completely non-signifying ... There's no content in them, except the act of making an artwork."

The drawings perform a kind of lifecycle. She is a child as she makes them and in the instant she decides they are finished she is an adult again. In that moment she becomes the artist.

"Finished" is the fundamental choice of Newman's work. The other word for this is "enough," which can be both an admonishment and validation. For a child, the decision is how much juice should be in the glass, how much cereal in the bowl. The phrase is "say when."

Newman calls this the inscription of limit. Previously she has described it as the place where language divides being. Her skill is in being able to return to that juncture, to work at the fork of knowledge. The drawings are this skill in the extreme.

"I do it as a non-thinking, infantile person," she says. "And then a bit later on, I become like an adult artist, a connoisseur, and I go: 'That's art. I'm going to show that. That's useful.'"

P.100 *Untitled*, 2018, gouache on paper, 42 × 29.7 cm.
P.101 *Untitled*, 2019, conte crayon on paper, 42 × 29.7 cm.
Untitled, 2009, pencil on paper, 21 × 14.5 cm.
P.102 *Untitled*, 2009, watercolour on paper, 29.5 × 21 cm.
Untitled, 1990, texta on paper, 30 × 21 cm.
P.103 *Untitled*, 2018, charcoal on paper, 42 × 29.7 cm.
P.104 *Untitled*, 2019, found paper, 48.5 × 35 cm.
P.105 *Untitled*, 2012, cardboard on paper, 32 × 21.5 cm.
P.106 *Untitled*, 2011, gouache, 76 × 57 cm.
P.107 *Untitled*, 2009, gouache, 44.5 × 31.5 cm.
P.108 *Untitled*, 1987, watercolour on paper, 47 × 32.5 cm.
P.109 *Untitled*, 2013, texta on paper, 43.5 × 32.5 cm.
P.110 *Untitled*, 2011, oil pastel and pencil on paper, 38 × 28.5 cm.
P.111 *Untitled*, 2011, gouache on paper, 29.5 × 21 cm.
P.112 *Untitled*, 2015, gouache on paper, 29.5 × 21 cm.
Untitled, 2015, gouache on paper, 29.5 × 21 cm.
Untitled, 2015, gouache and pencil on paper, 29.5 × 21 cm.
Untitled, 2015, gouache and pencil on paper, 29.5 × 21 cm.
P.113 *Untitled*, 2015, watercolour and pencil on paper, 29.5 × 21 cm.
Untitled, 2015, gouache and pencil on paper, 29.5 × 21 cm.
Untitled, 2015, watercolour on paper, 29.5 × 21 cm.
P.114 *Untitled*, 2012, pencil on paper, 29.5 × 21 cm.
Untitled, 2012, pencil on paper, 29.5 × 21 cm.
P.115 *Untitled*, 2012, pencil on paper, 29.5 × 21 cm.
P.116 *Untitled*, 1984, watercolour on paper, 41 × 59 cm.
P.117 *Untitled*, 1984, gouache on paper, 28.5 × 19 cm.
P.118 *Untitled*, 1985, watercolour on paper, 28 × 33 cm.
P.119 *Untitled*, 1985, pencil on paper, 35.5 × 47 cm.
Untitled, 1985, pencil on paper, 35.5 × 47 cm.
P.120 *Untitled*, 1985, pastel on paper, 20.5 × 29 cm.
Untitled, 1985, pastel on paper, 24.5 × 20.5 cm.
P.121 *Untitled*, 1985, pastel on paper, 20.5 × 29 cm.
Untitled, 1985, pastel on paper, 20.5 × 29 cm.
P.122 *Untitled*, 1985, watercolour on paper, 20 × 14.5 cm.
Untitled, 1985, watercolour on paper, 20 × 14.5 cm.
Untitled, 1985, conte crayon on paper, 20 × 14.5 cm.
P.123 *Untitled*, 1985, conte crayon on paper, 29 × 41.5 cm.
Untitled, 1985, pencil on paper, 20 × 14.5 cm.
P.124 *Untitled*, 1985, pencil on paper, 29 × 41.5 cm.
Untitled, 1985, pencil on paper, 14.5 × 20 cm.
P.125 *Untitled*, 1985, pencil on paper, 41.5 × 59 cm.
P.126 *Untitled*, 1985, conte crayon, gouache, and pencil on paper, 28 × 38 cm.
P.127 *Untitled*, 1986, pastel and pencil on paper, 35.5 × 47 cm.
Untitled, 1986, conte crayon and pastel on paper, 35.5 × 47 cm. Private collection.
P.128 *Untitled*, 1987, charcoal on paper, 60 × 48 cm.
P.129 *Untitled*, 1986, charcoal on paper, 35.5 × 47 cm.
Untitled, 1987, pencil on paper, 30 × 21 cm.
P.130 *Untitled*, 1990, pastel on paper, 28 × 39 cm.
Untitled, 1990, pencil on paper, 12.5 × 20 cm.
P.131 *Untitled*, 1987, pencil on paper, 78 × 48 cm.
P.132 *Untitled*, 1990, collage and watercolour on paper, 34.5 × 24.5 cm.
P.133 *Untitled*, 1990, gouache on watercolour, 42 × 37 cm.
P.134 *Untitled*, 1992 stickers and ink on paper, 35 × 29 cm.
P.135 *Untitled*, 1992, stickers and ink on paper, 29.5 × 21 cm.
P.136 *Untitled*, 1992, stickers and ink on paper, 35 × 25 cm.
P.137 *Untitled*, 1992, stickers and ink on paper, 35 × 25.5 cm.
P.138 *Untitled*, 2011, pencil on paper, 21 × 20 cm.
P.139 *Untitled*, 2011, pencil on paper, 21 × 15 cm.
P.140 *Untitled*, 2011, pencil on paper, 21 × 15 cm.
P.141 *Untitled*, 2011, pencil on paper, 21 × 15 cm.
P.142 *Untitled*, 2011, pencil on paper, 21 × 15 cm.
P.143 *Untitled*, 2011, pencil on paper, 21 × 15 cm.
P.144 *Untitled*, 2011, pencil on paper, 21 × 15 cm.
P.145 *Untitled*, 2011, pencil on paper, 21 × 15 cm.
P.146 *Untitled*, 2011, pencil on paper, 21 × 15 cm.
P.147 *Untitled*, 2011, pencil on paper, 21 × 15 cm.

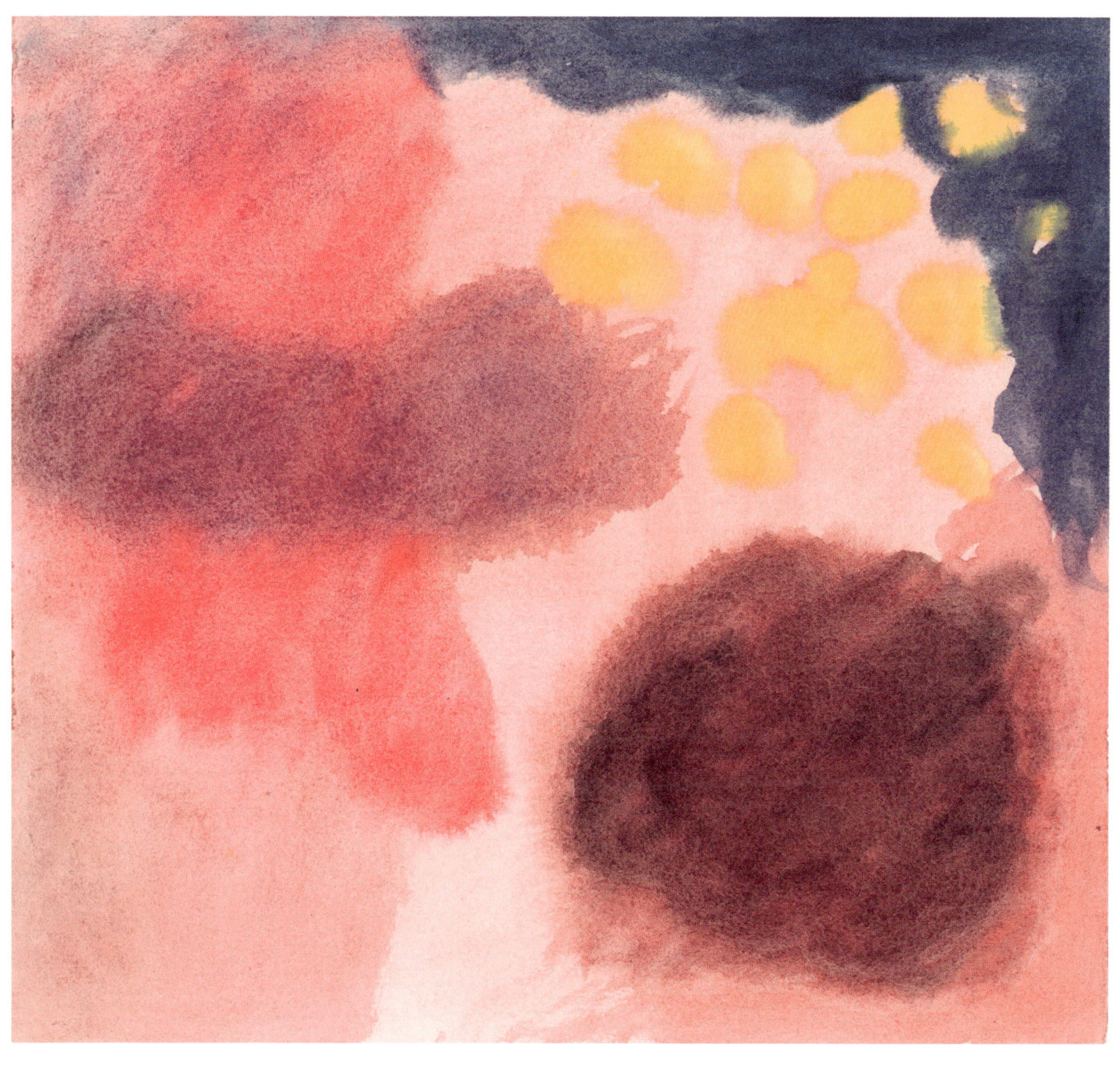

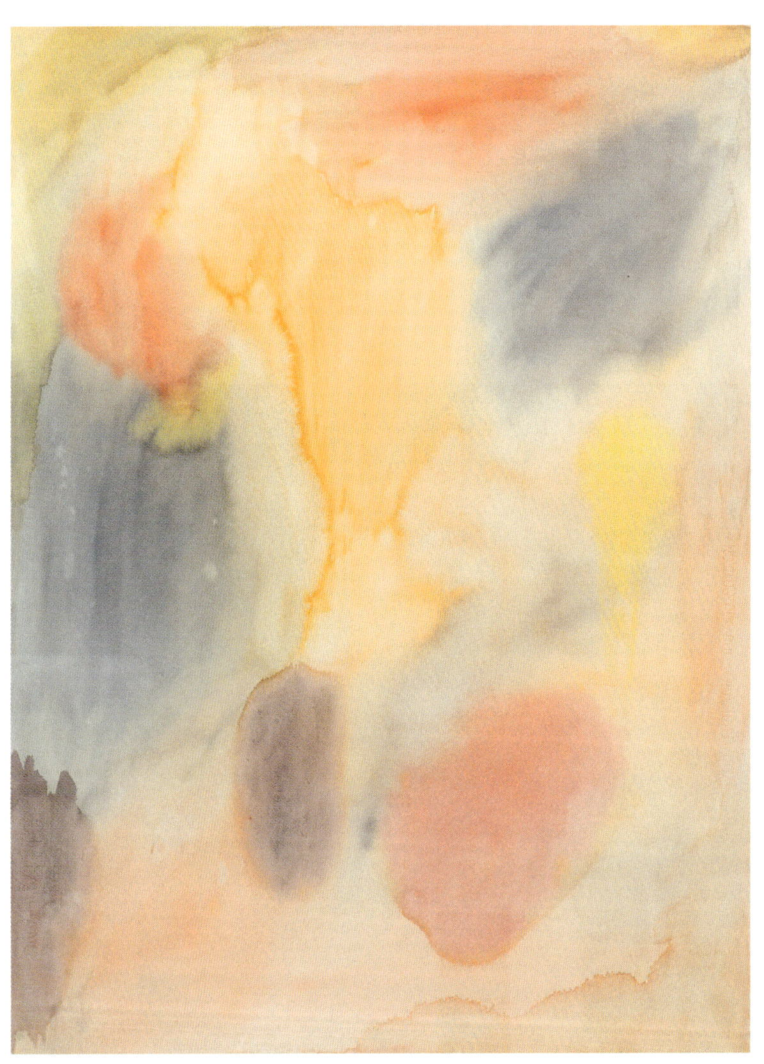

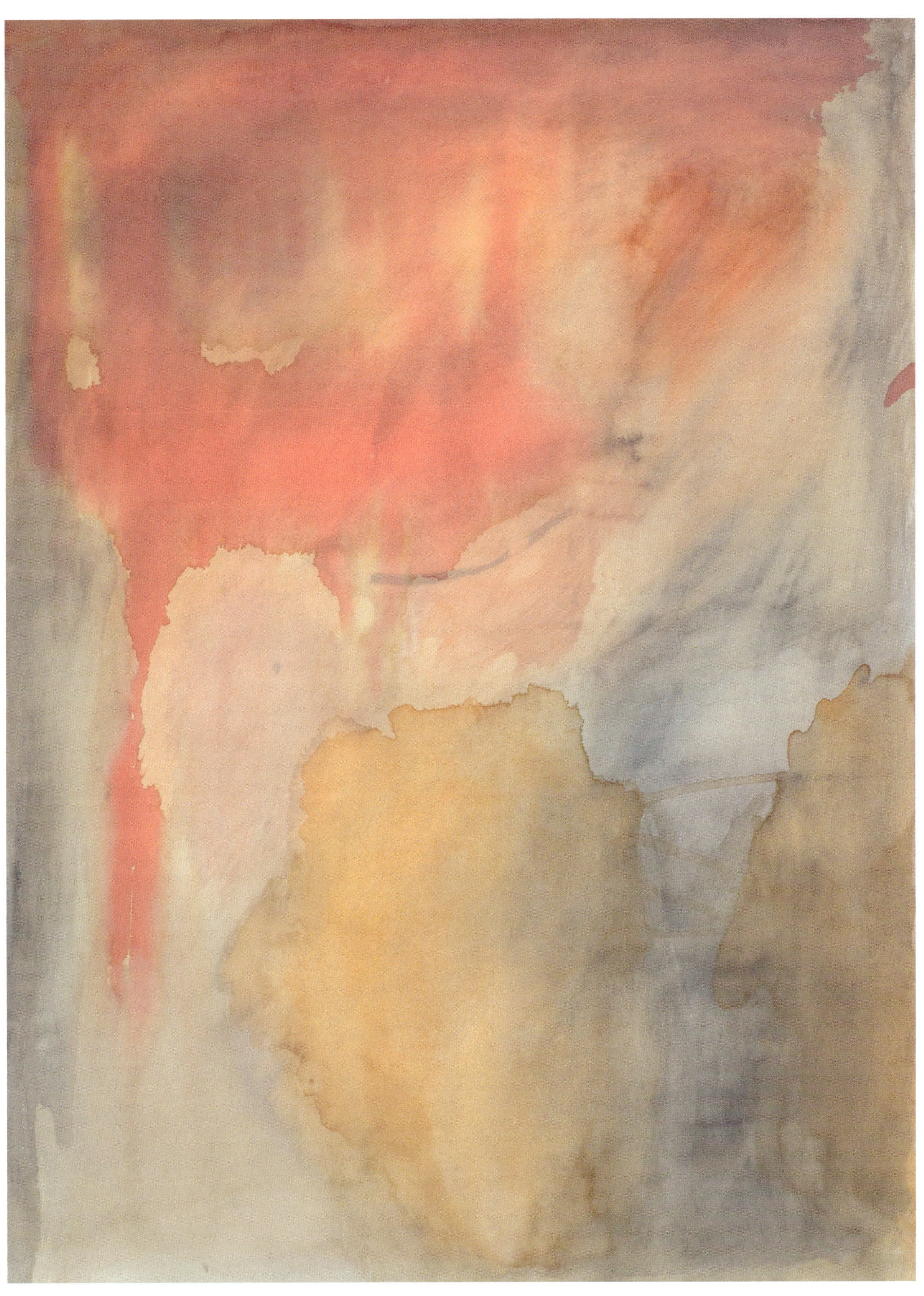

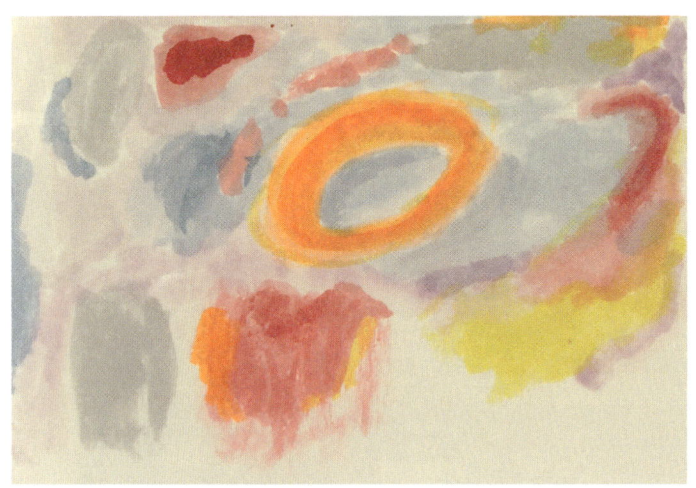

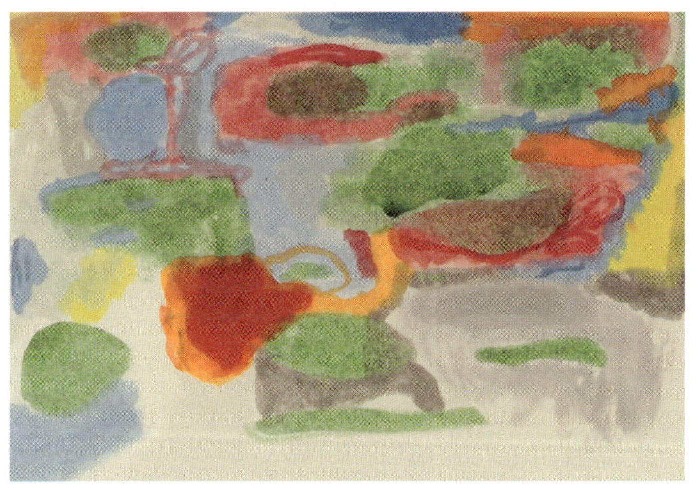

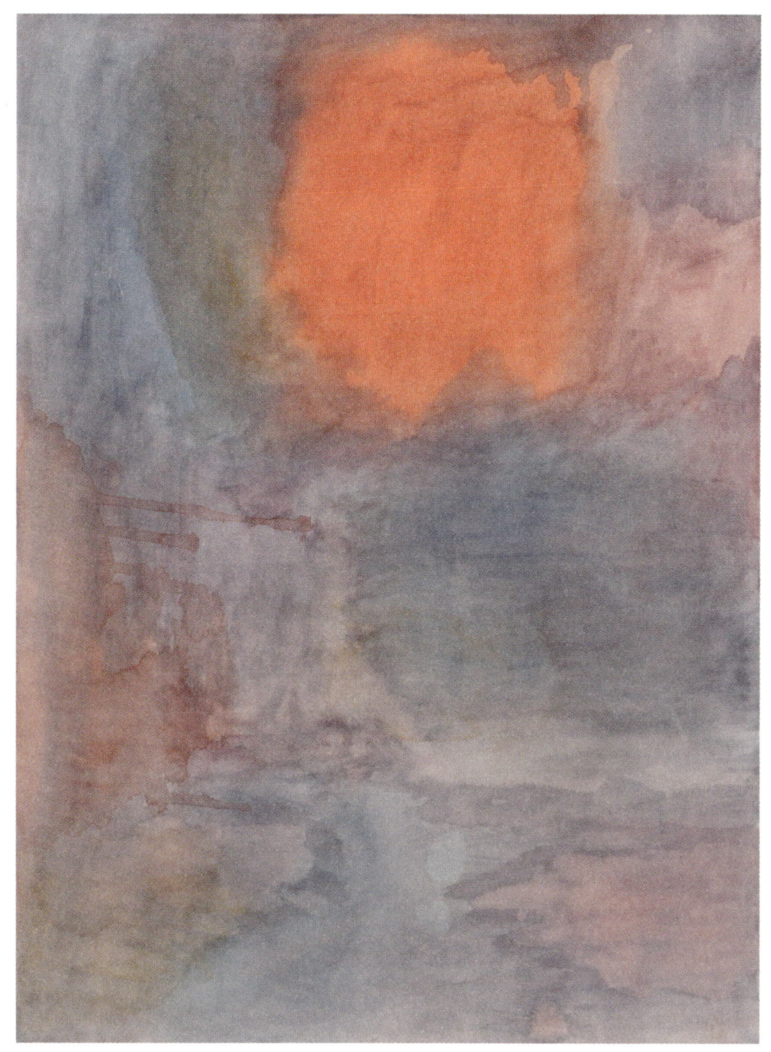

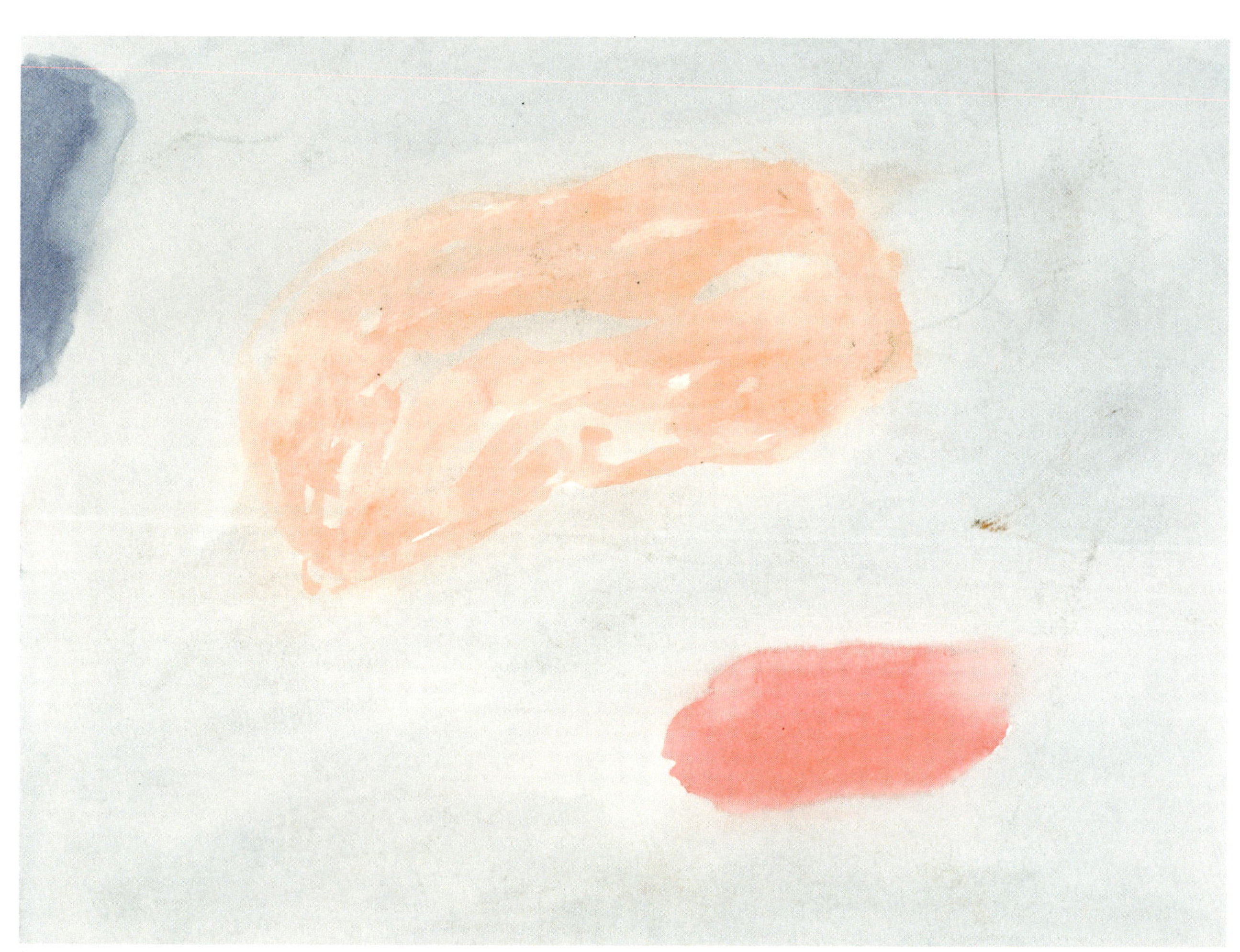

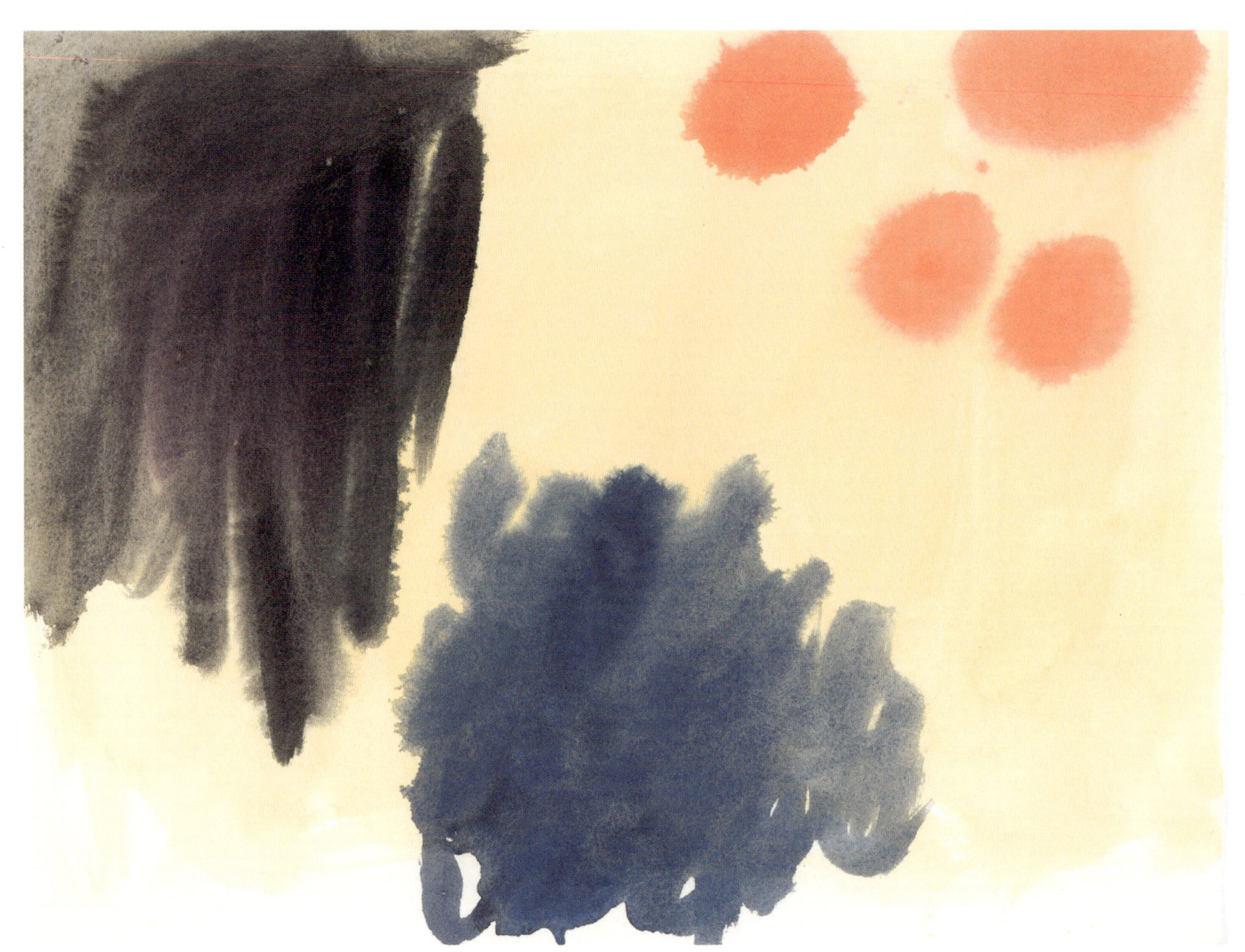

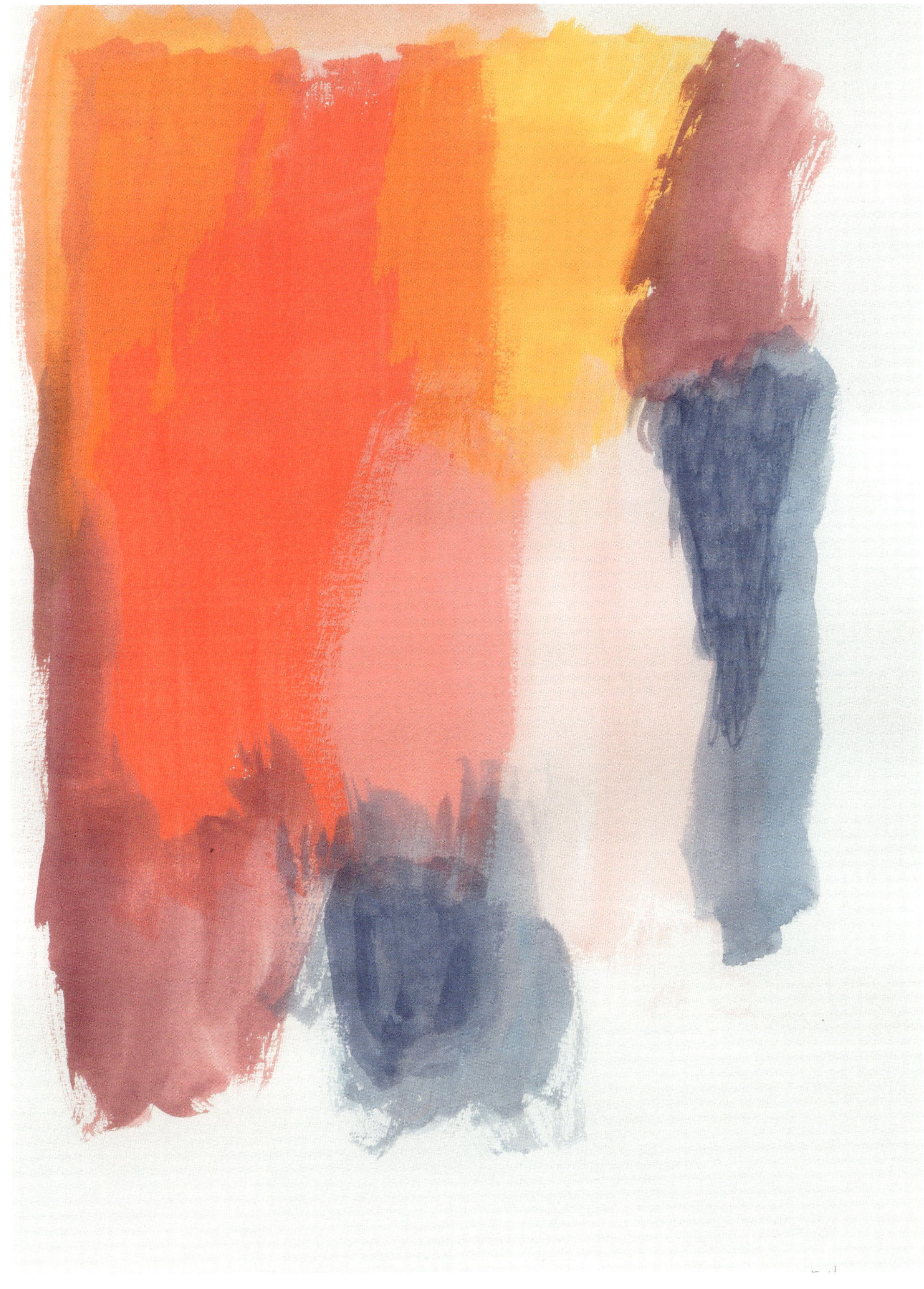

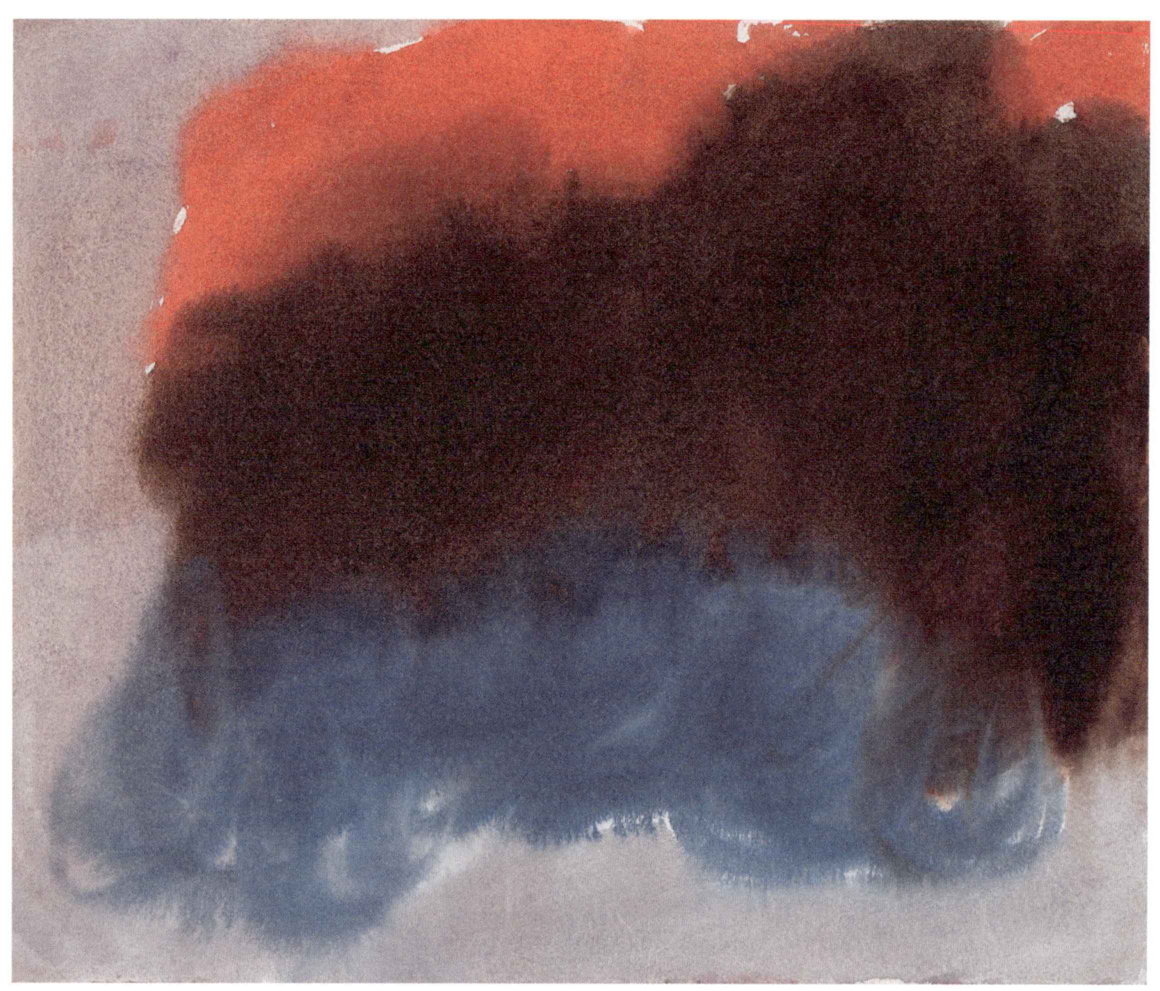

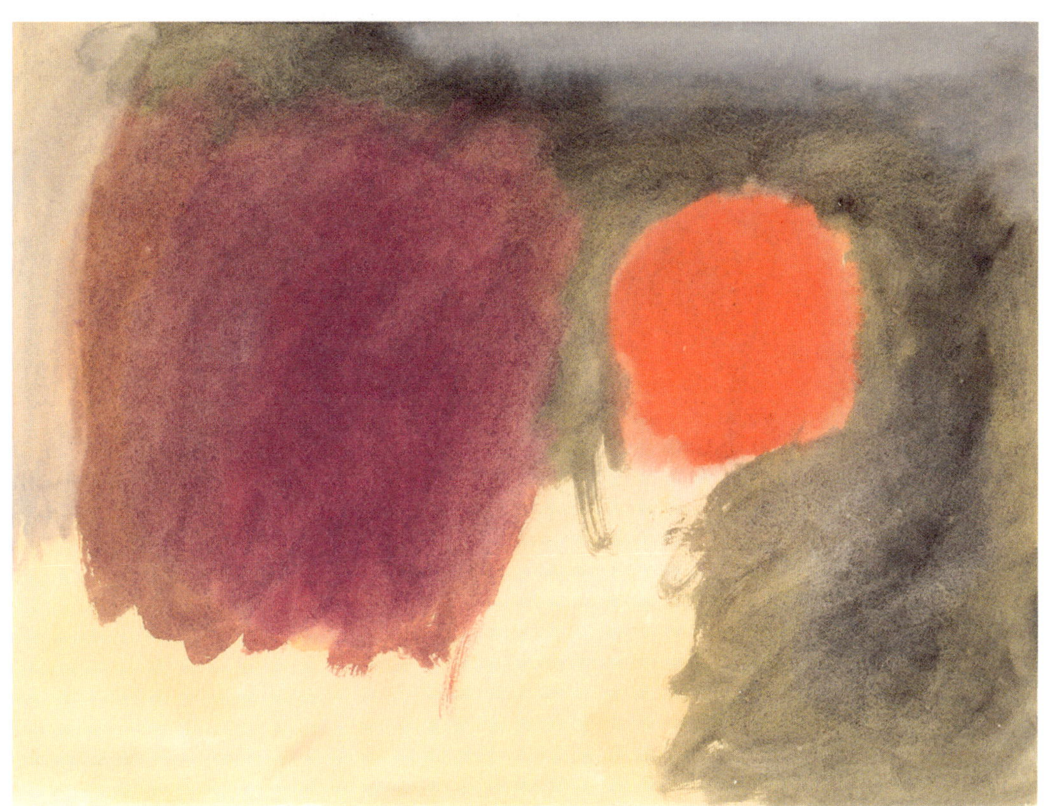

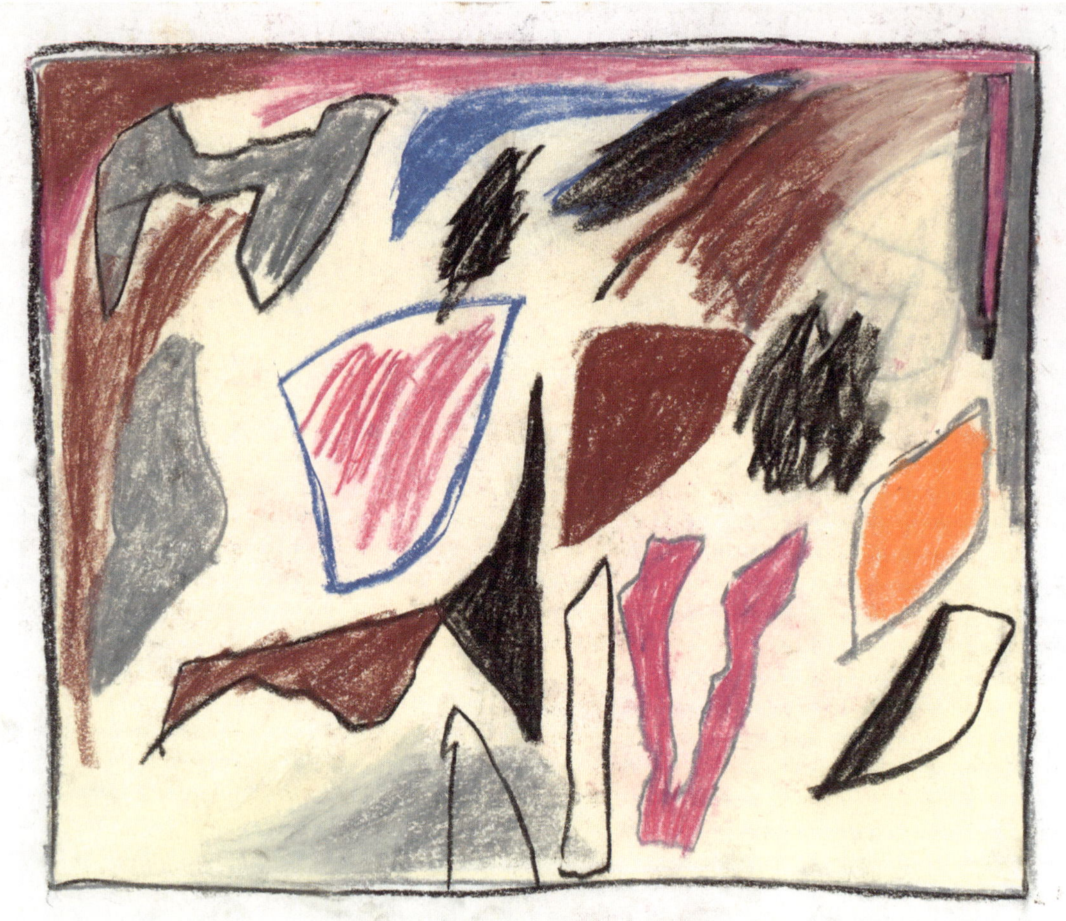

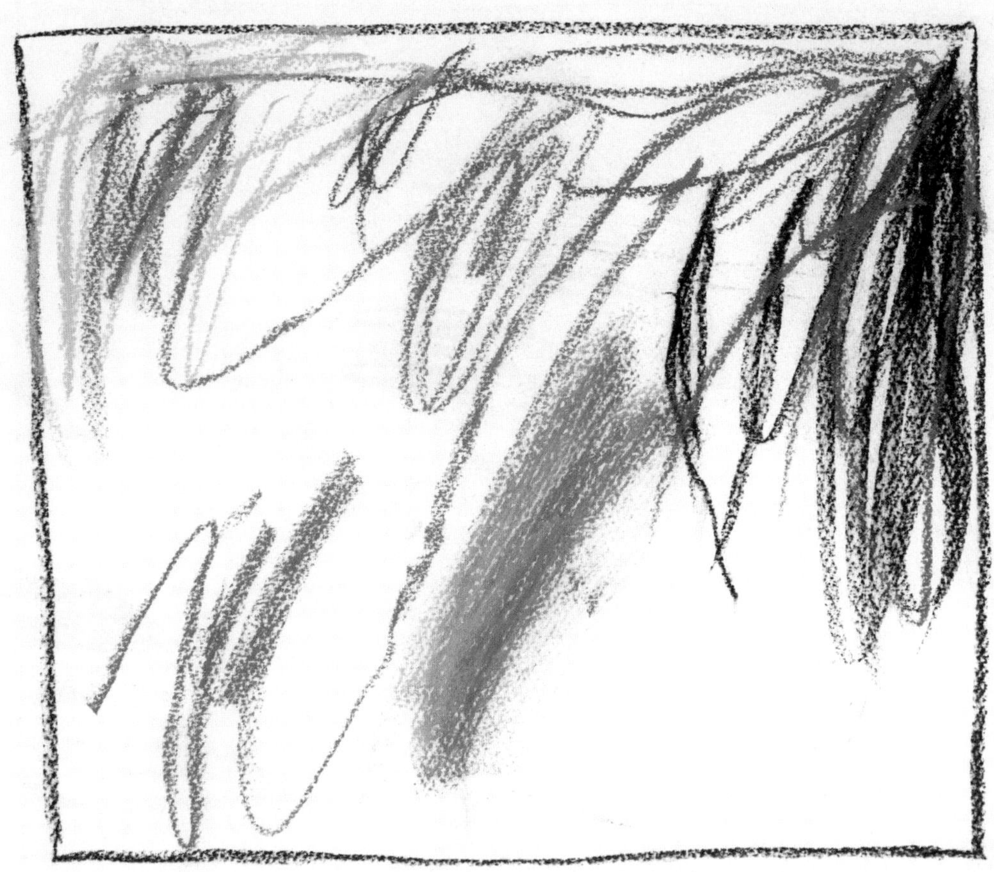

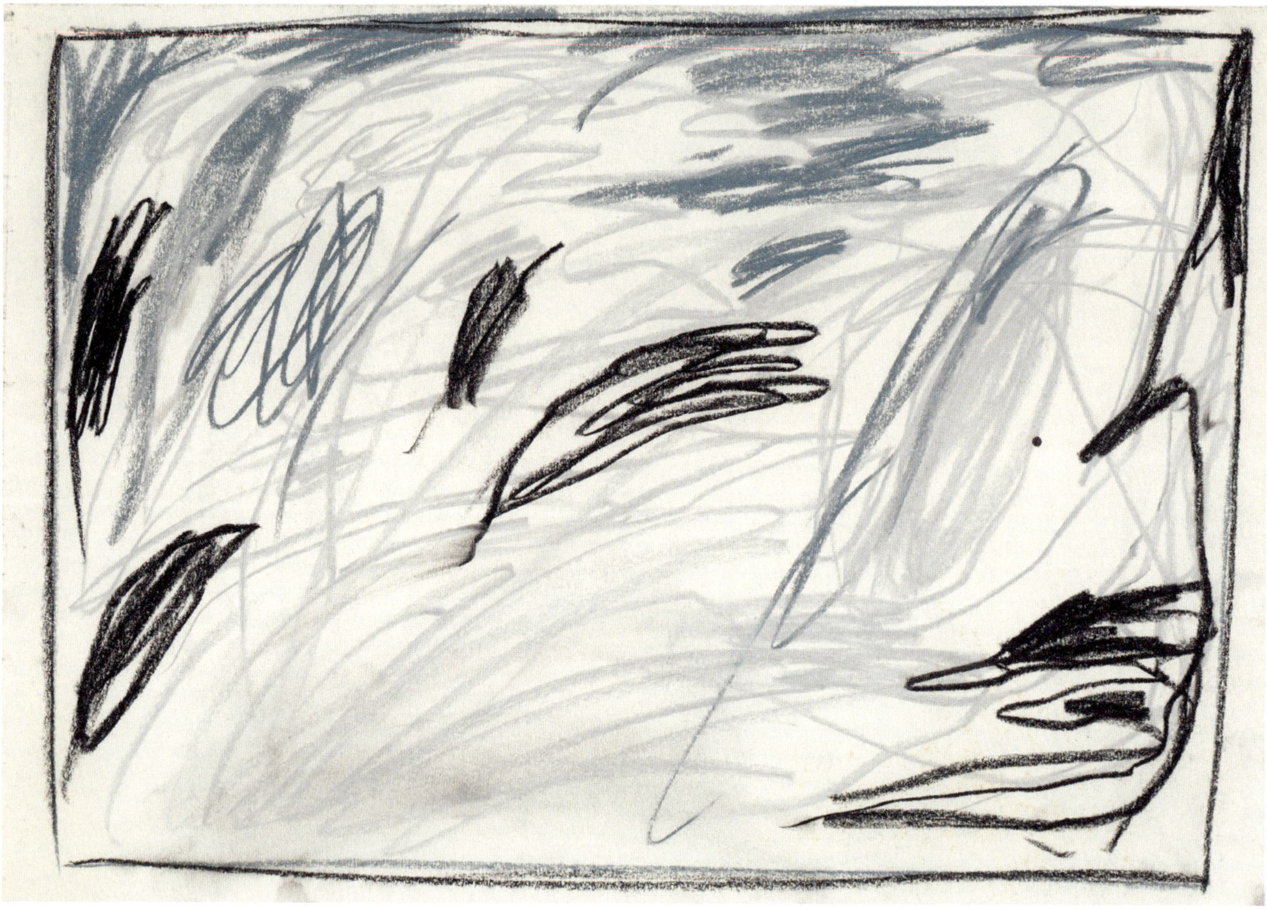

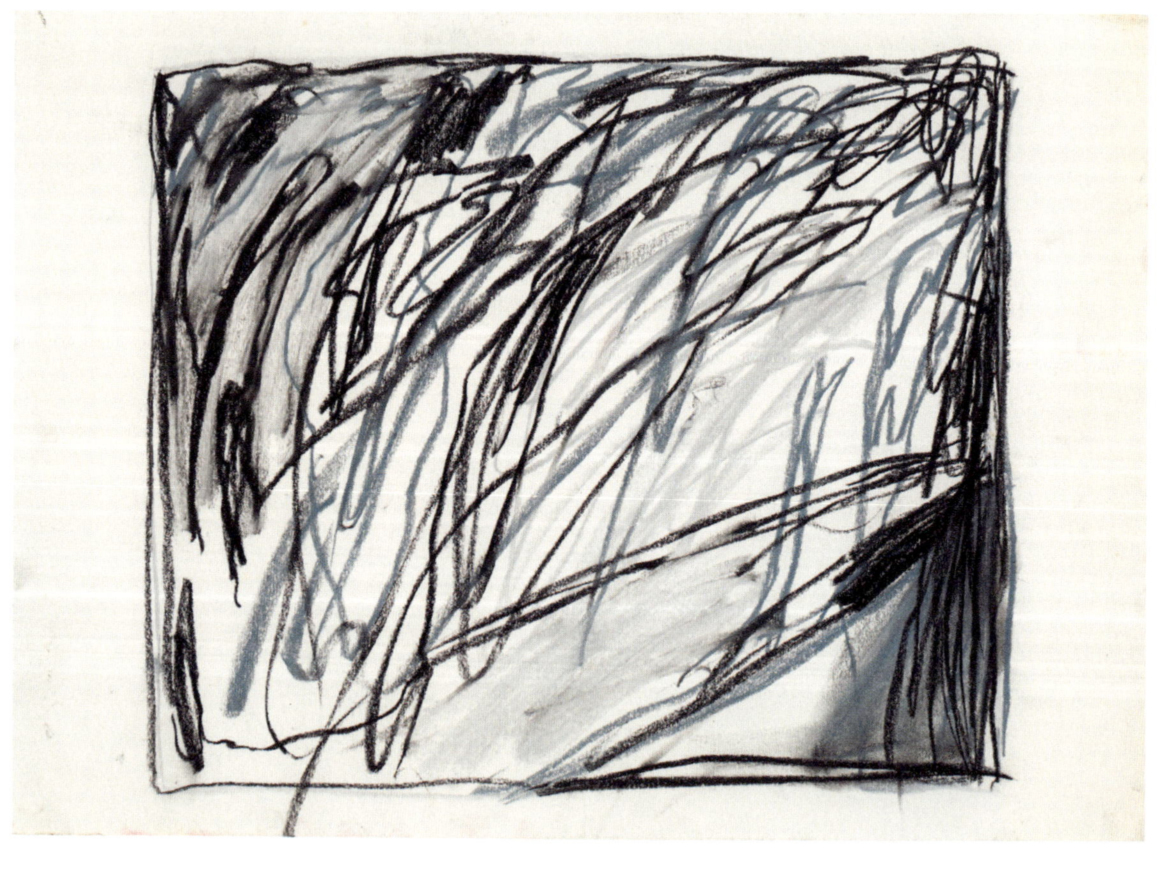

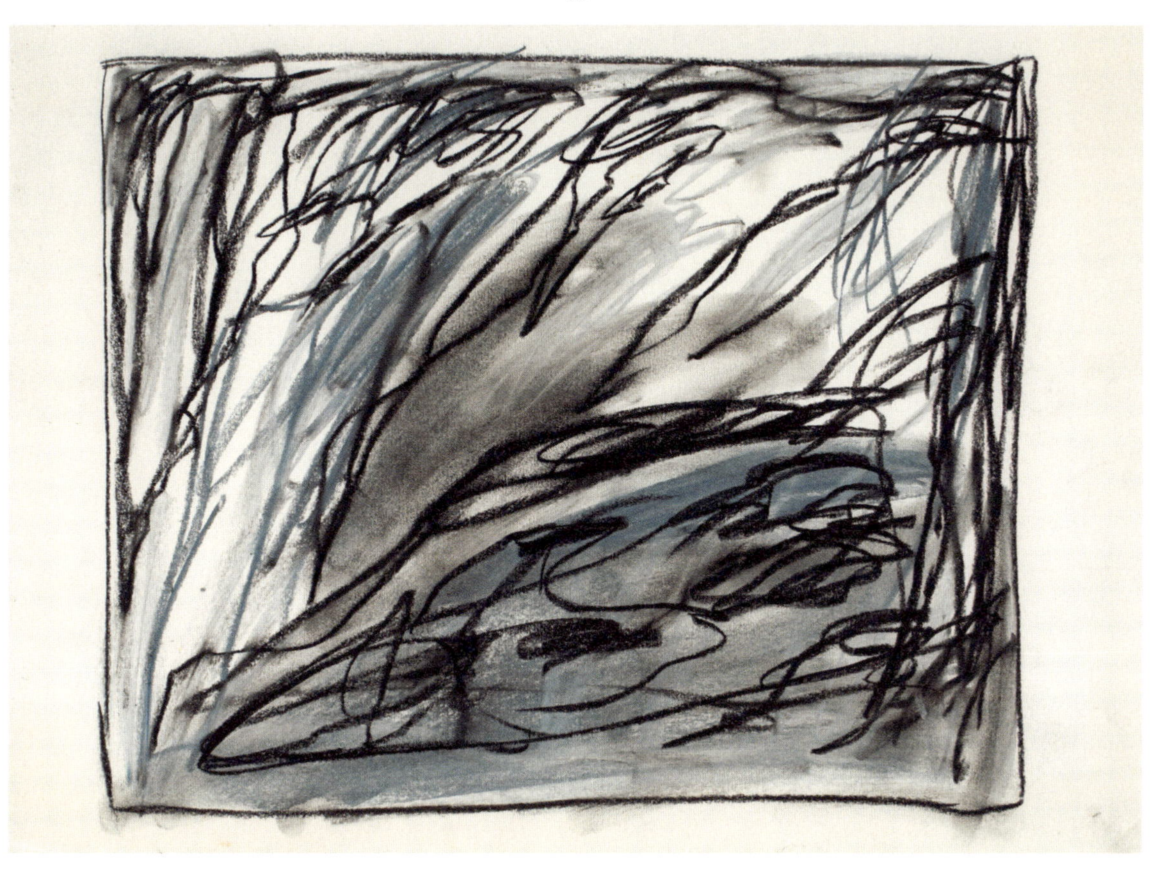

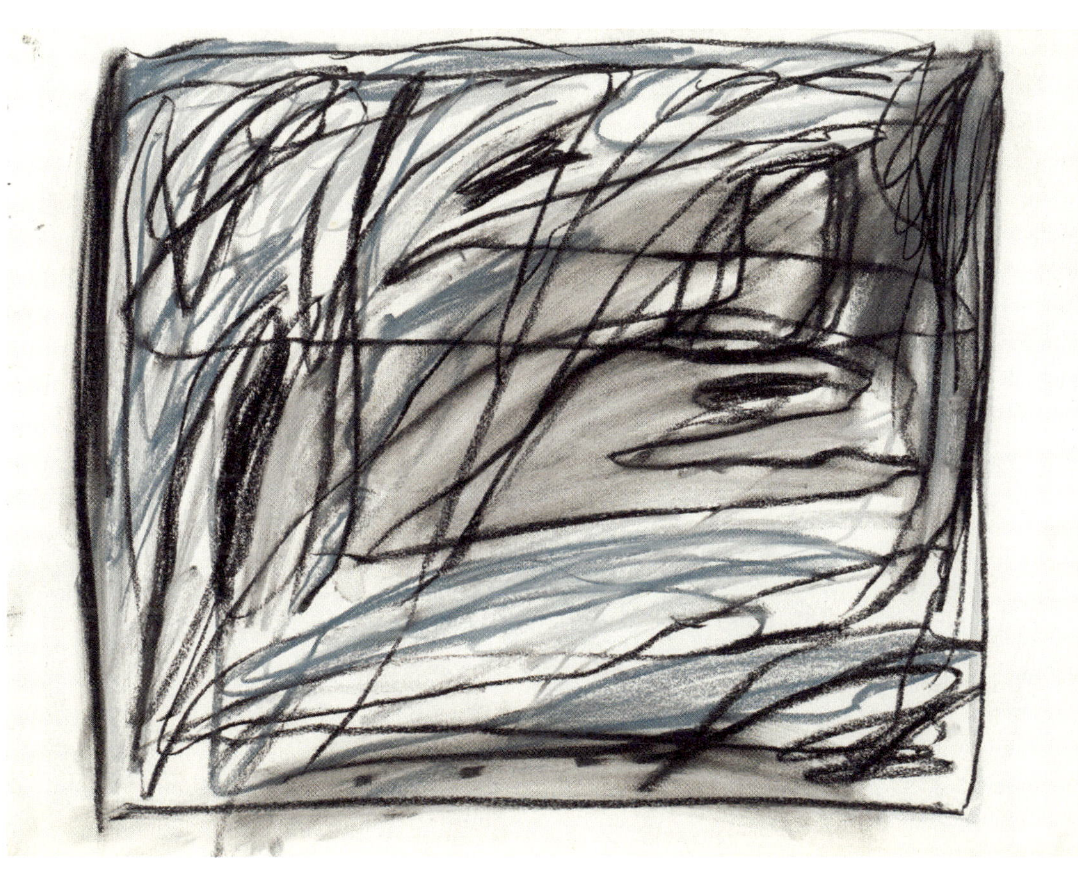

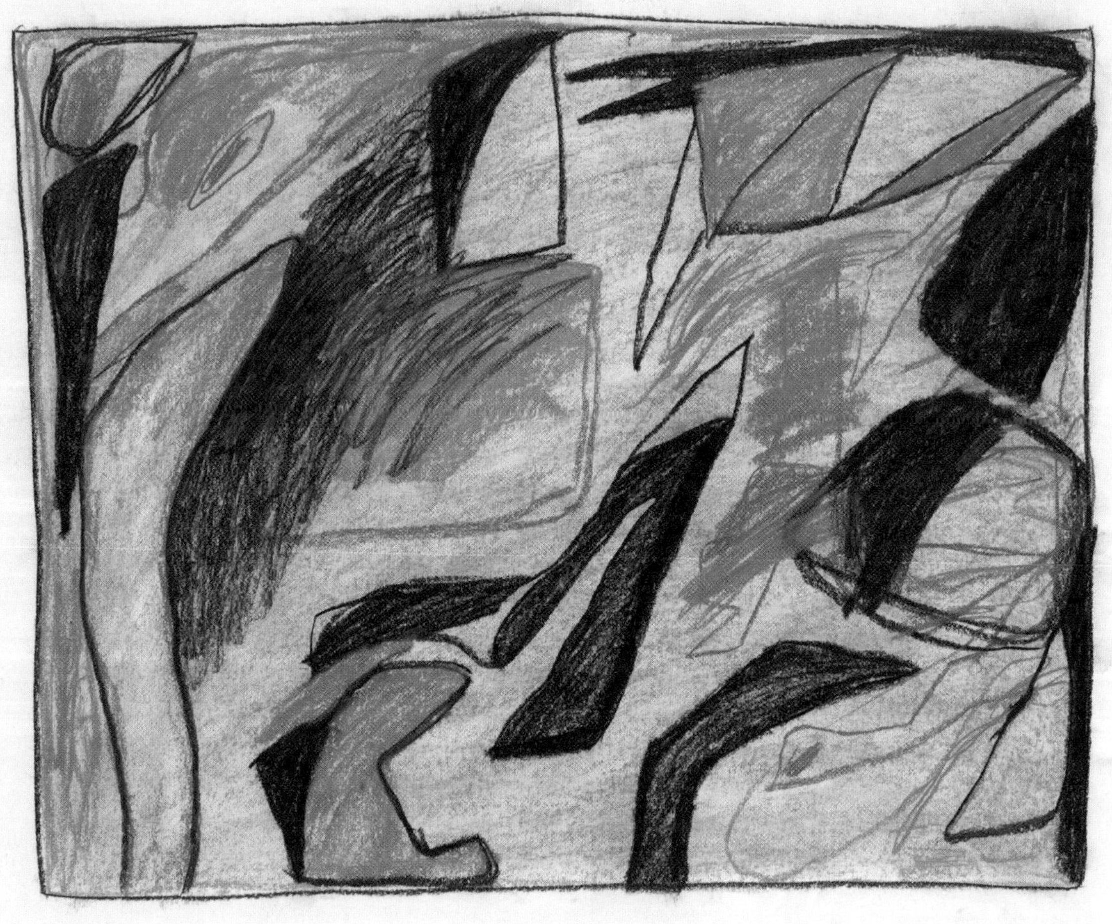

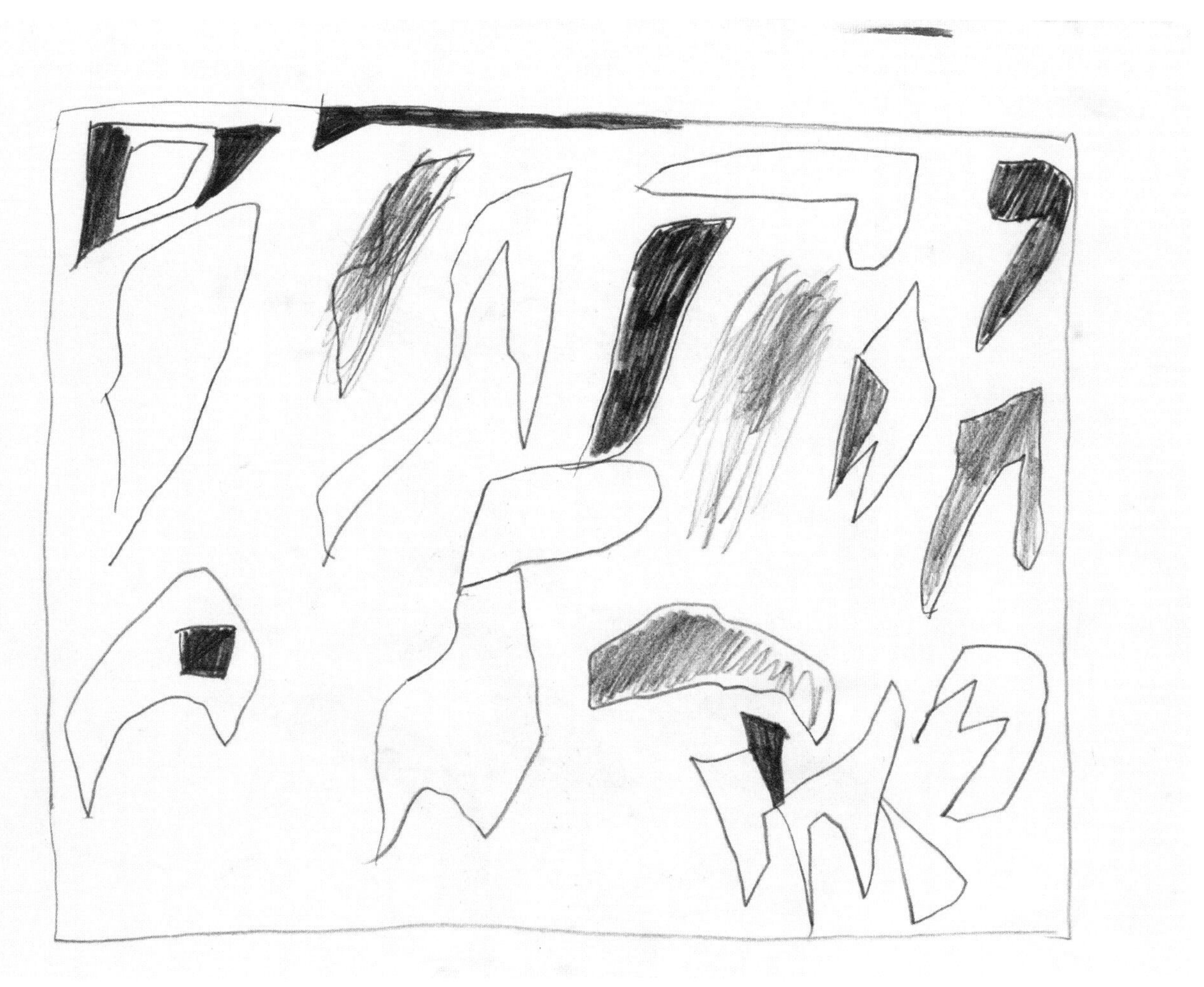

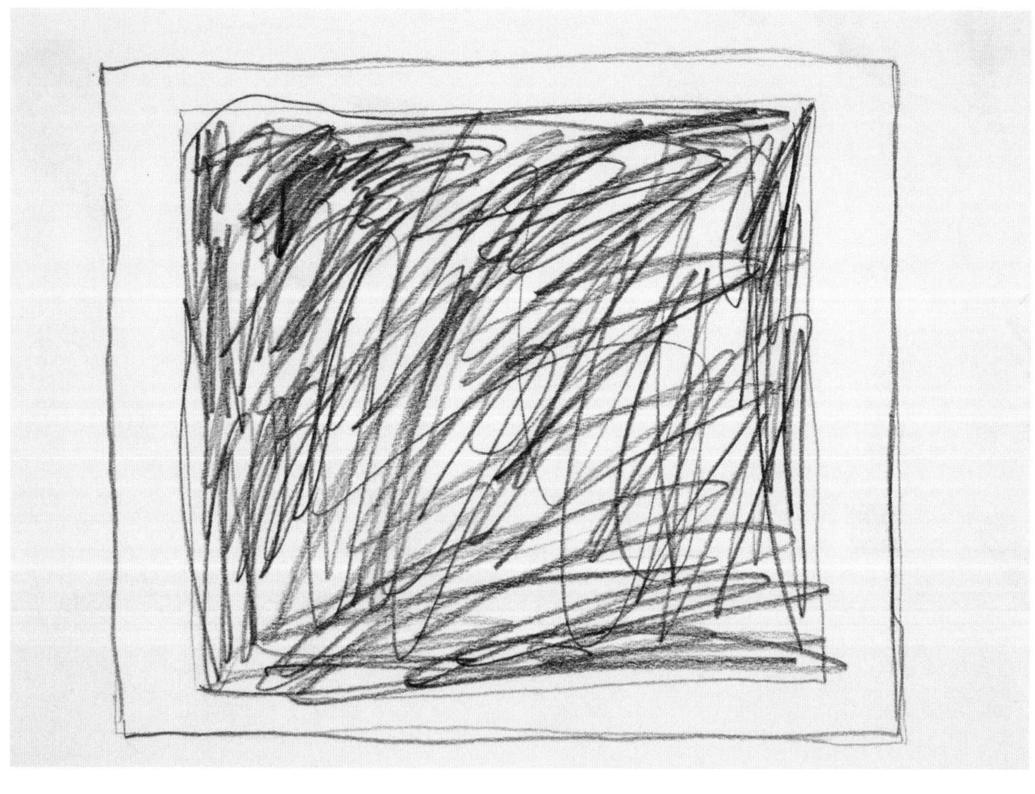

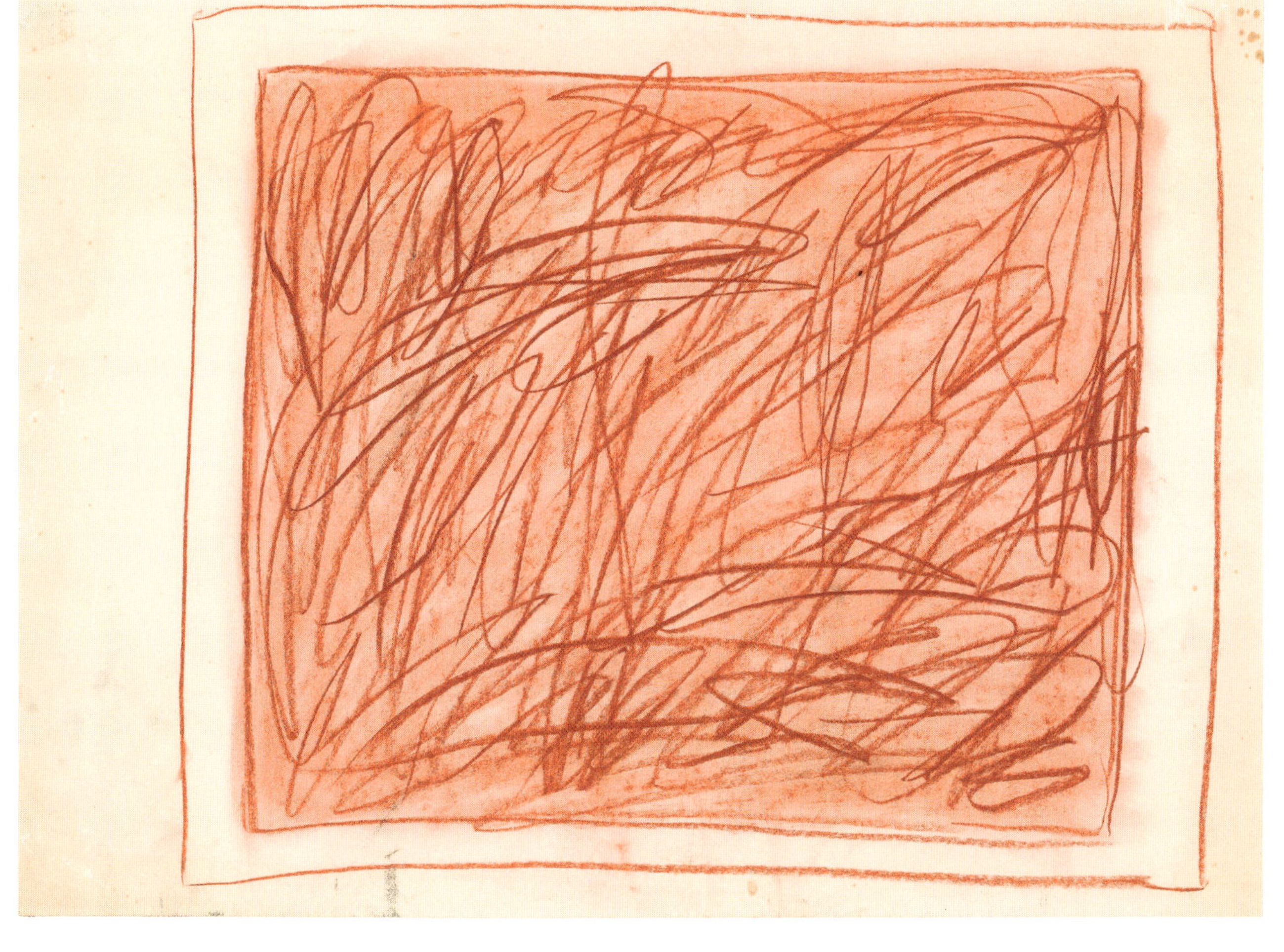

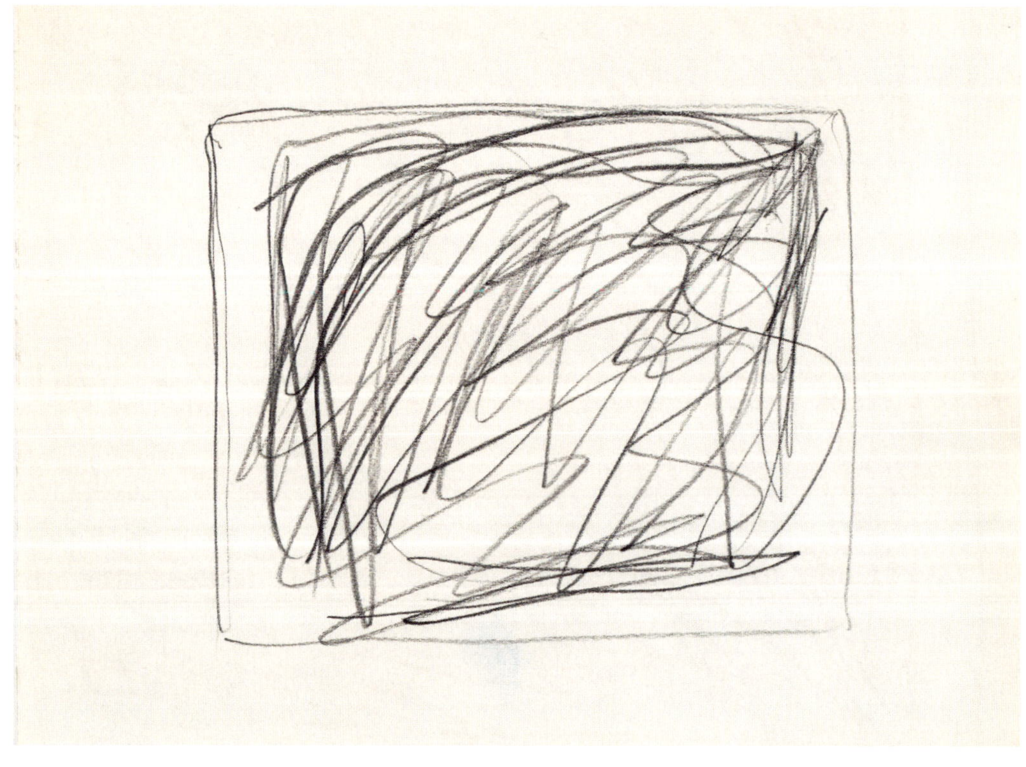

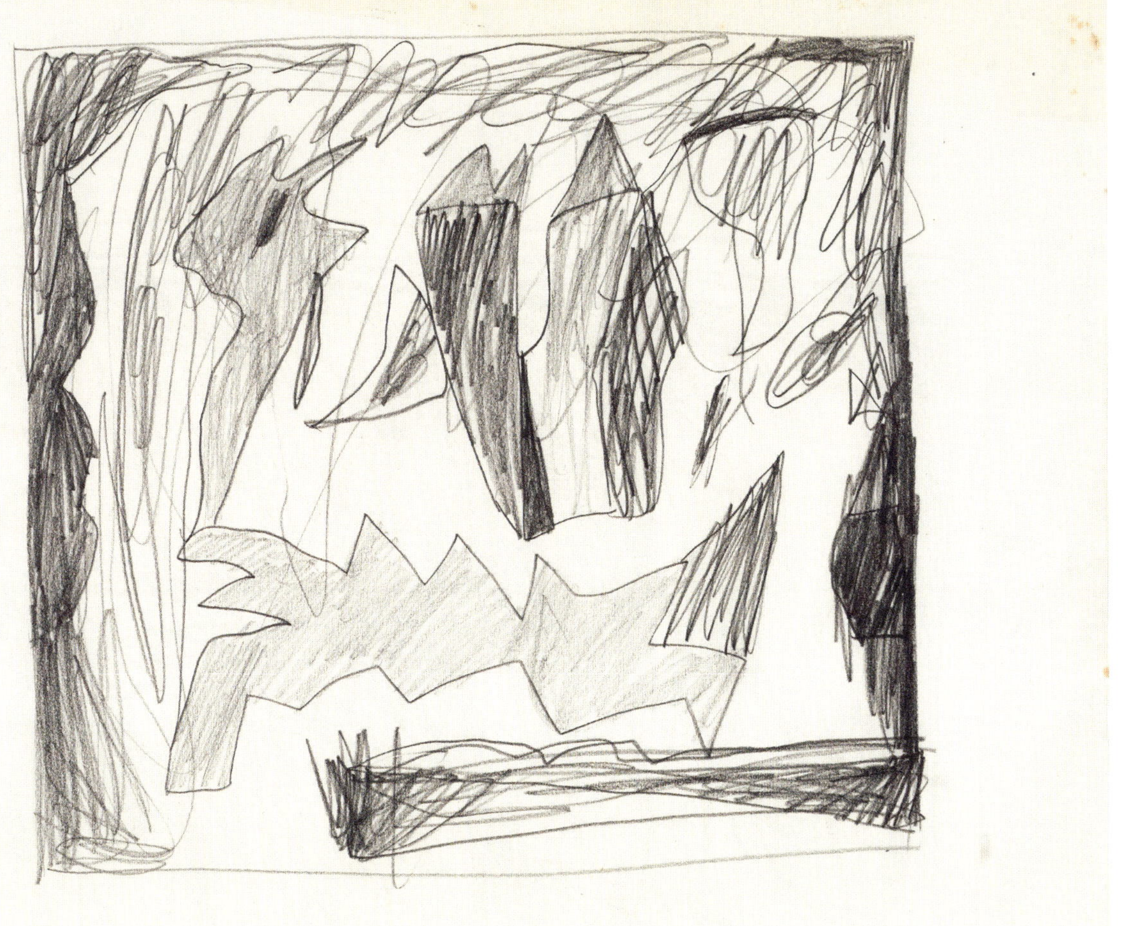

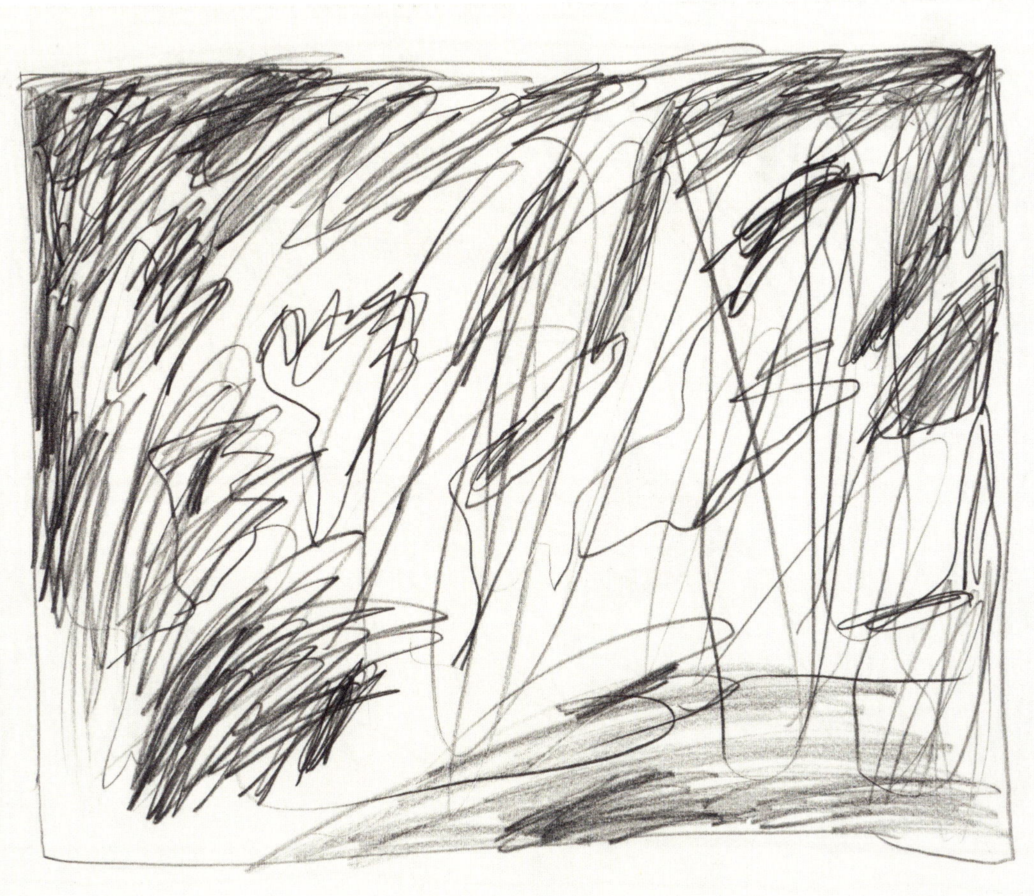

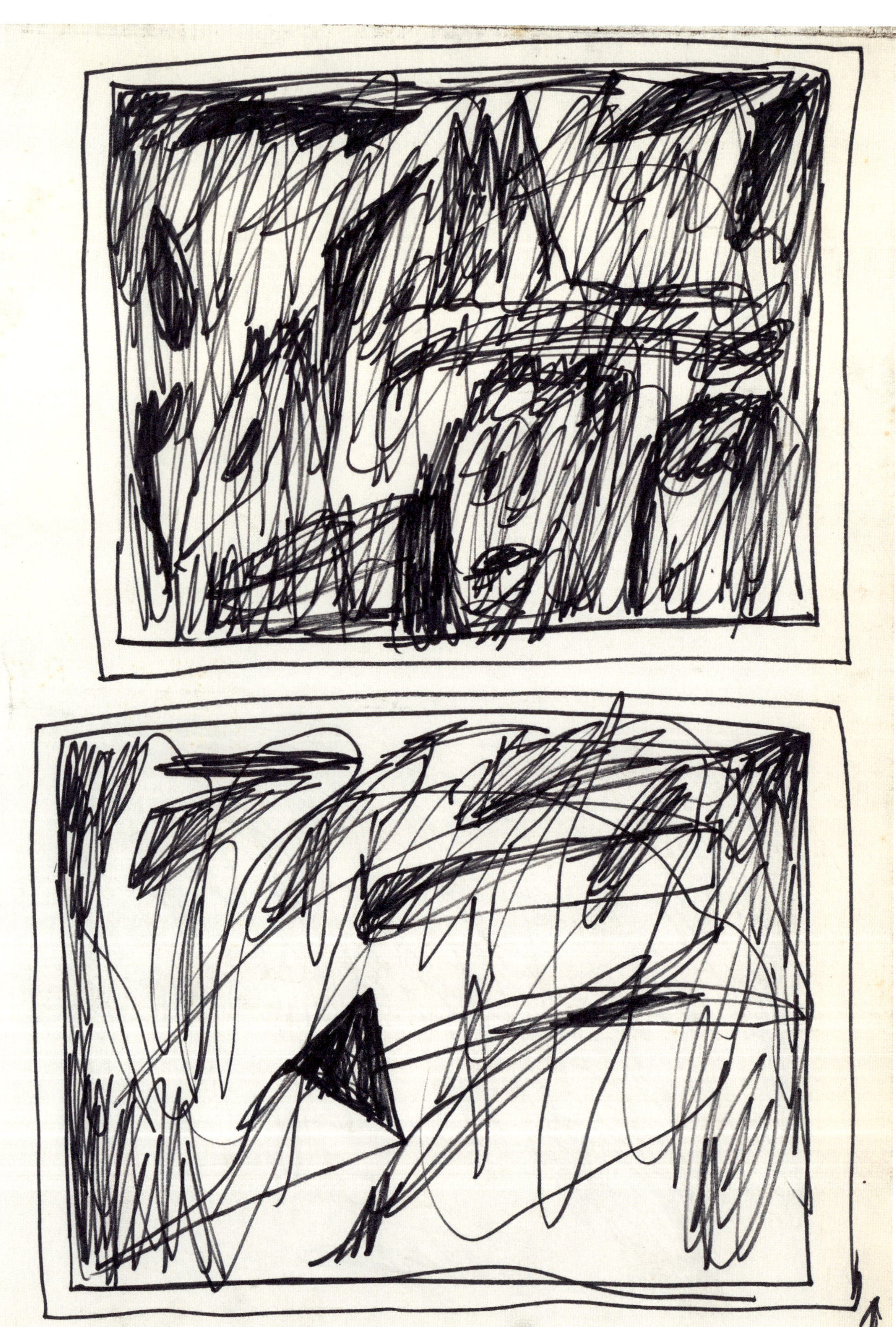

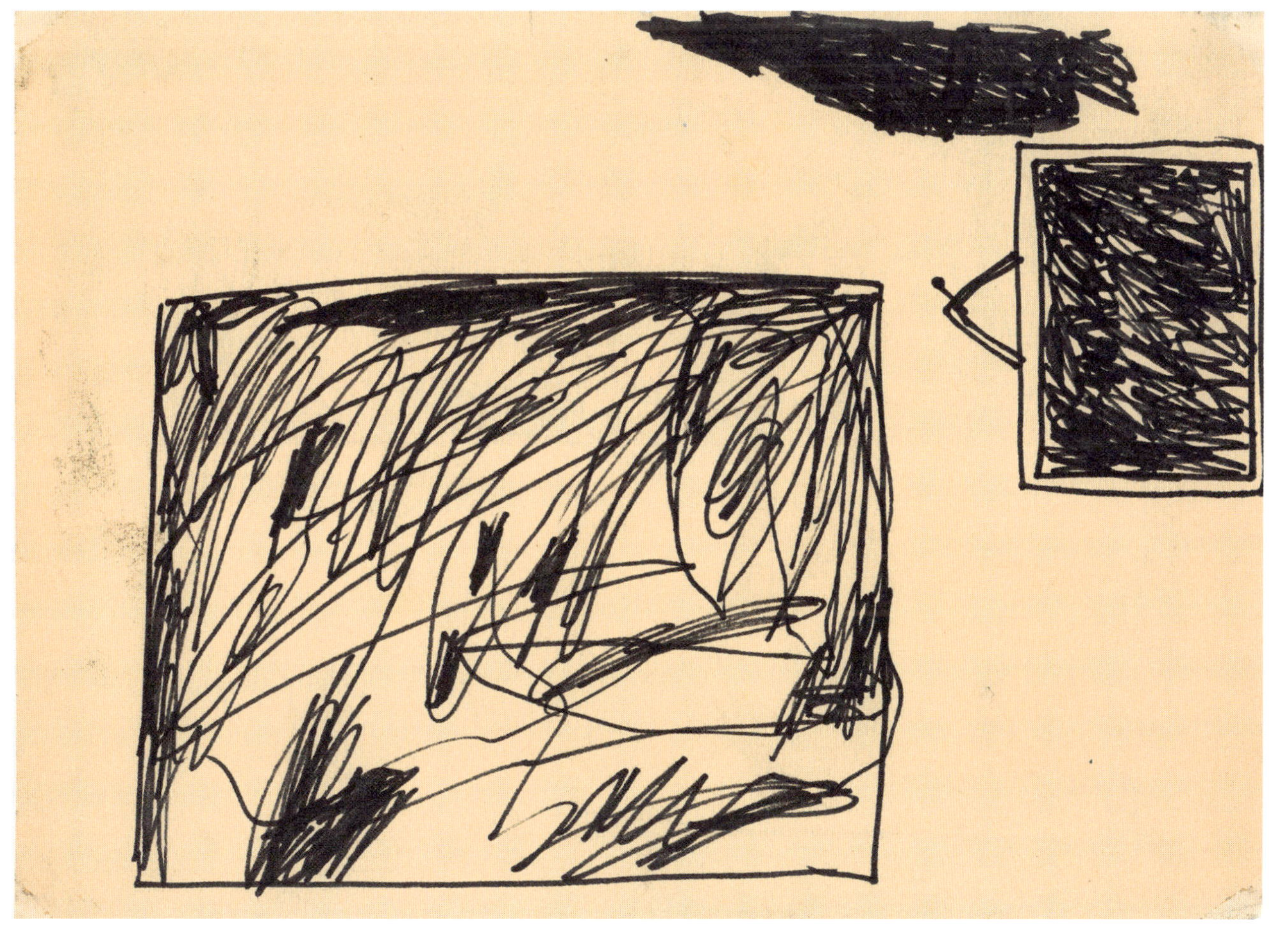

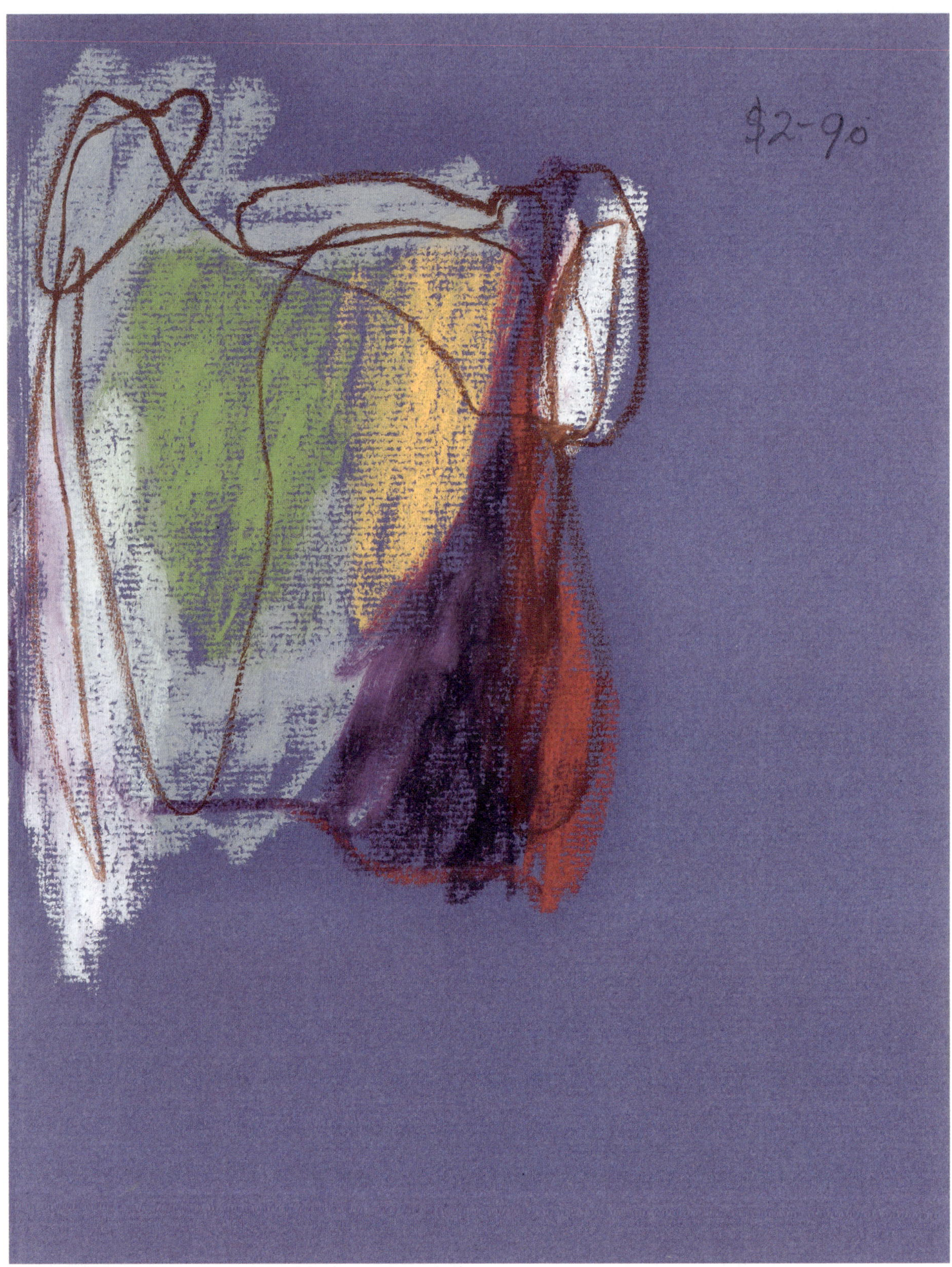
$2-90

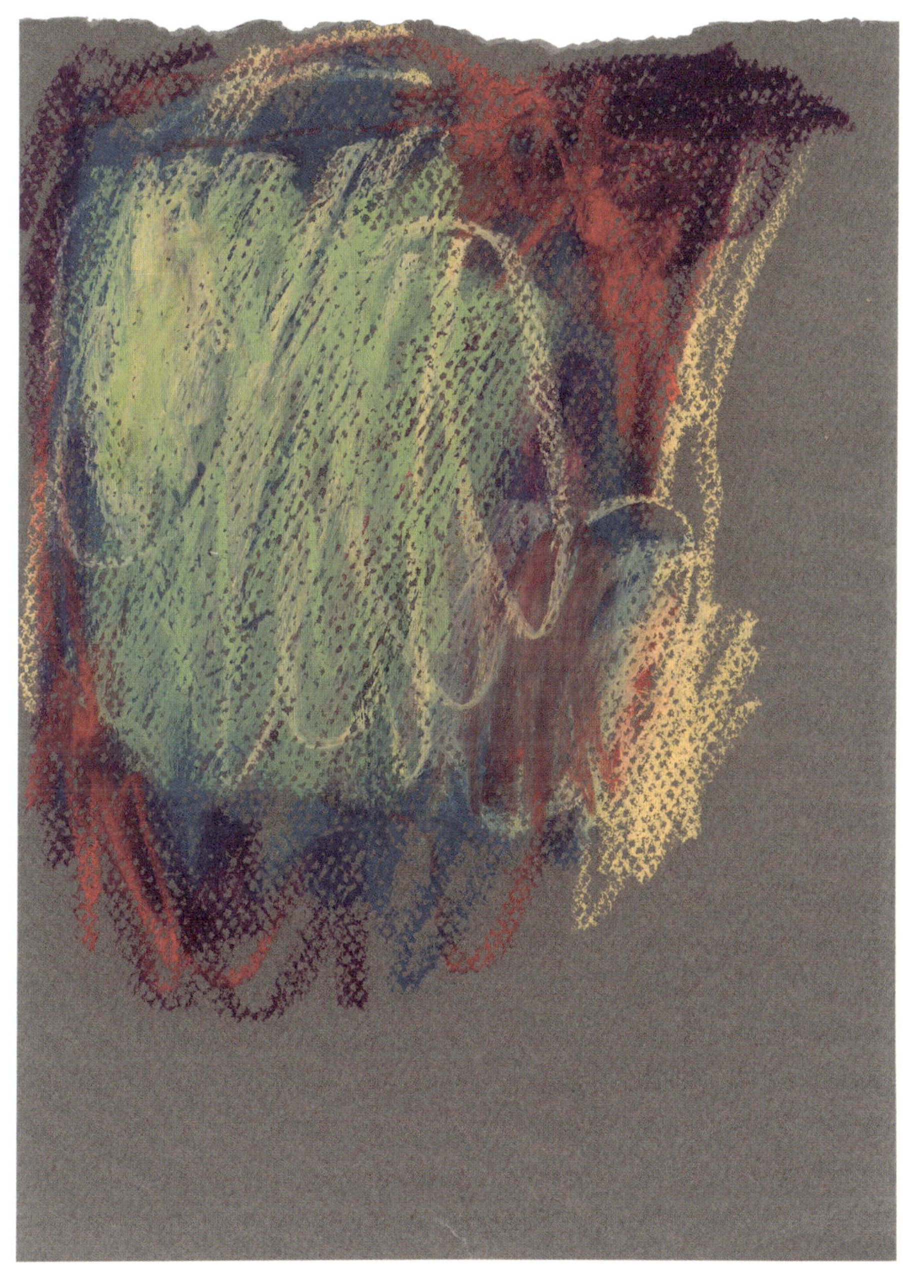

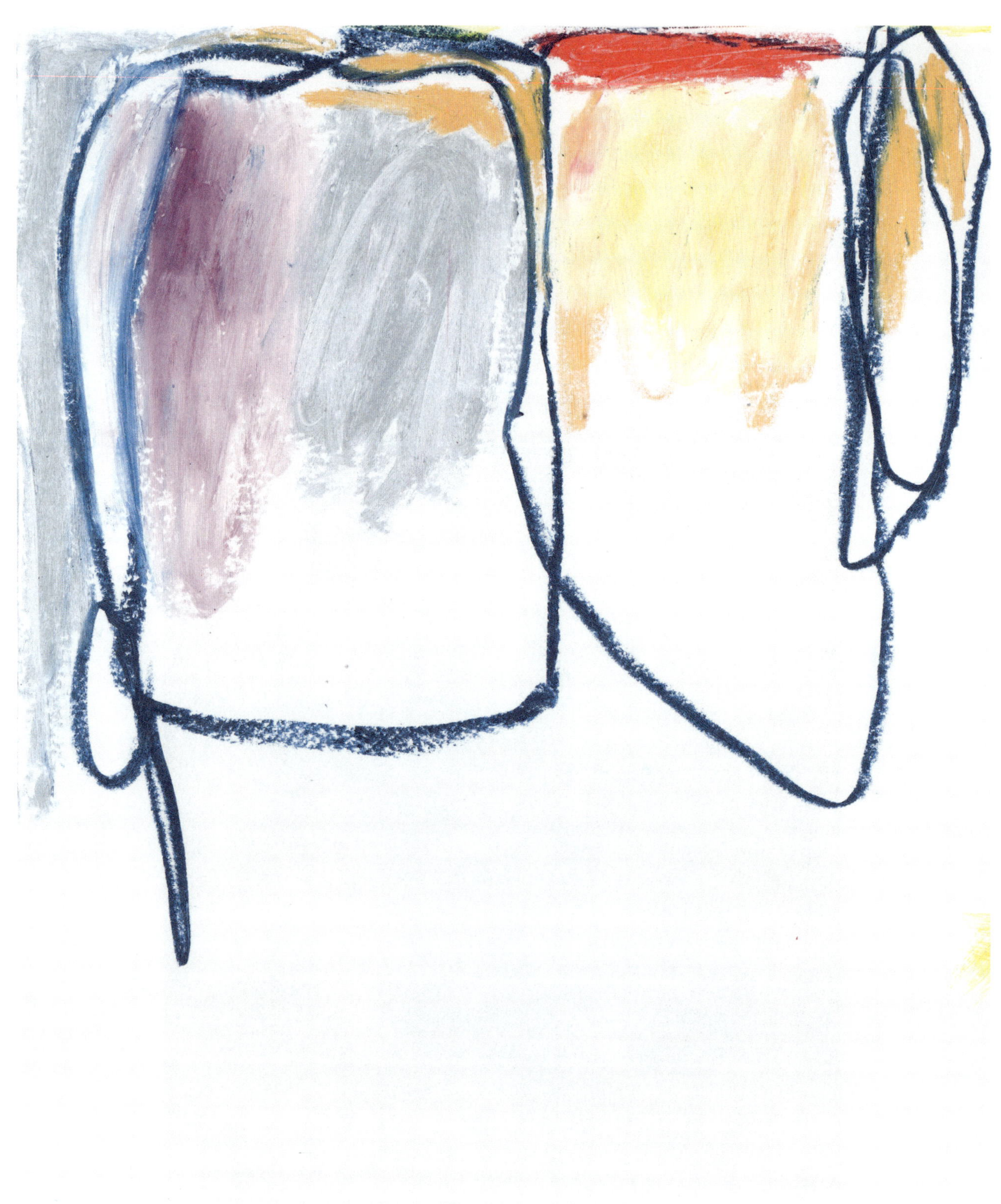

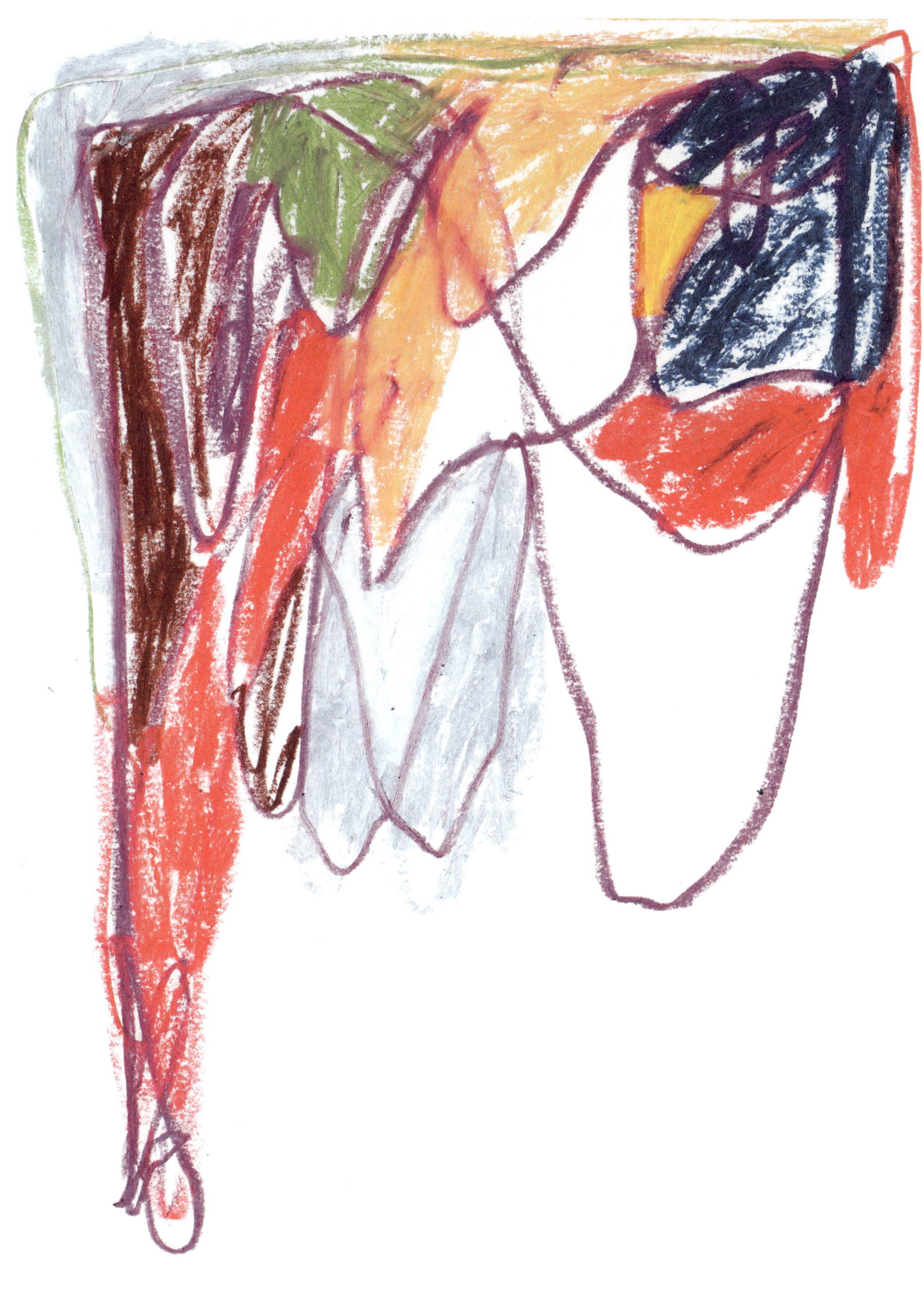

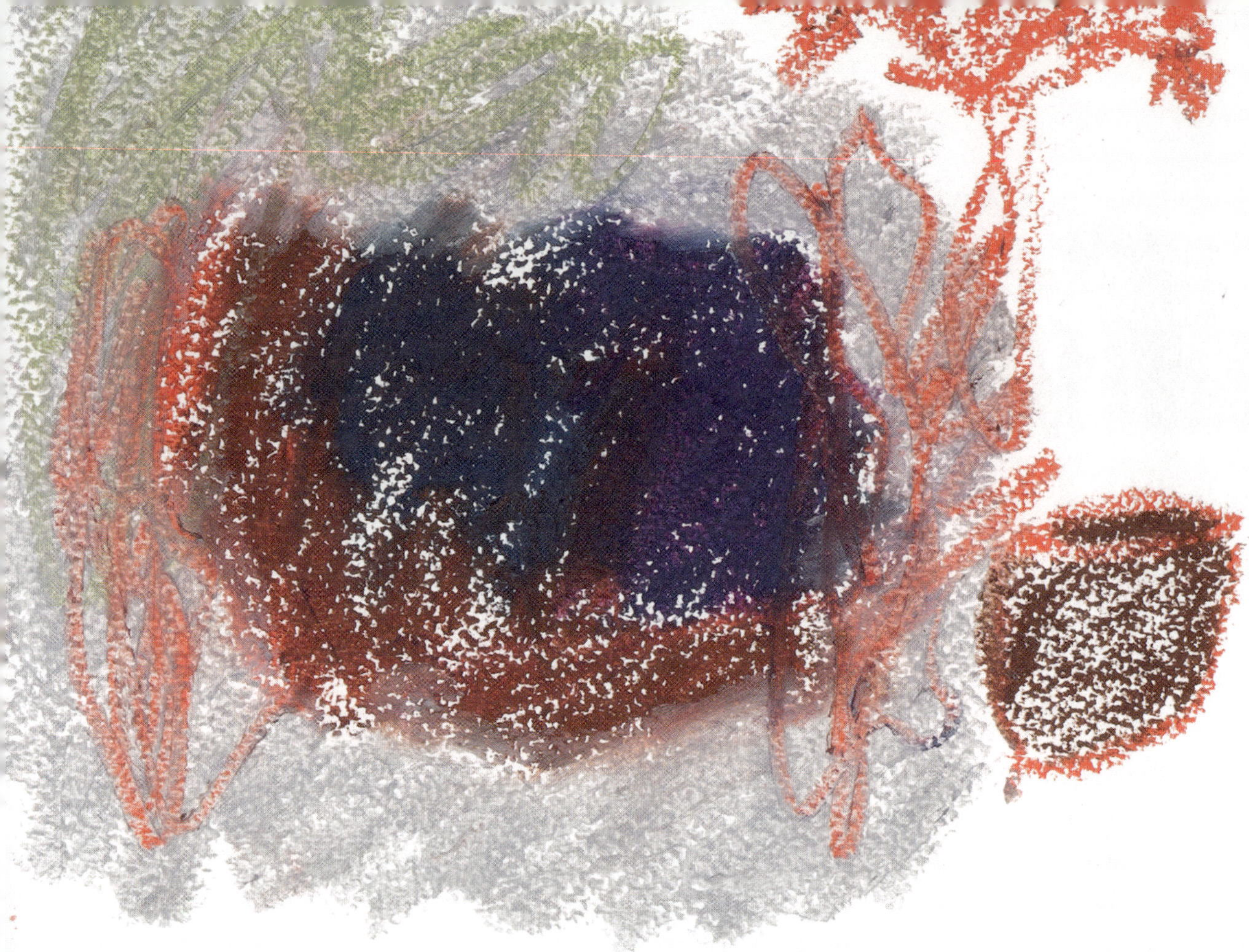

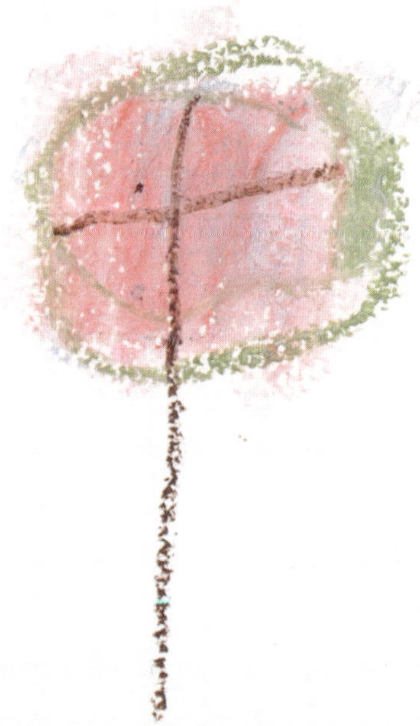

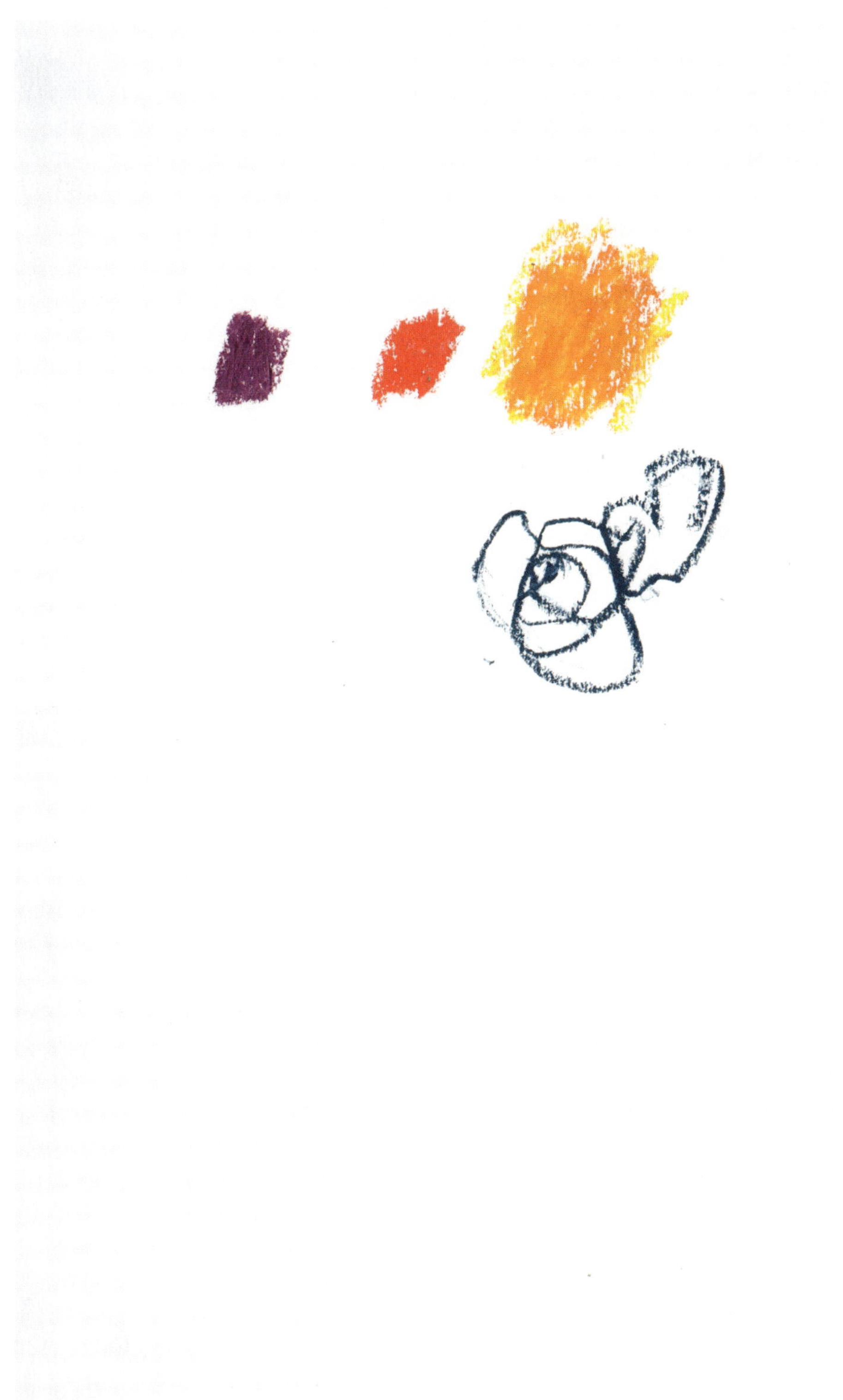

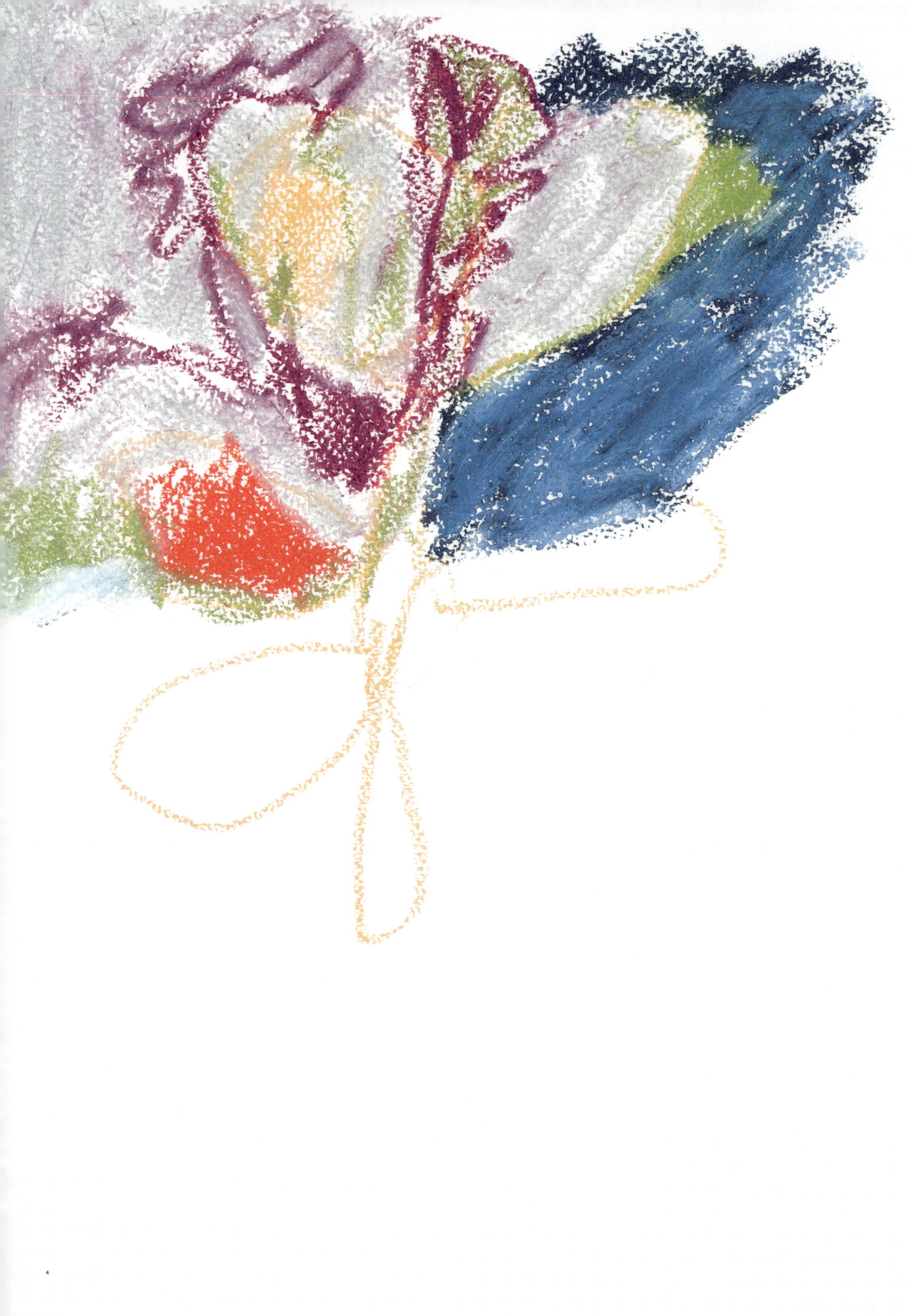

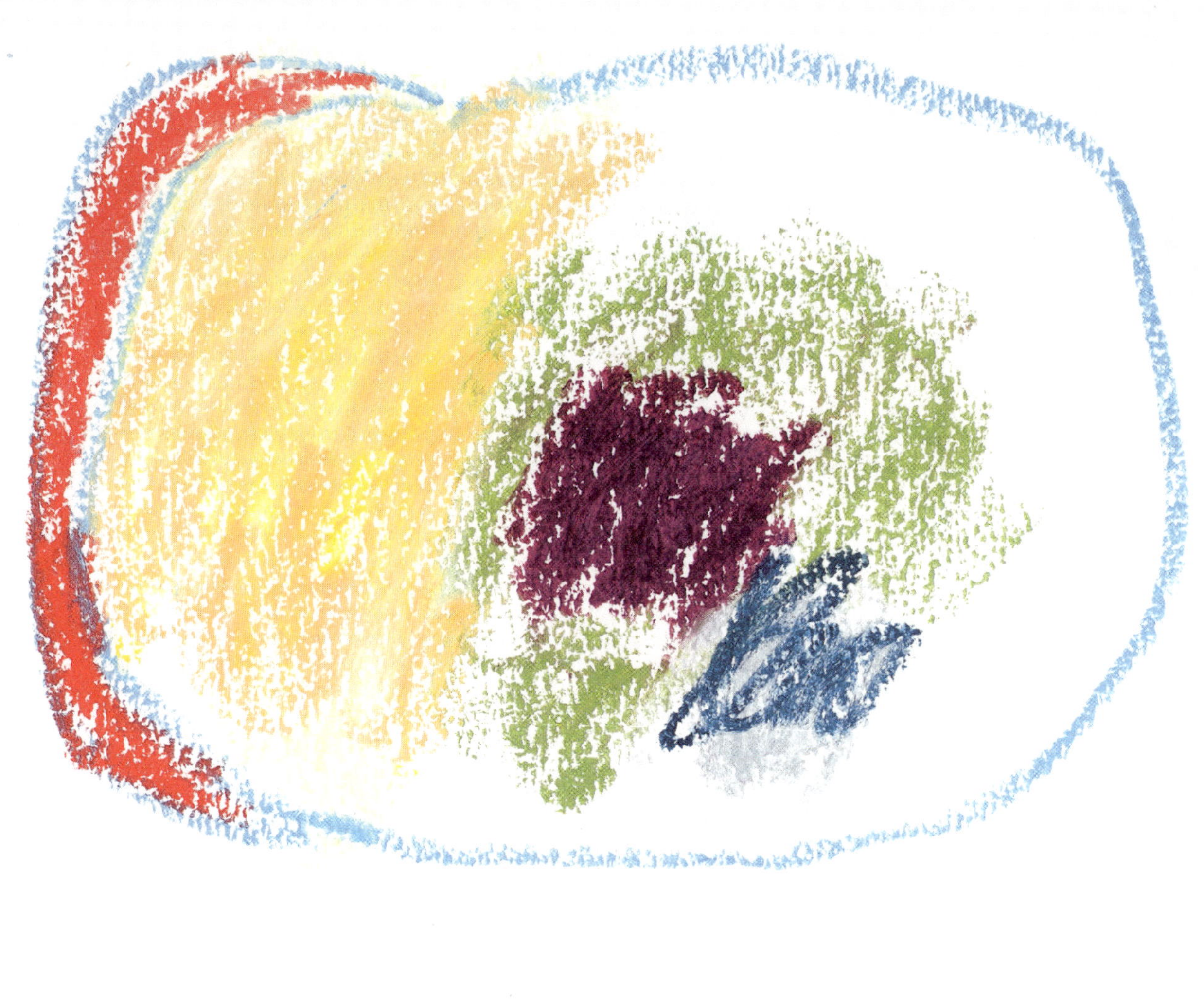

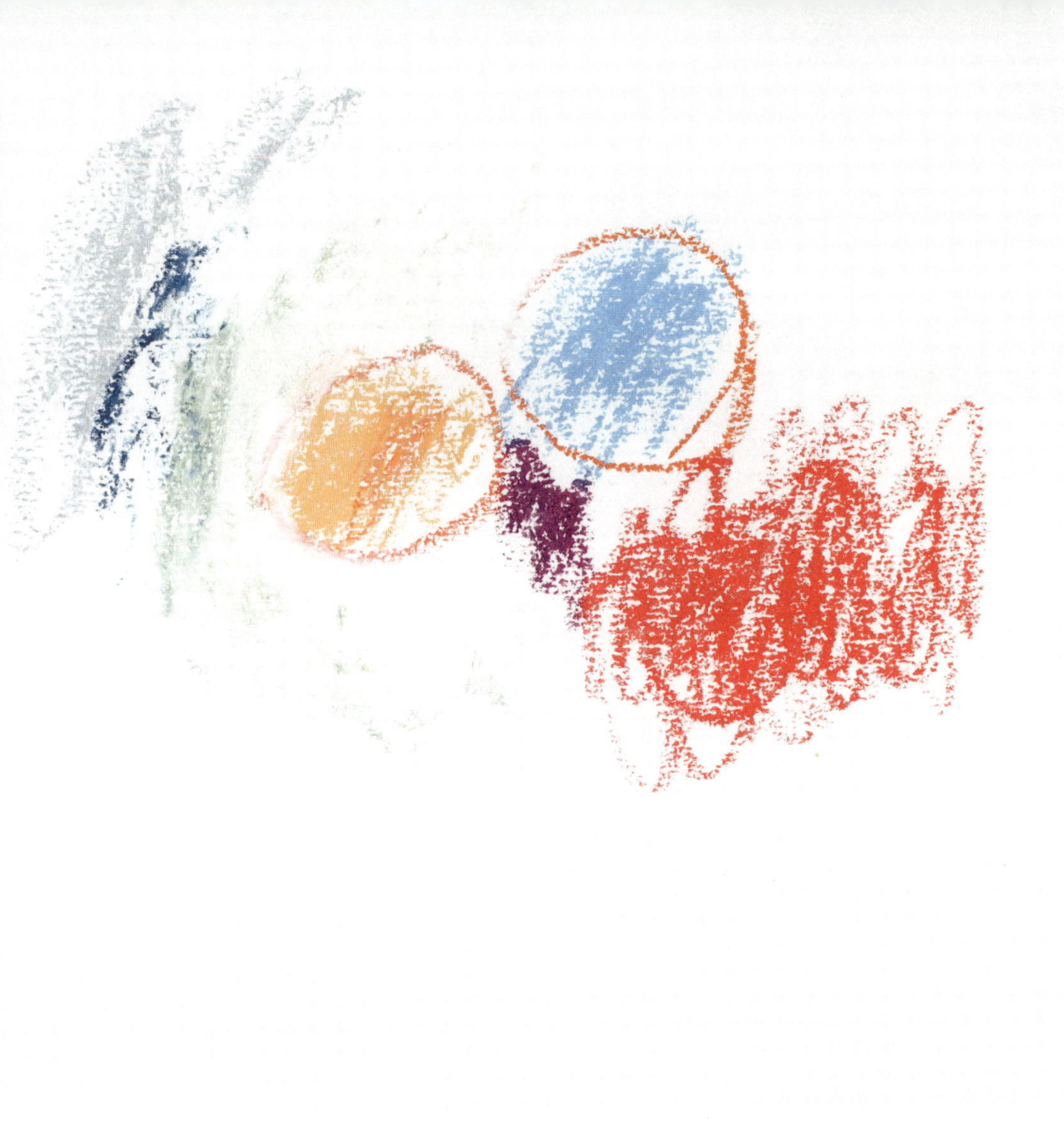

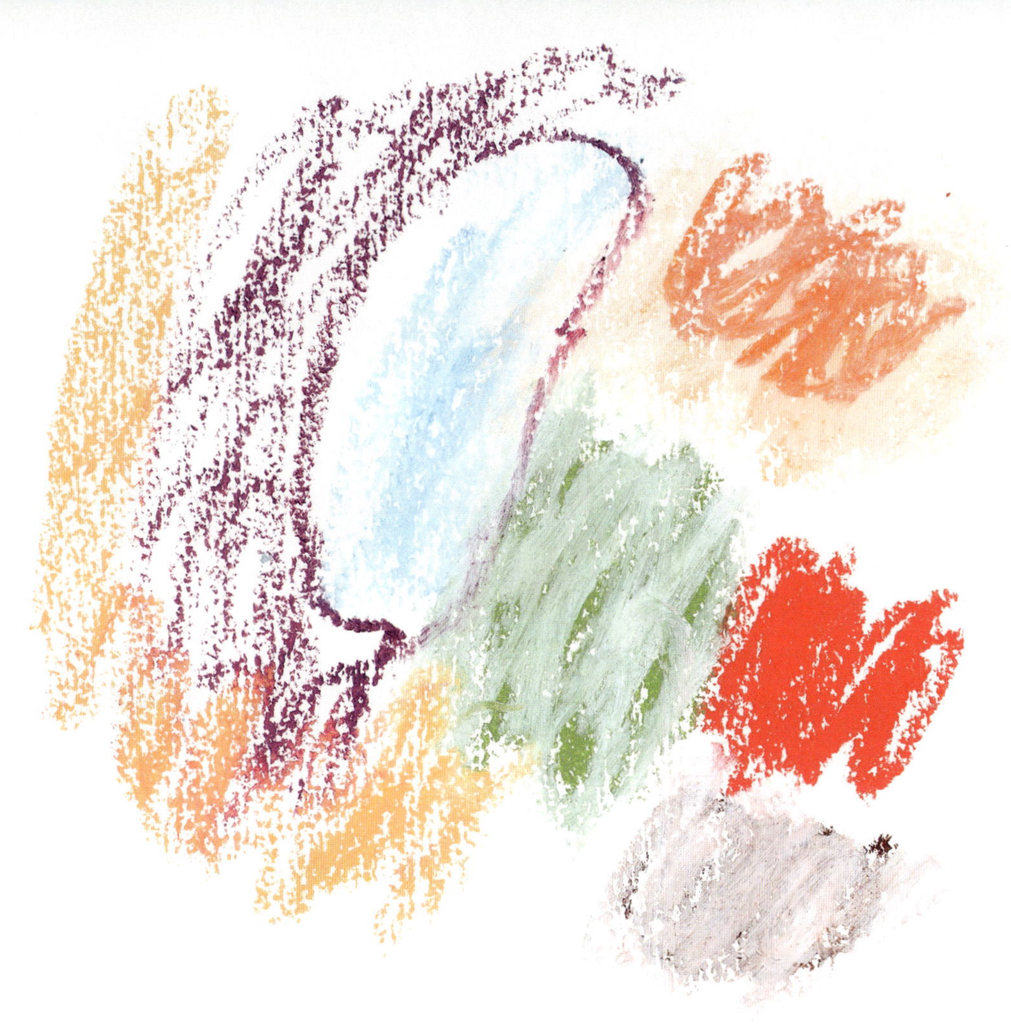

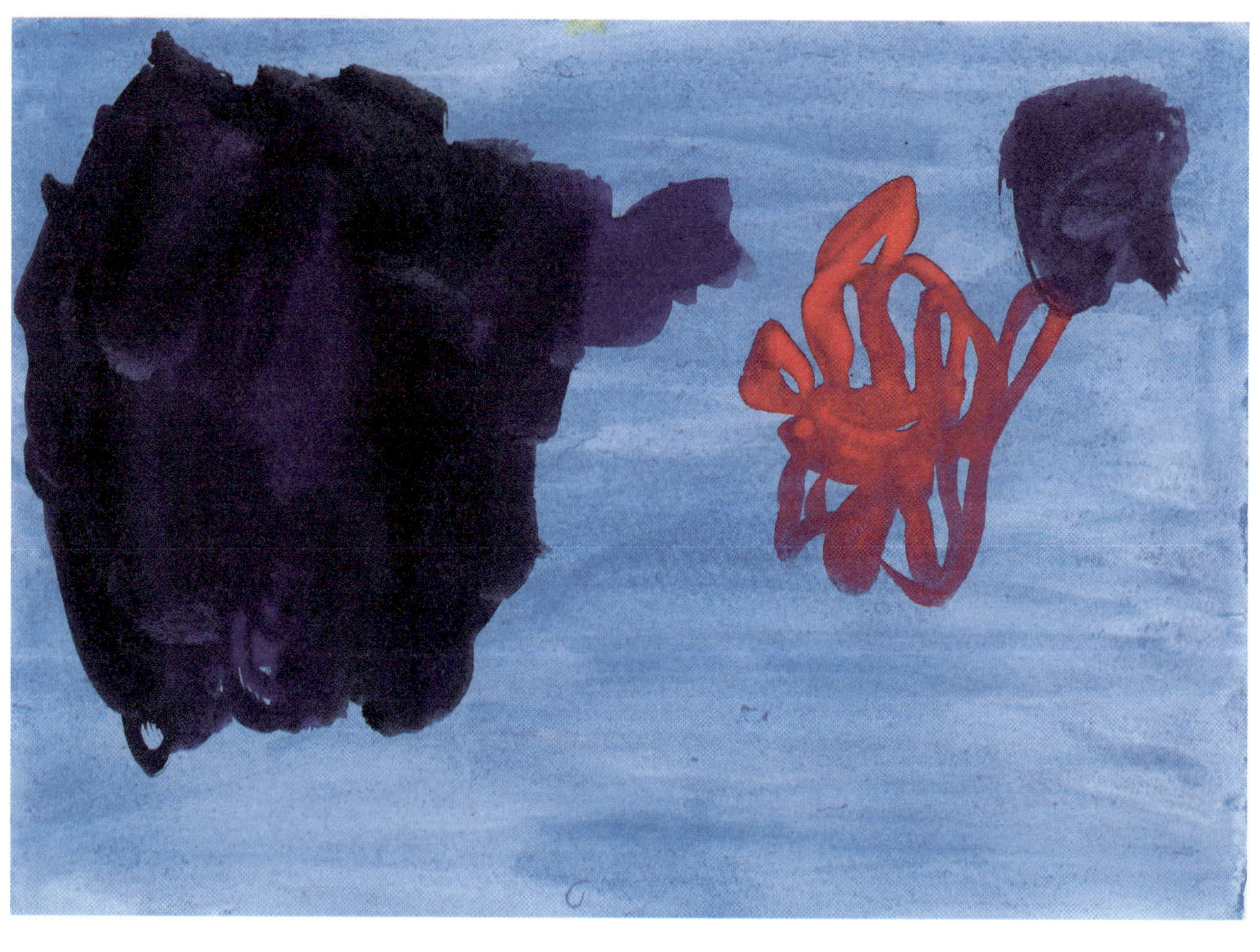

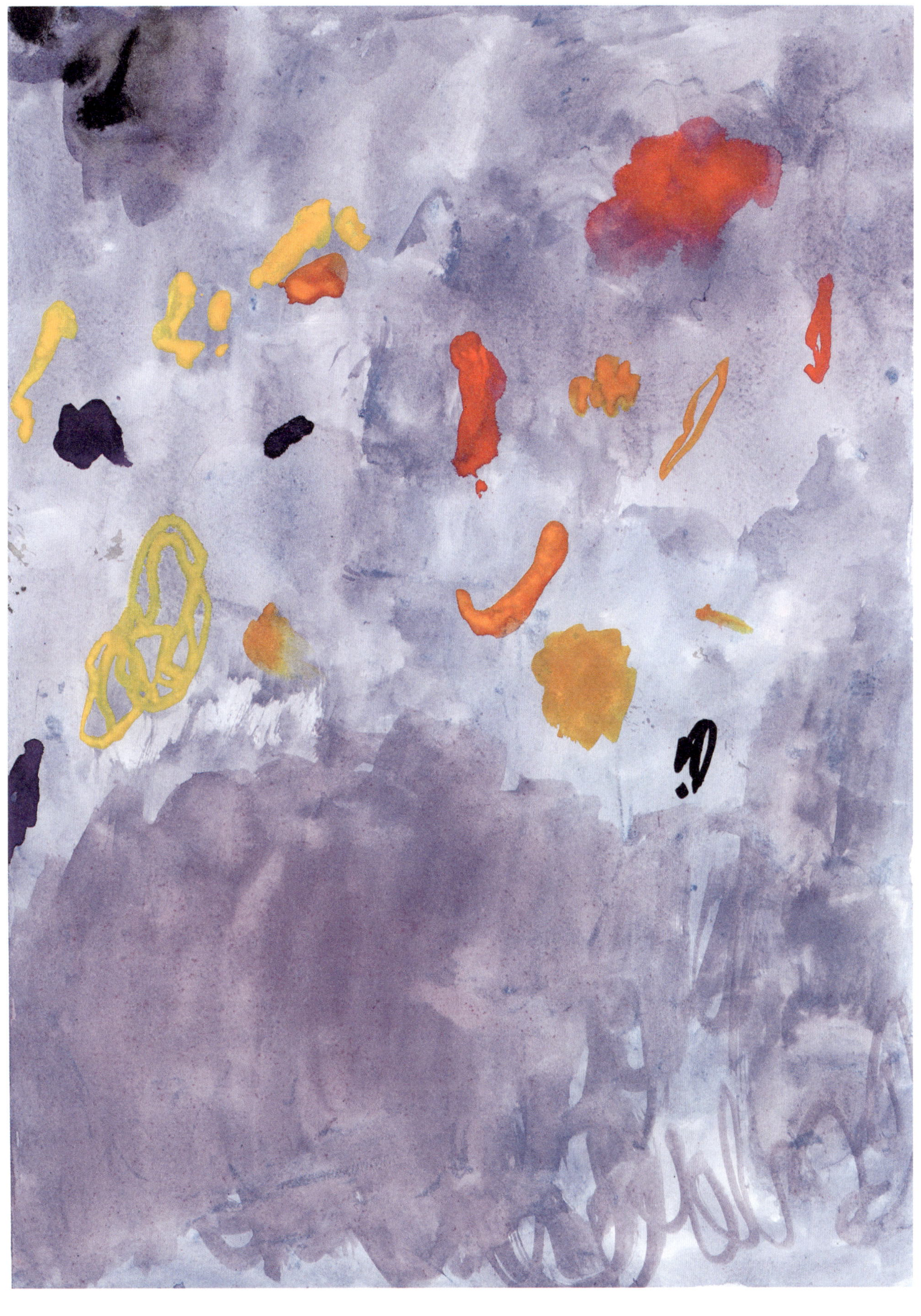

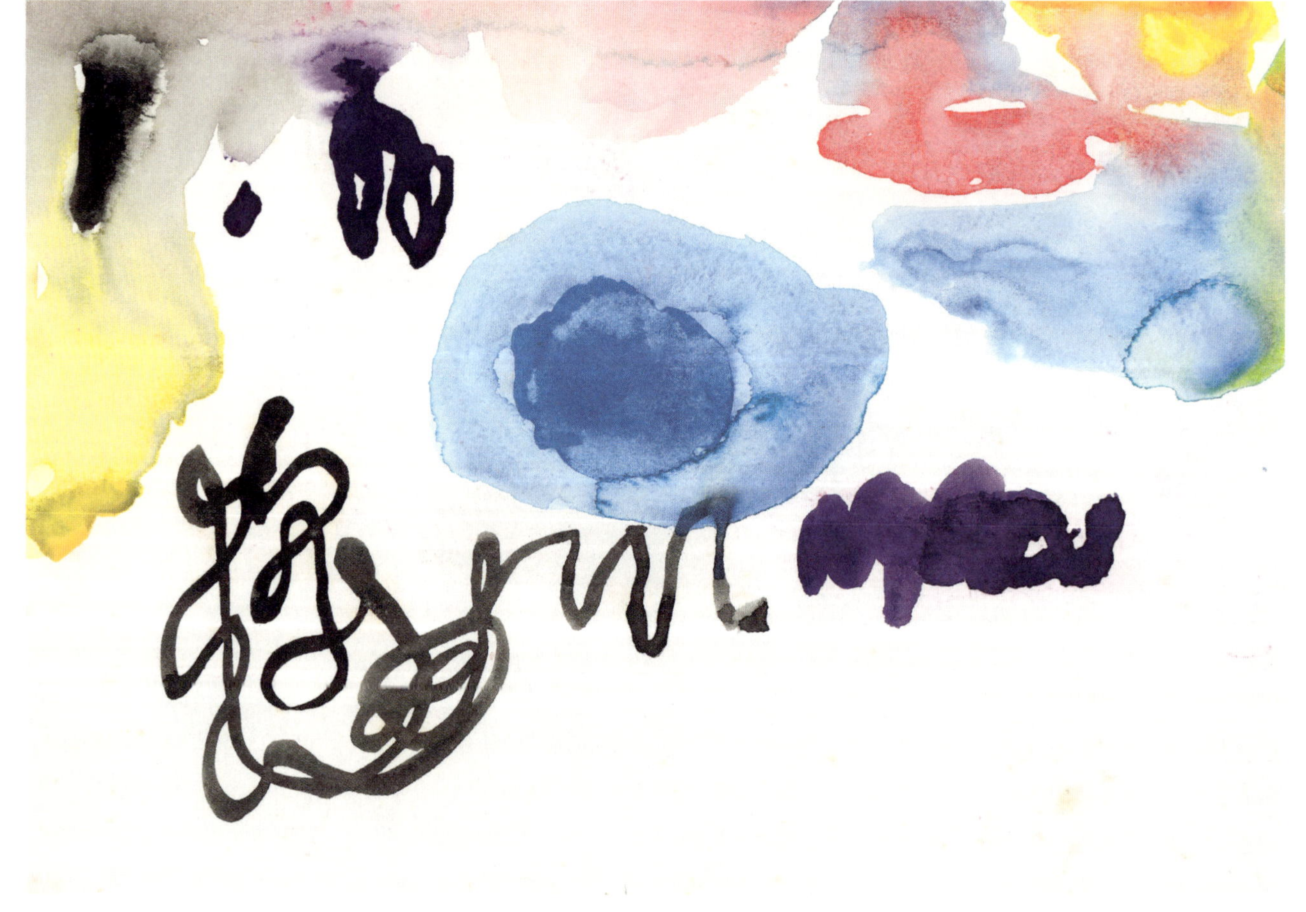

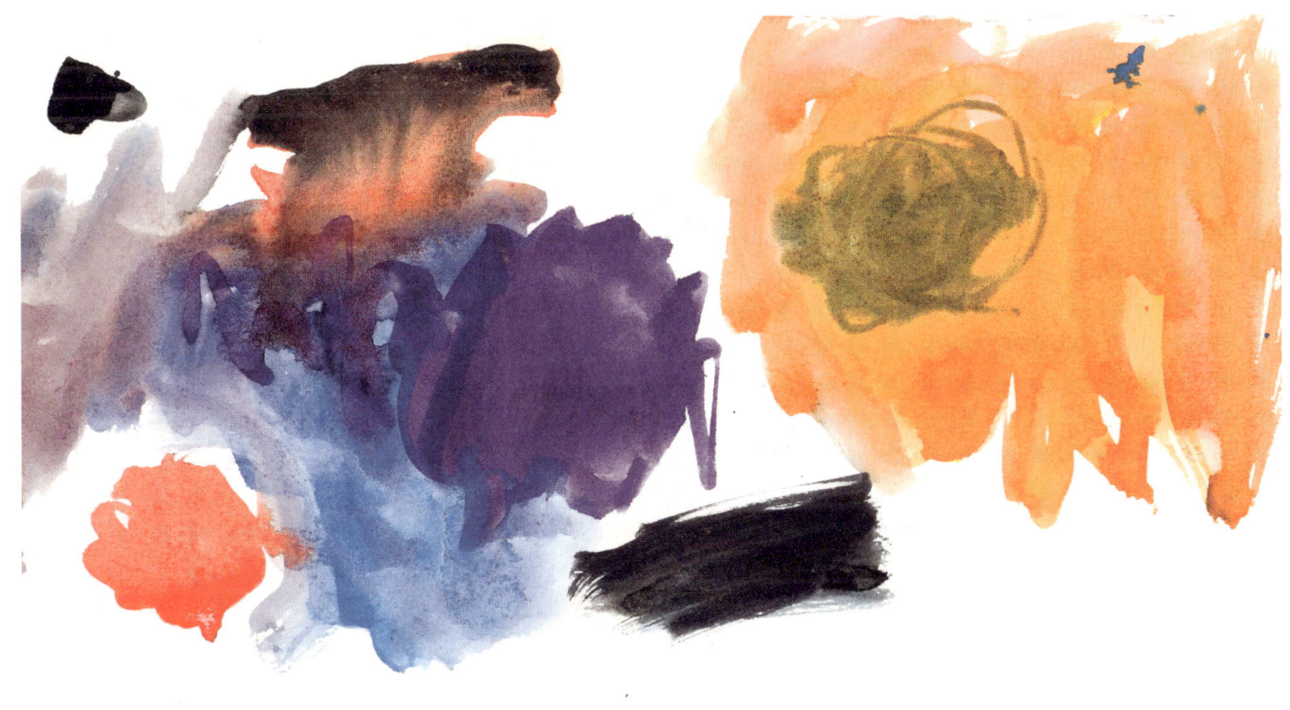

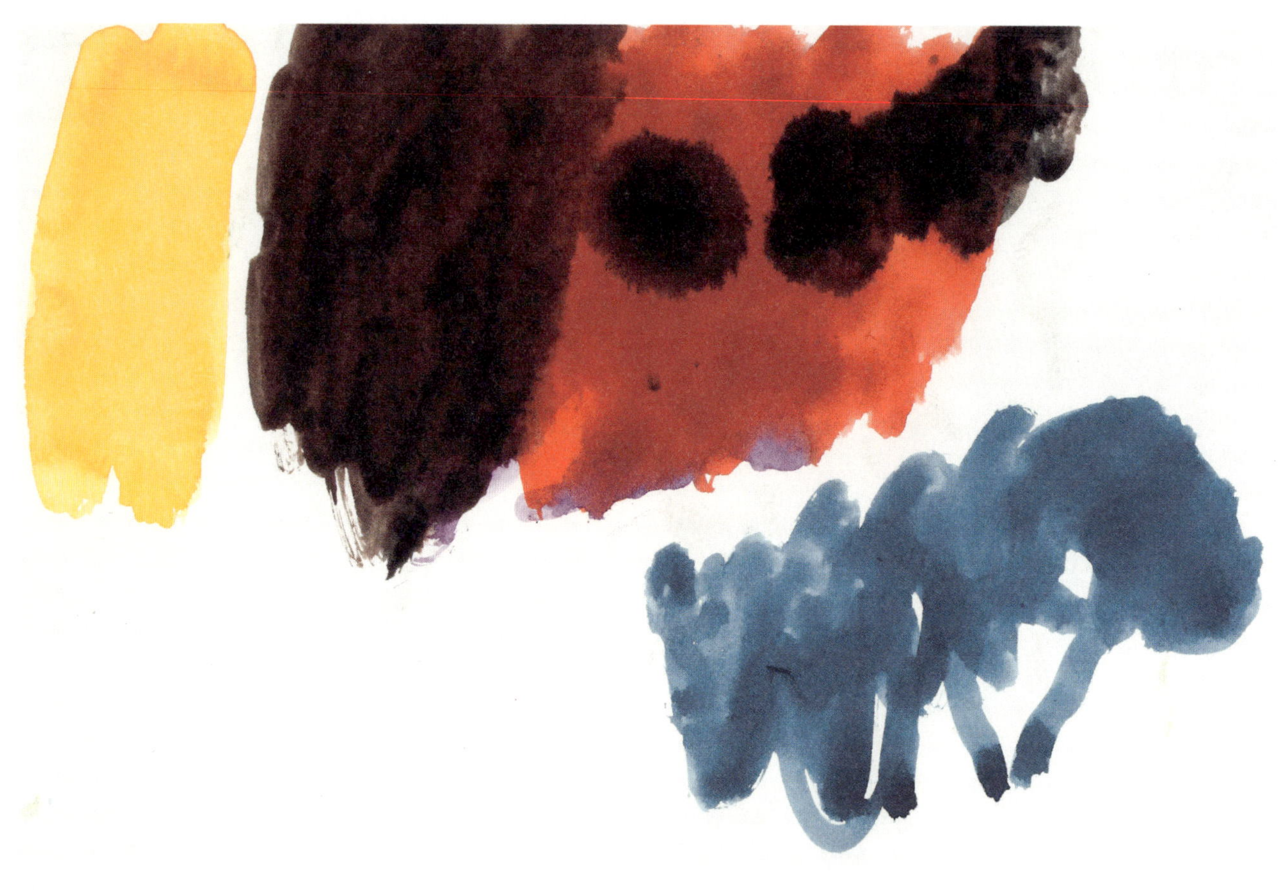

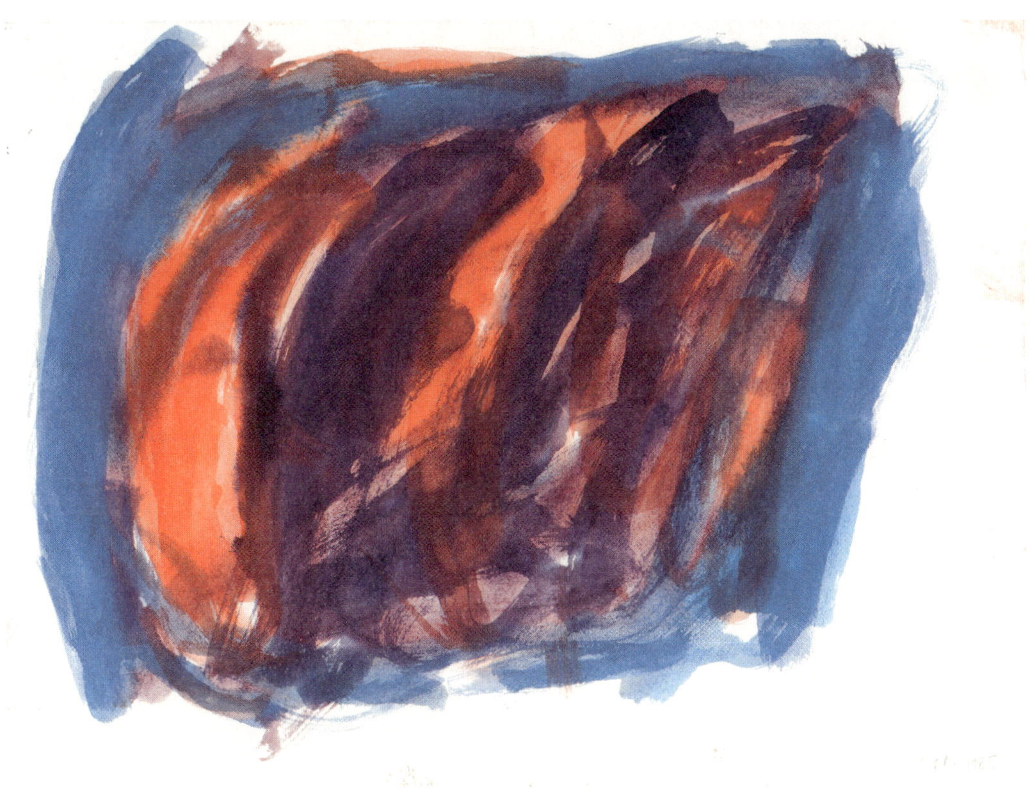

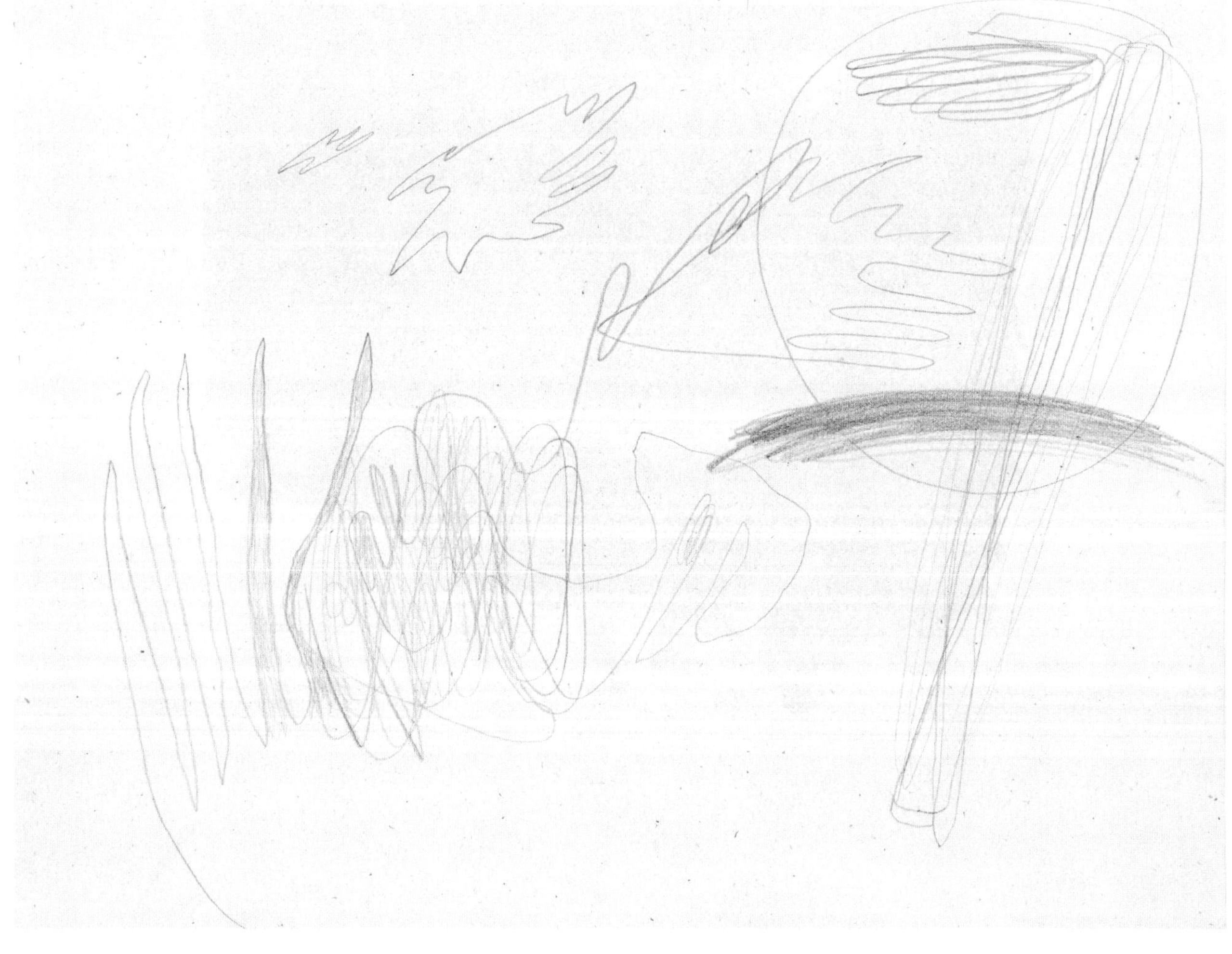

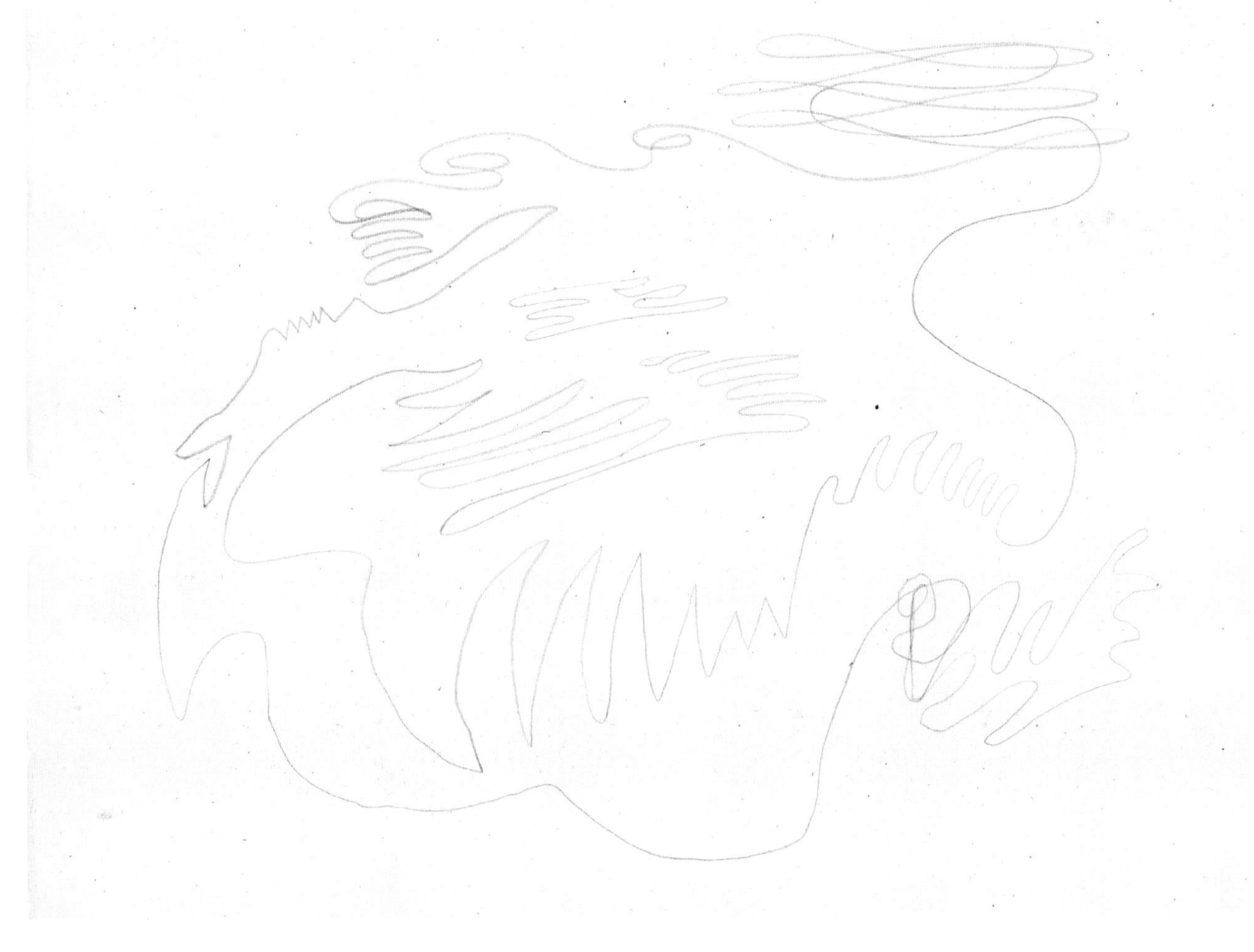

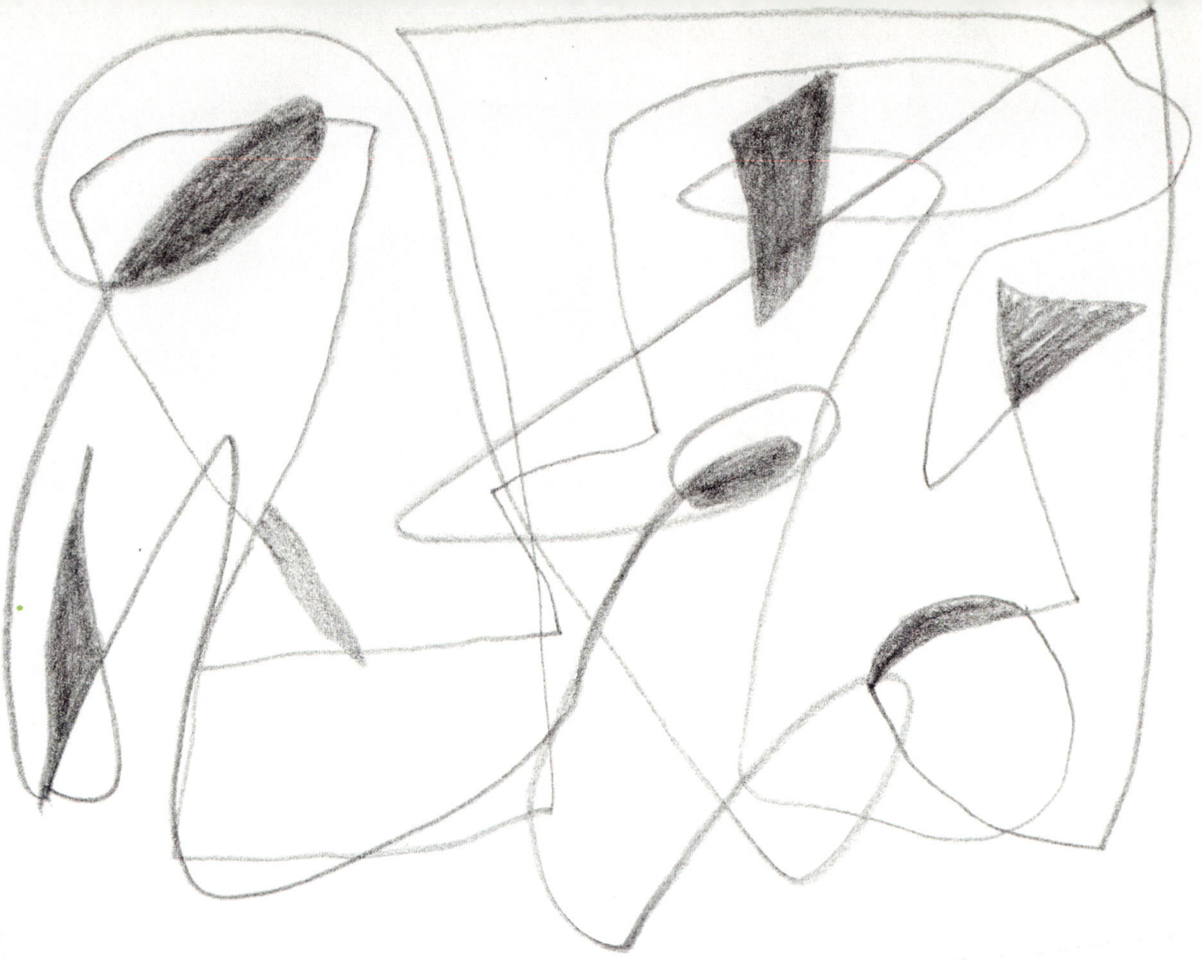

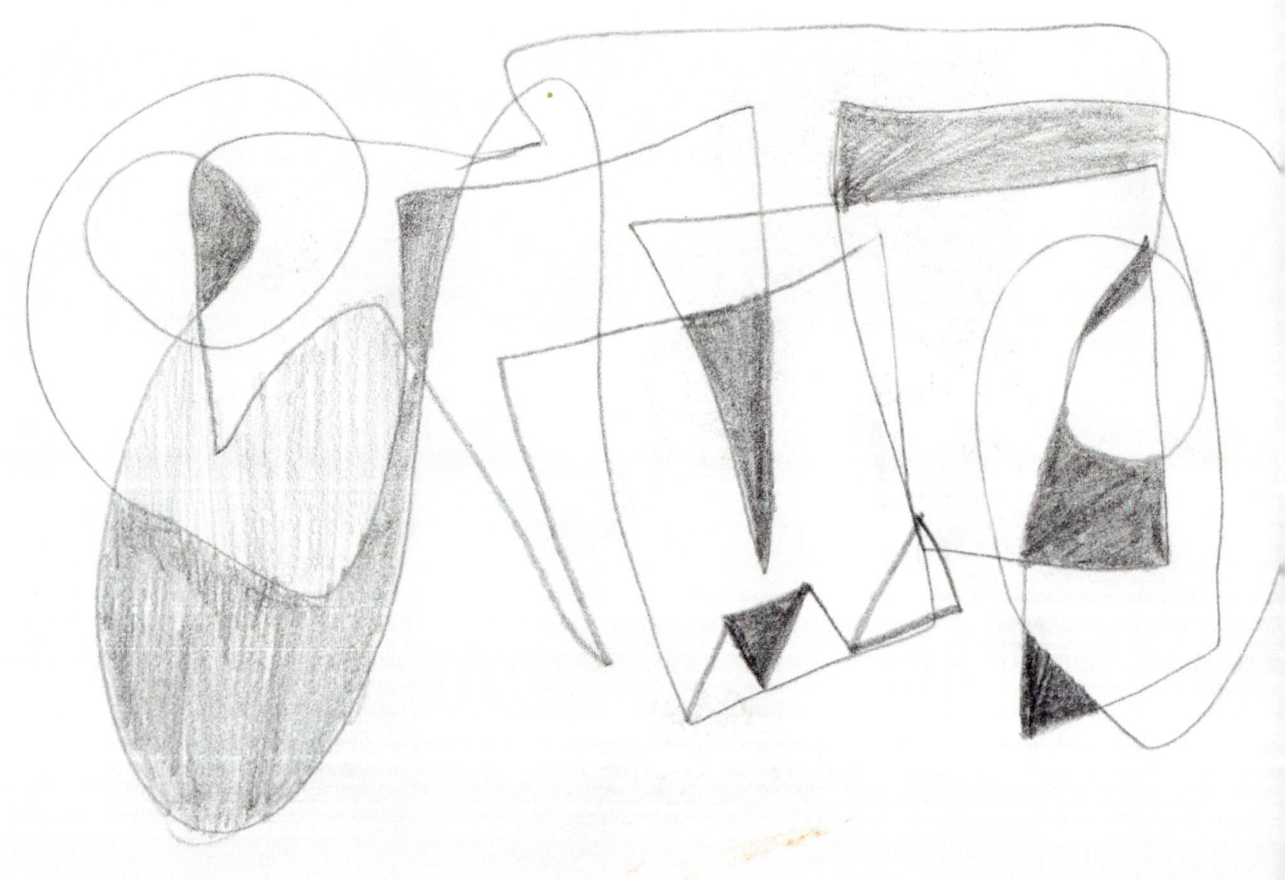

EN 1991

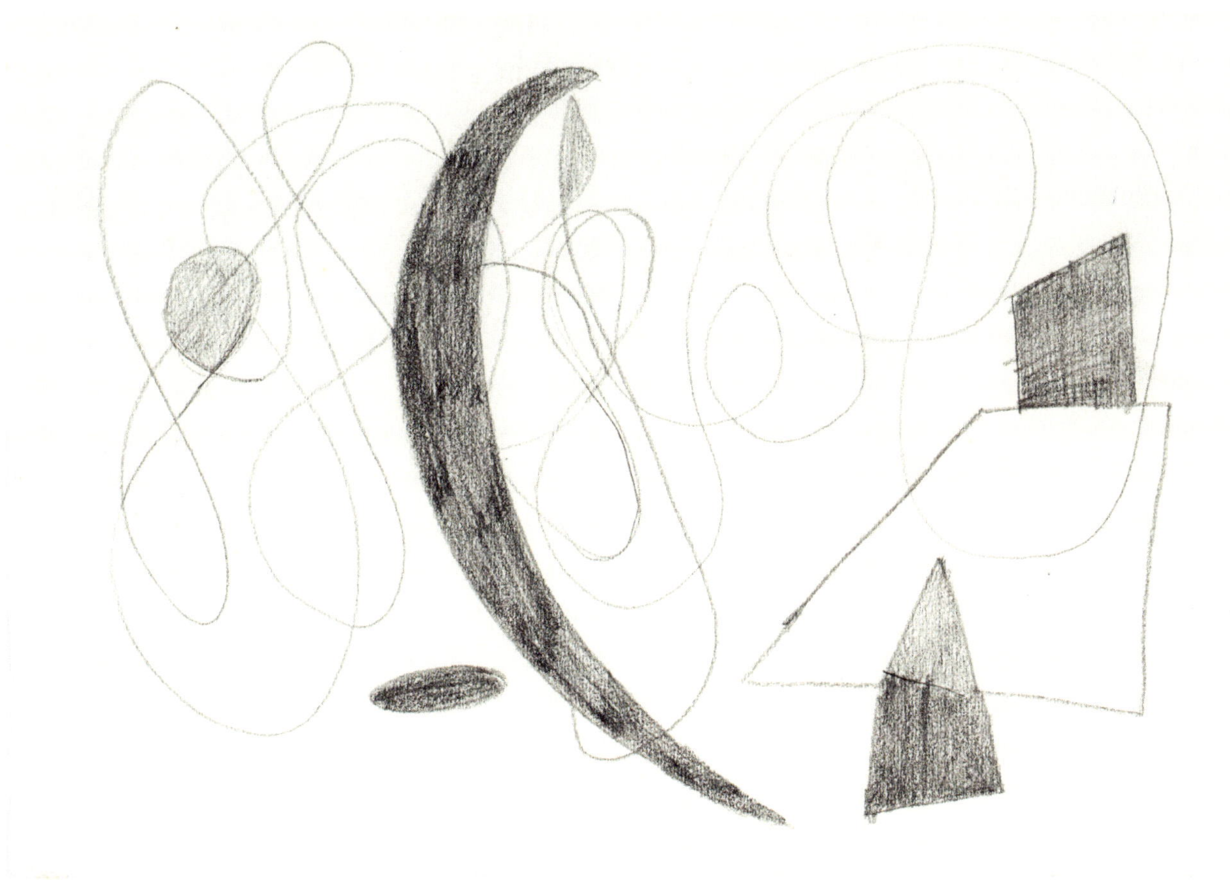

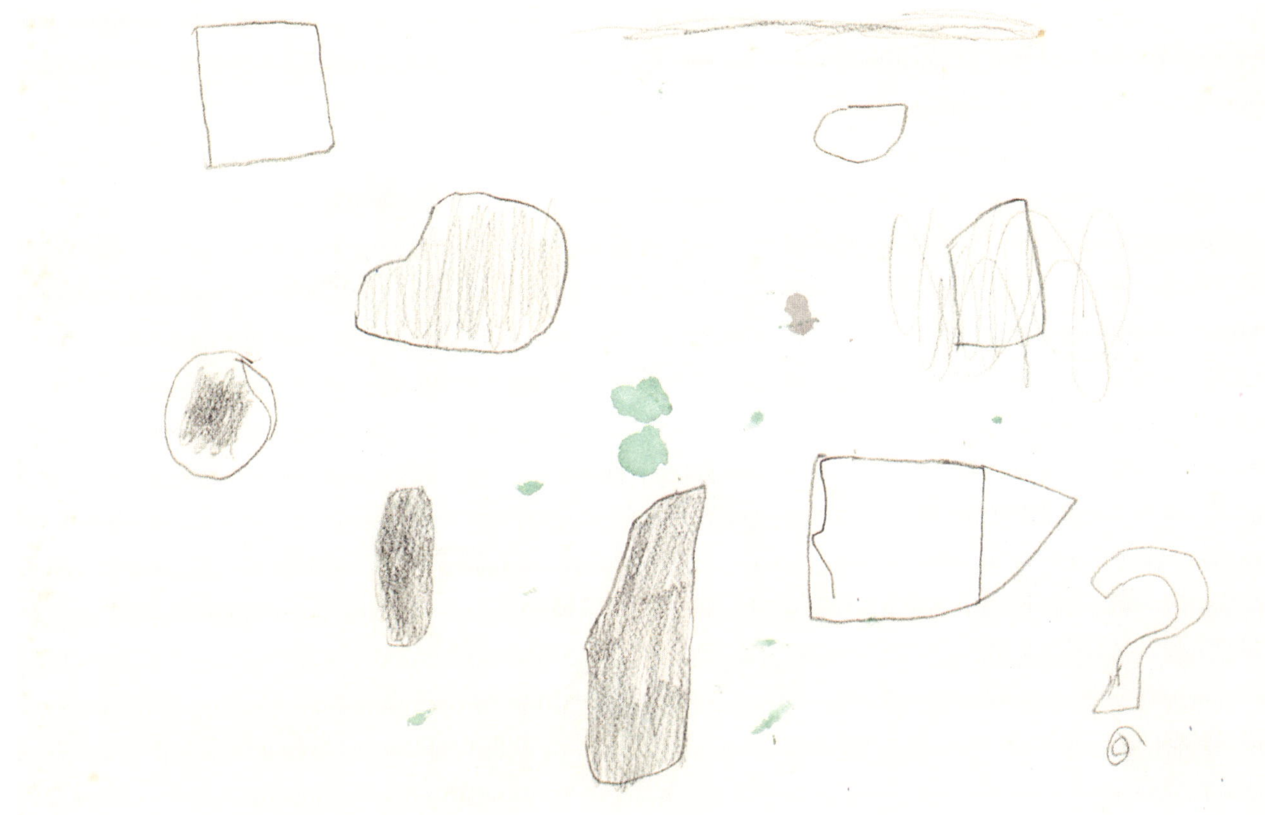
EN 1990

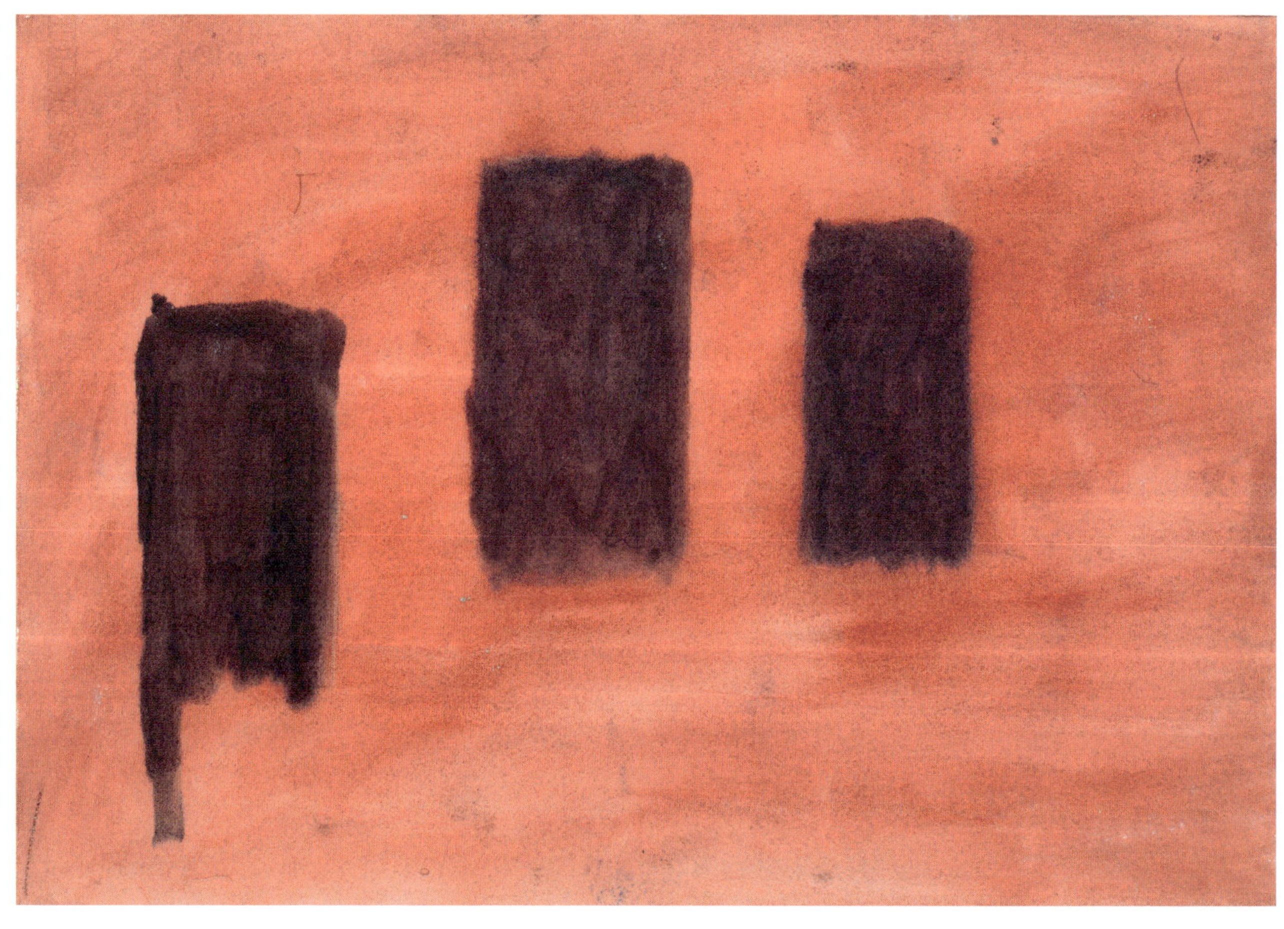

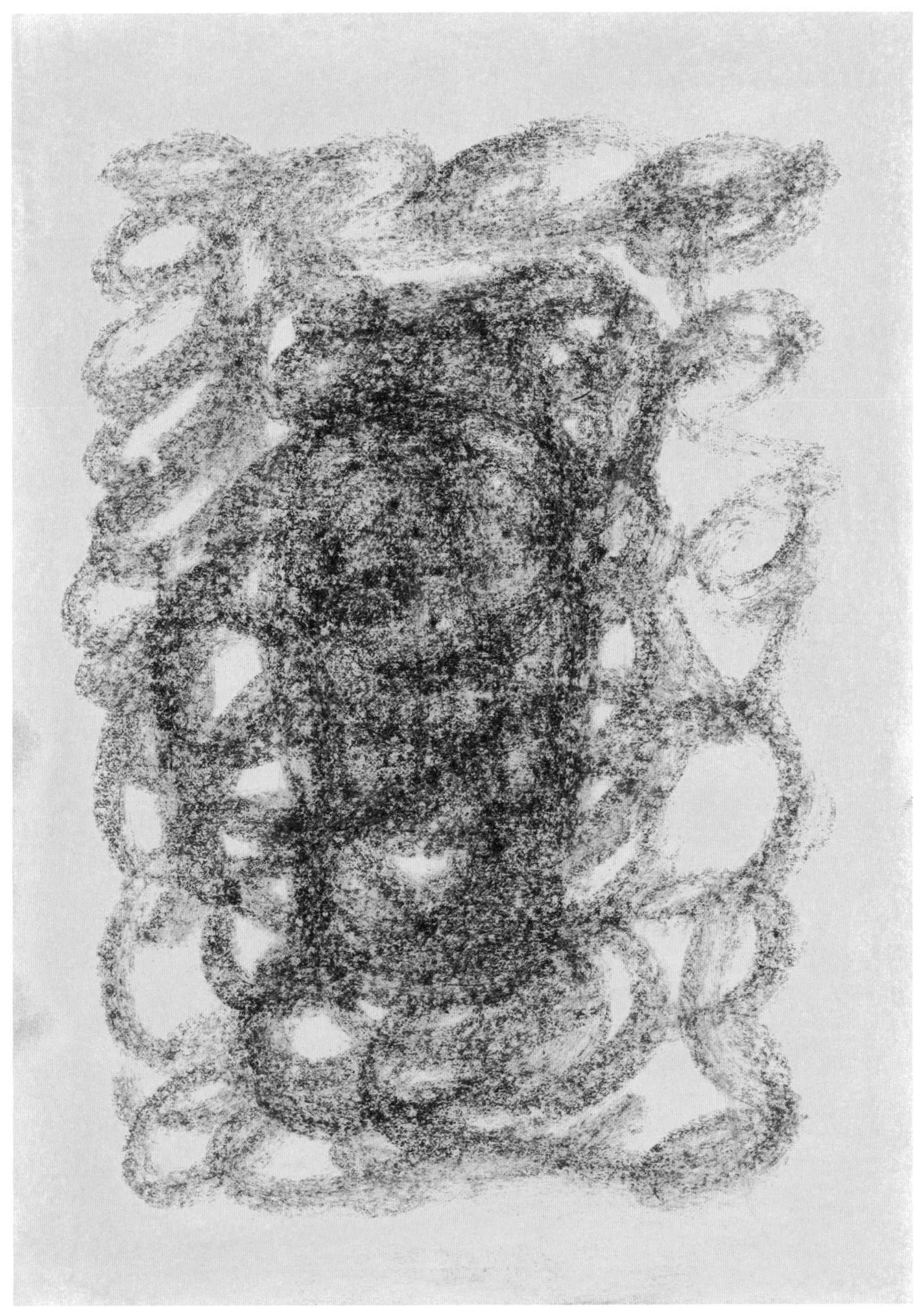

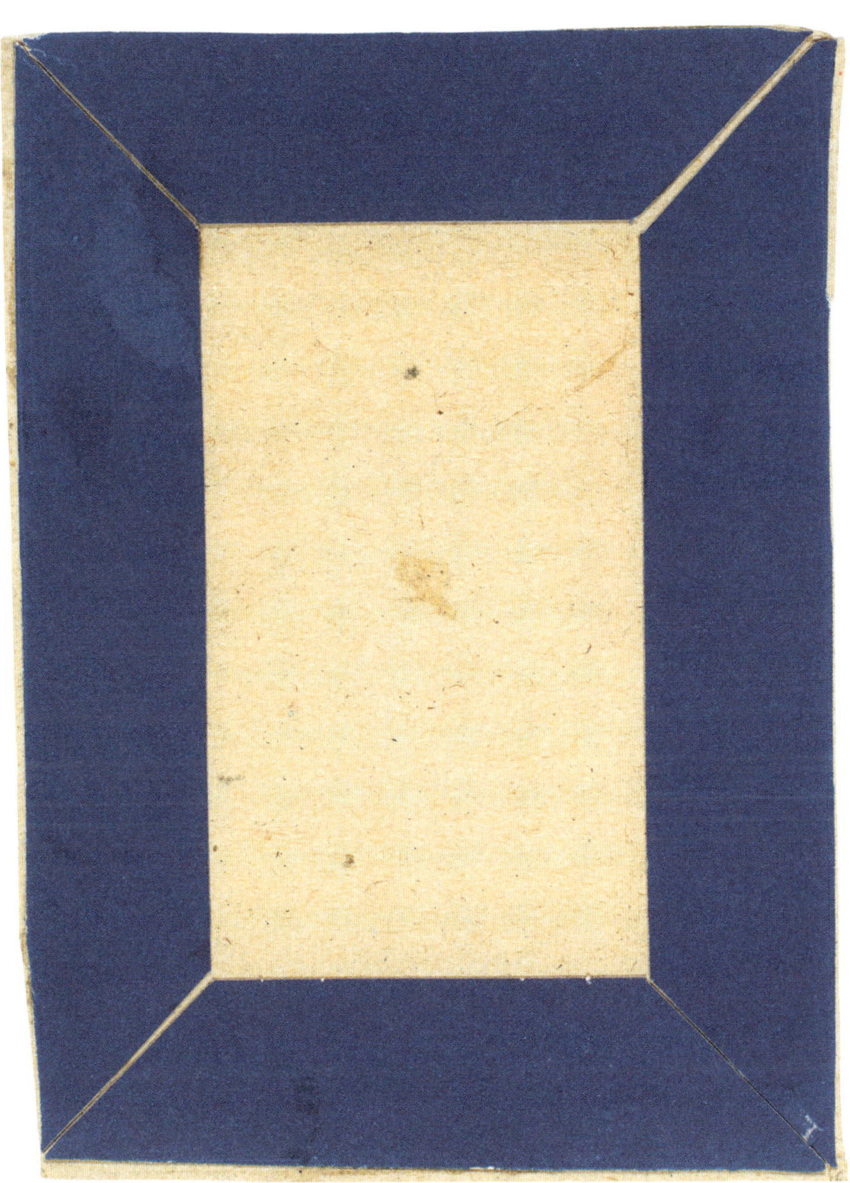

E.N 2009

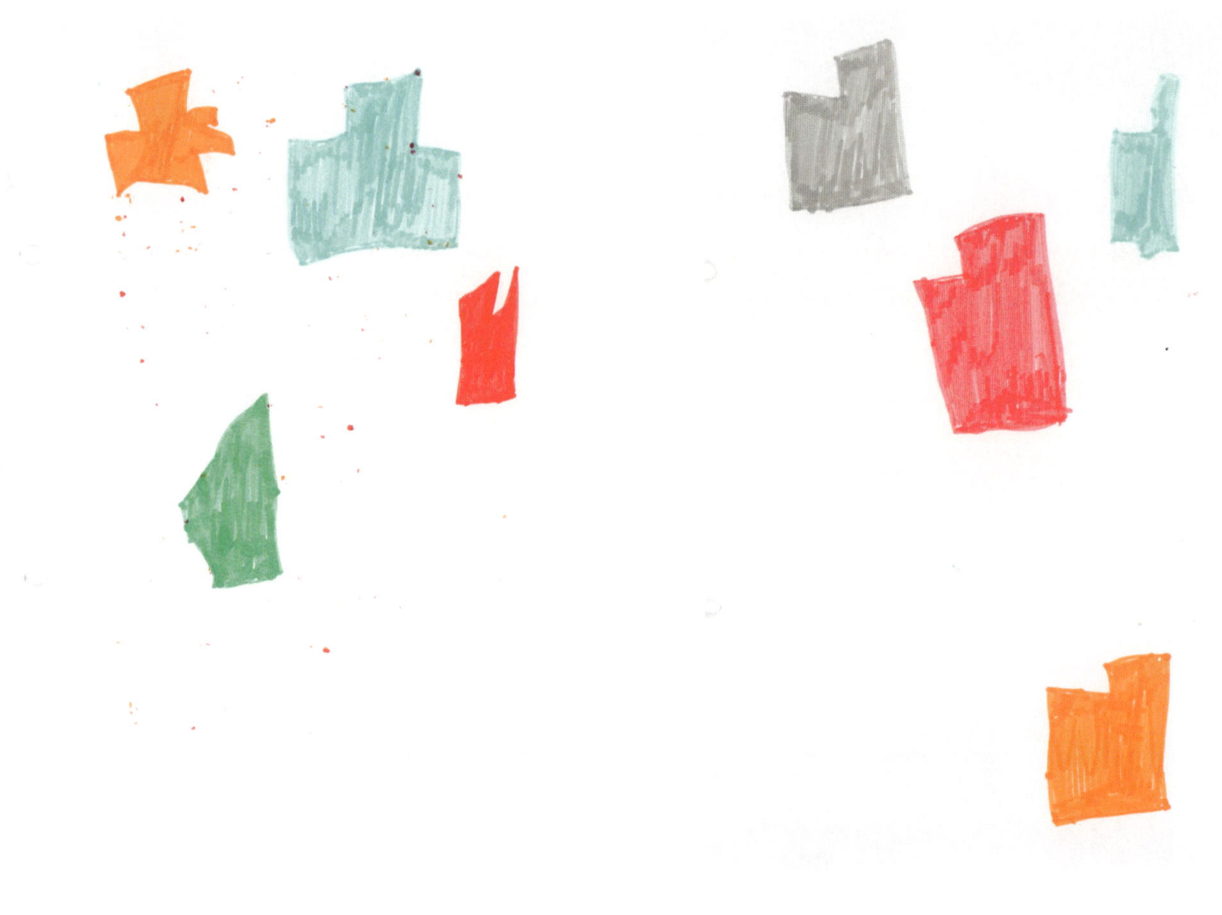

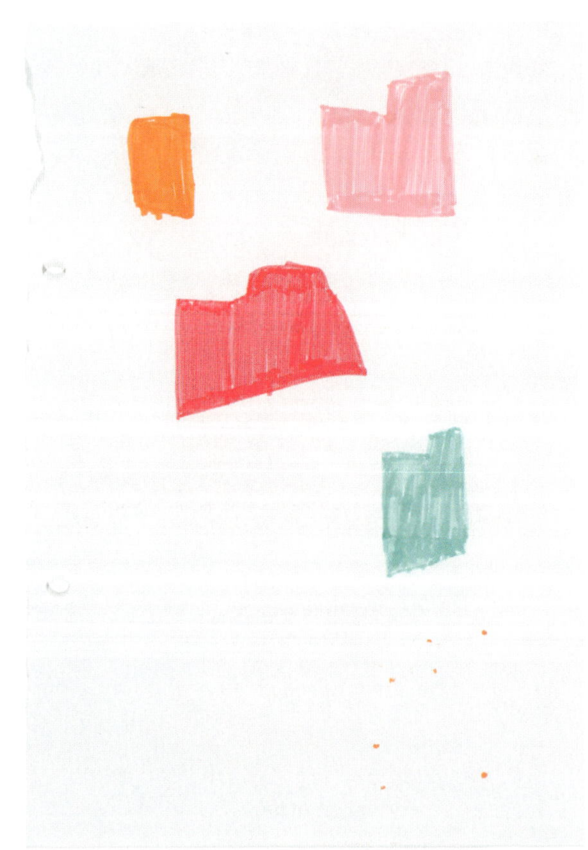

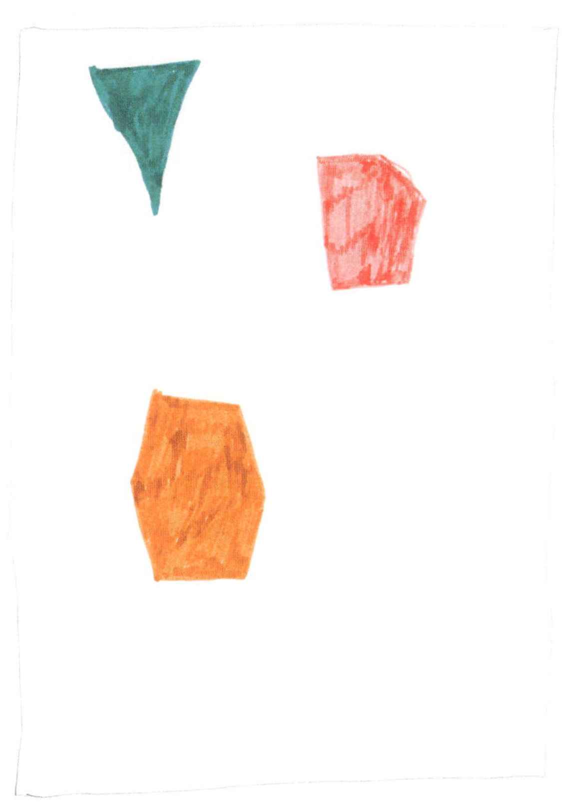

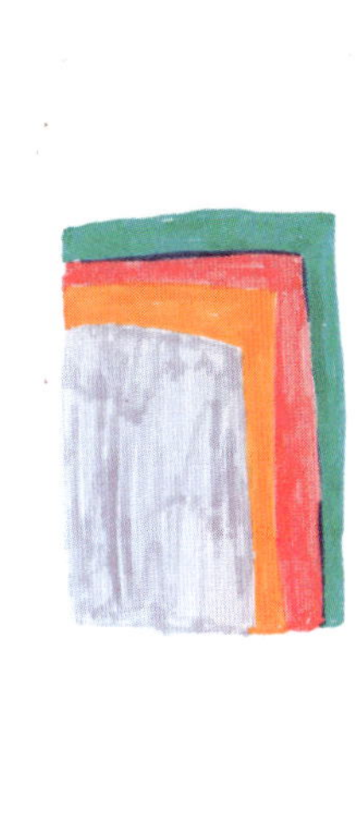

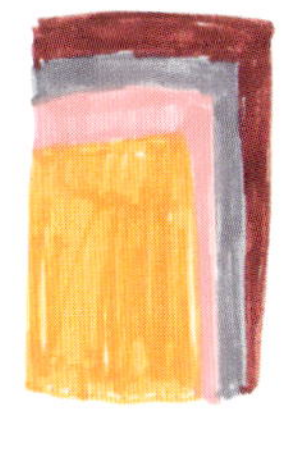

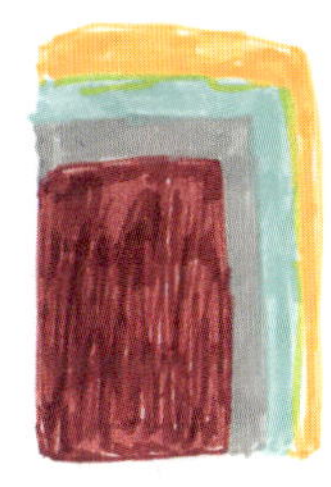

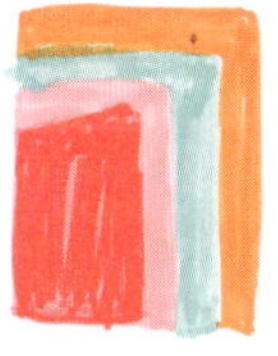

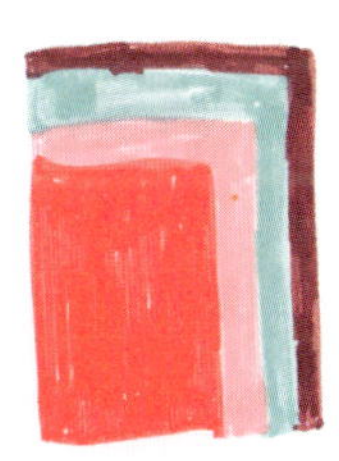

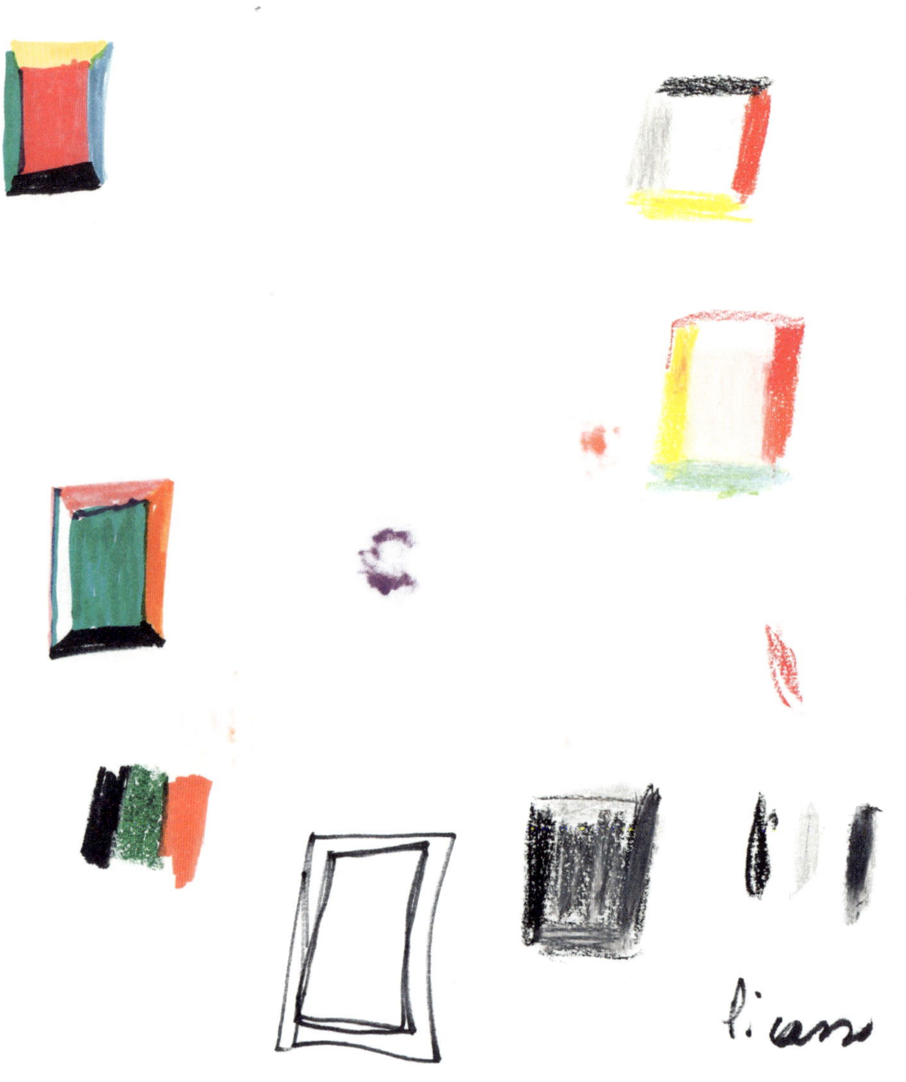

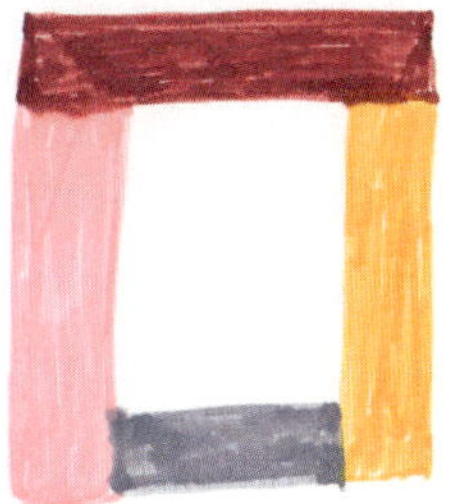

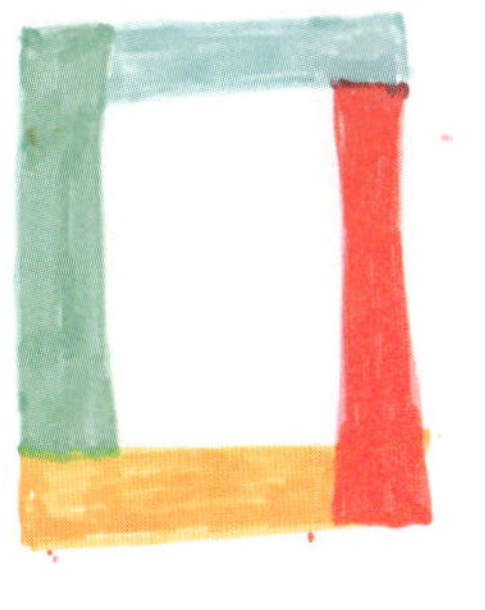

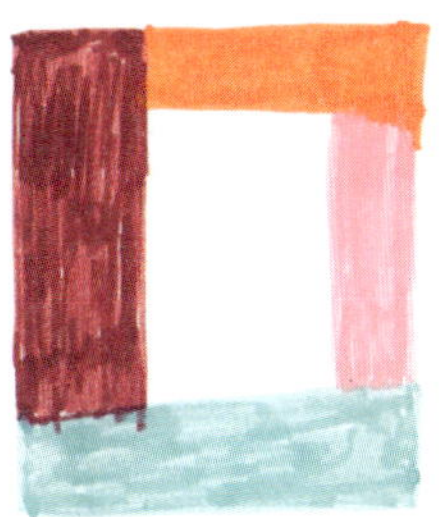

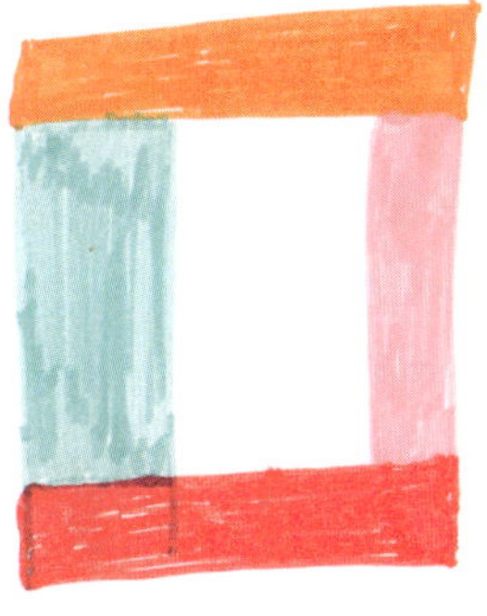

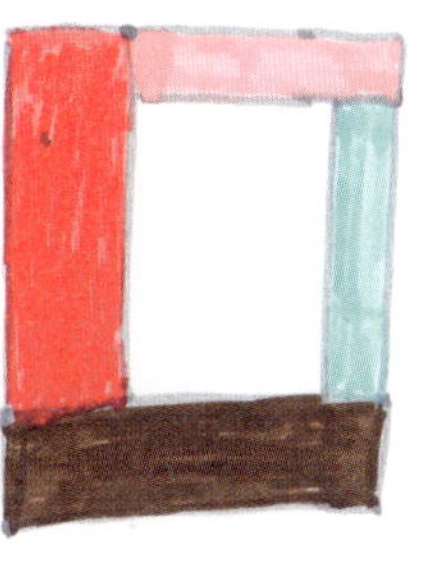

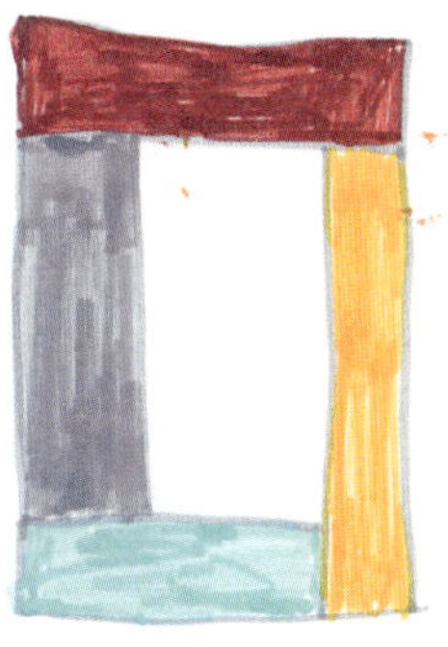

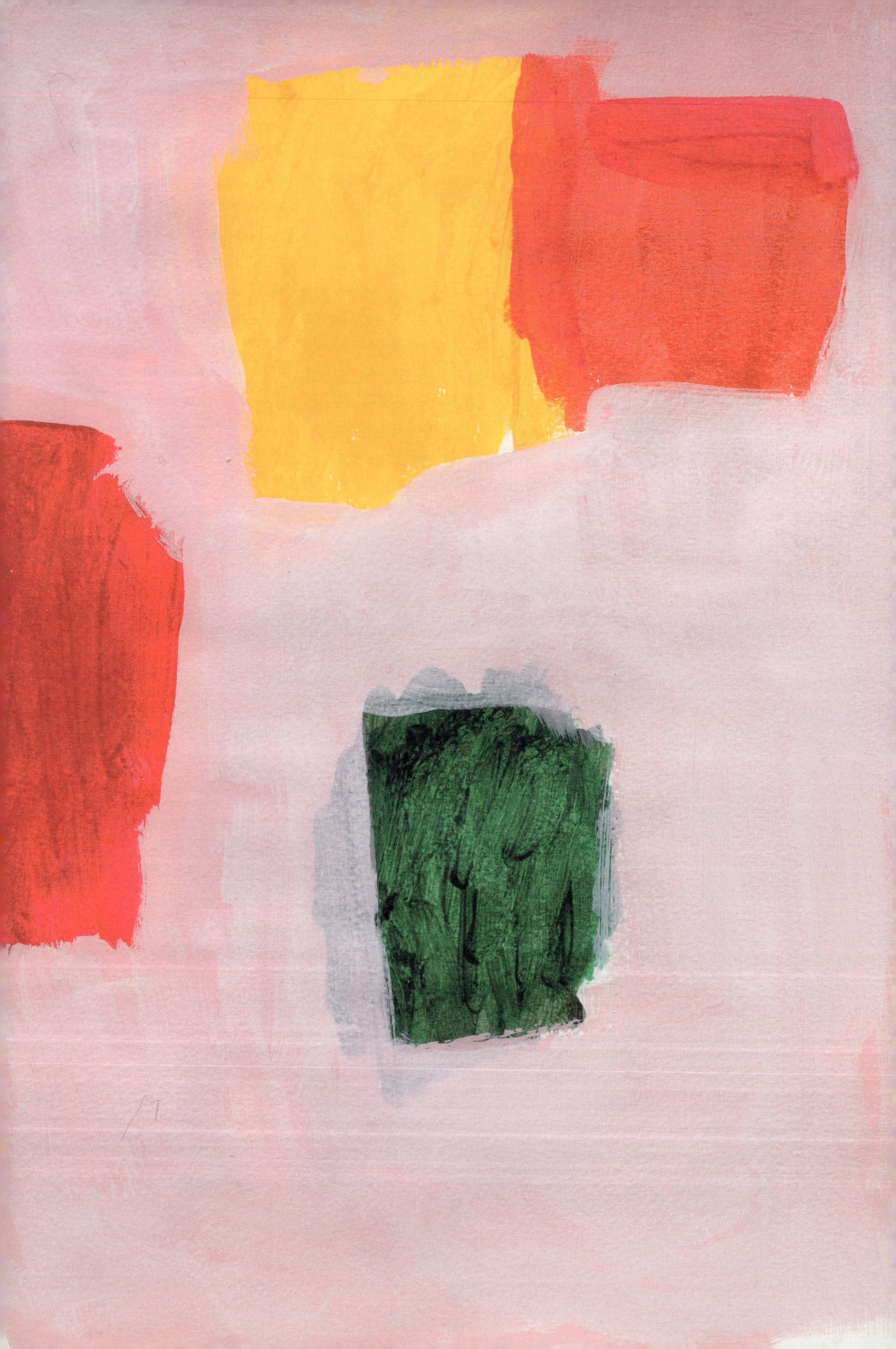

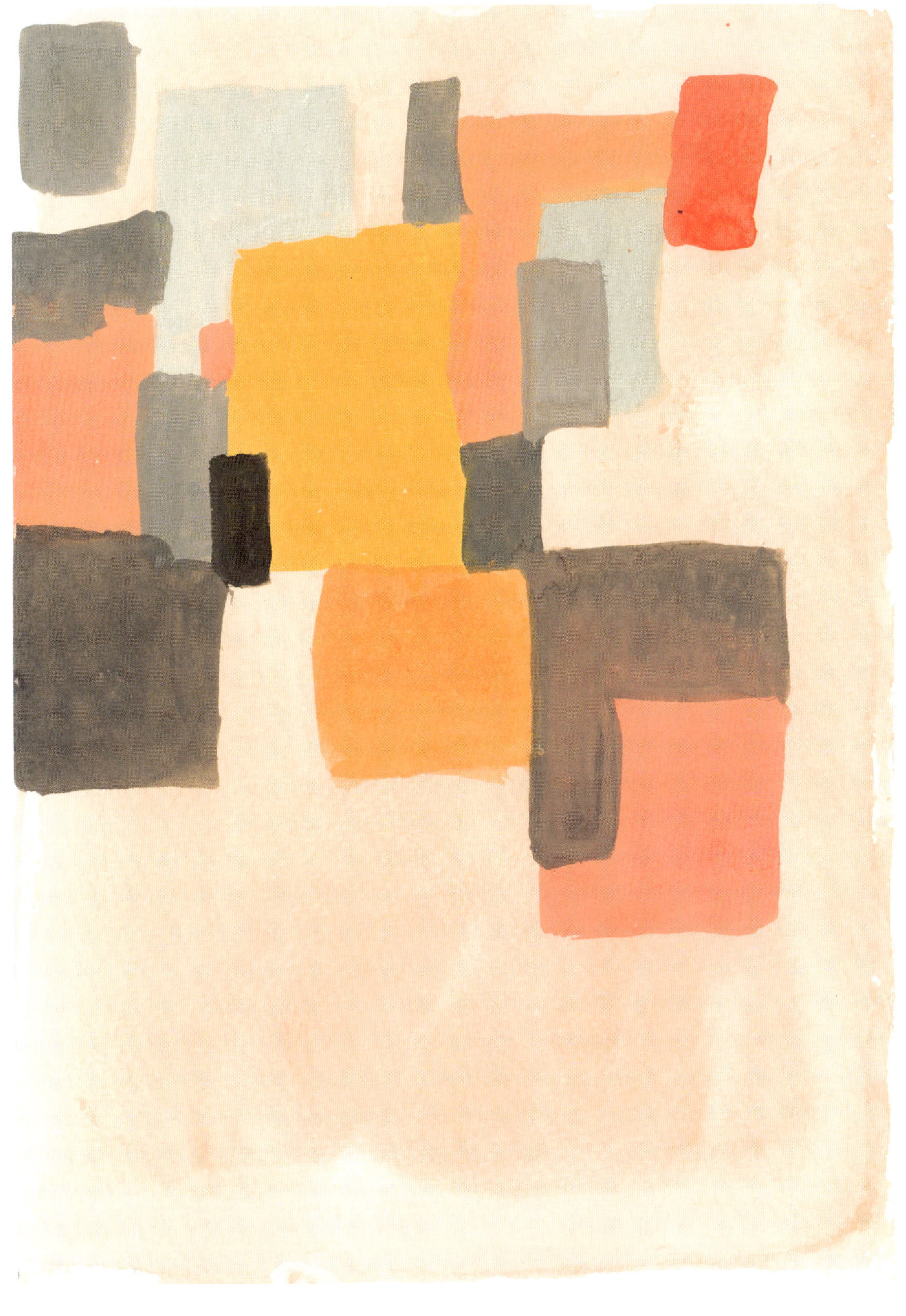

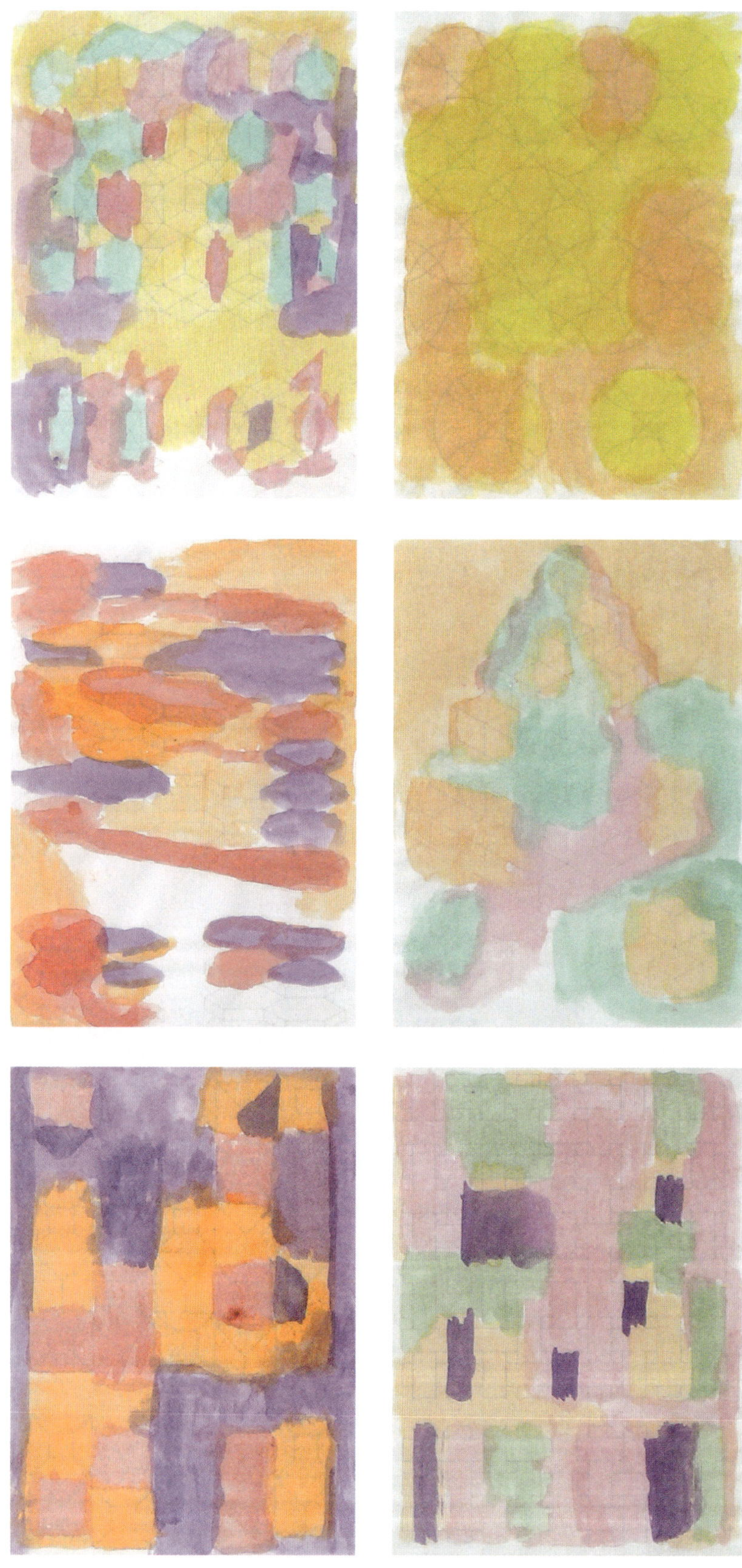

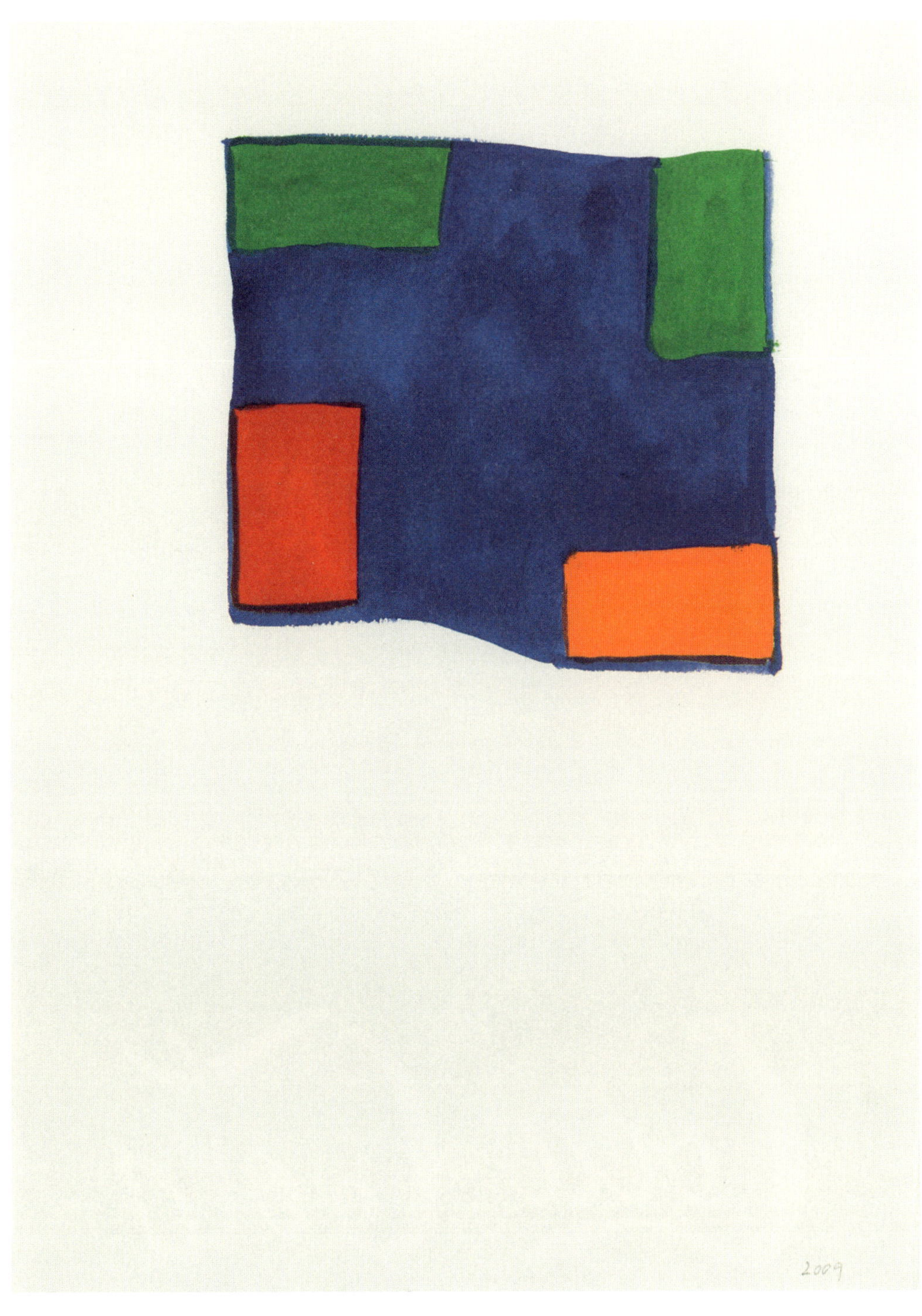
2009

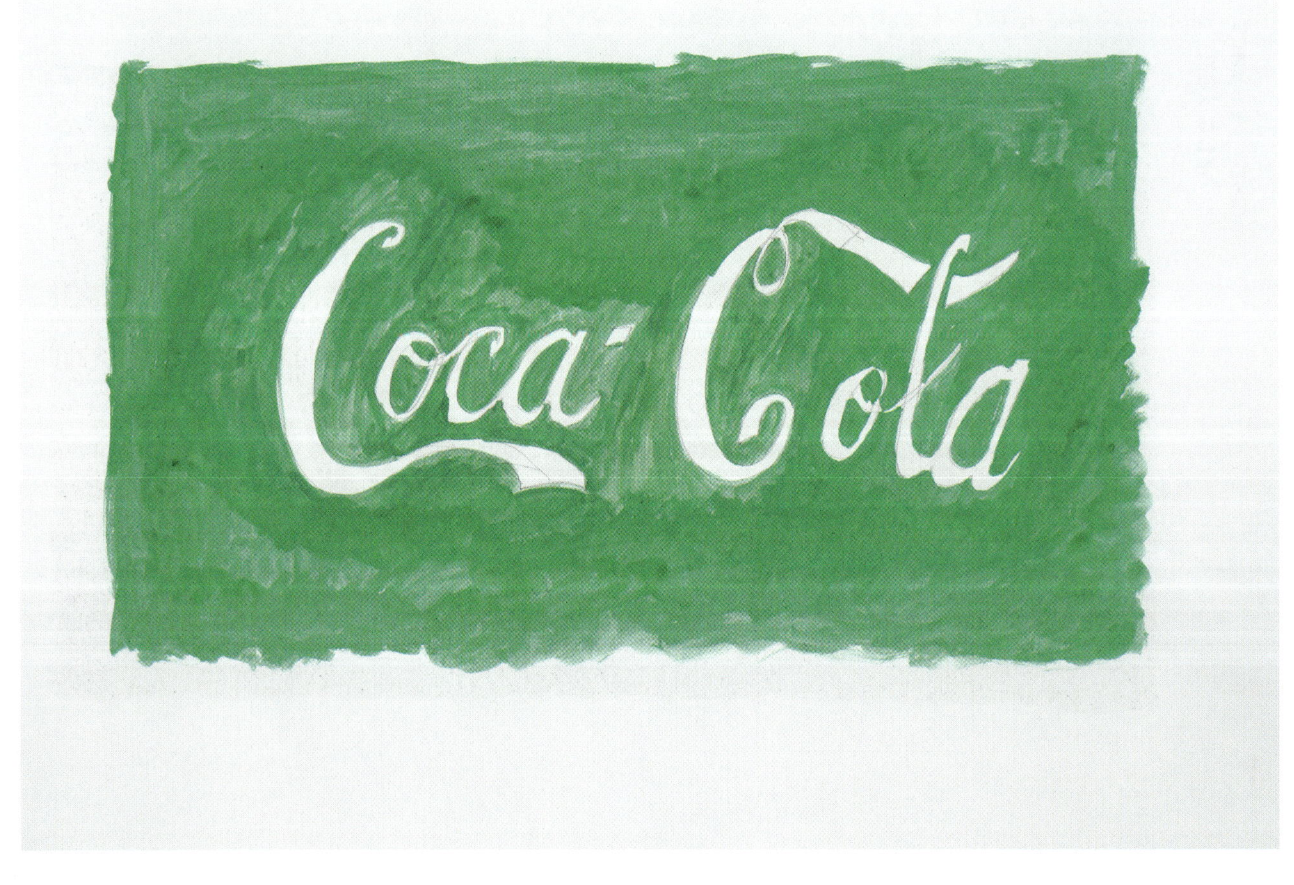
Coca-Cola

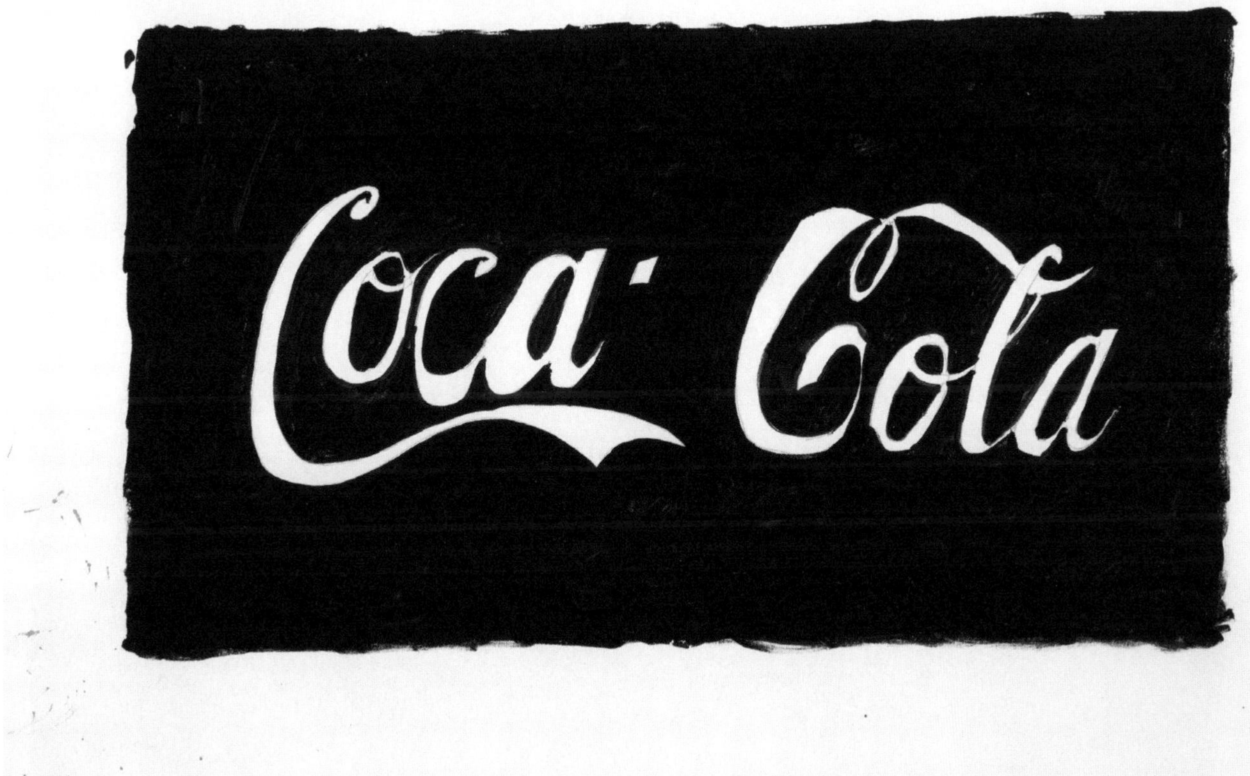
Coca-Cola

MILITANT
OF
TRUTH

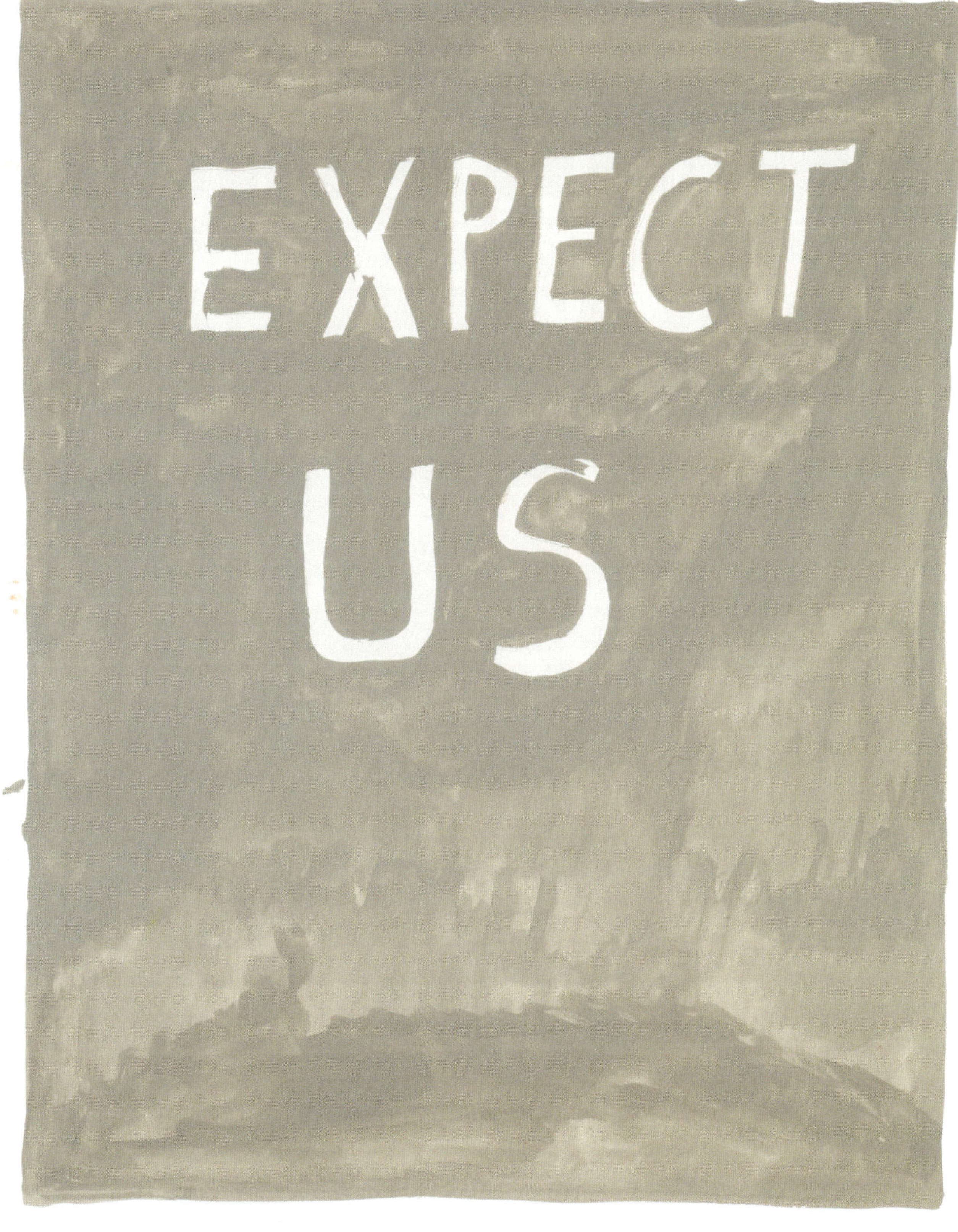
EXPECT
US

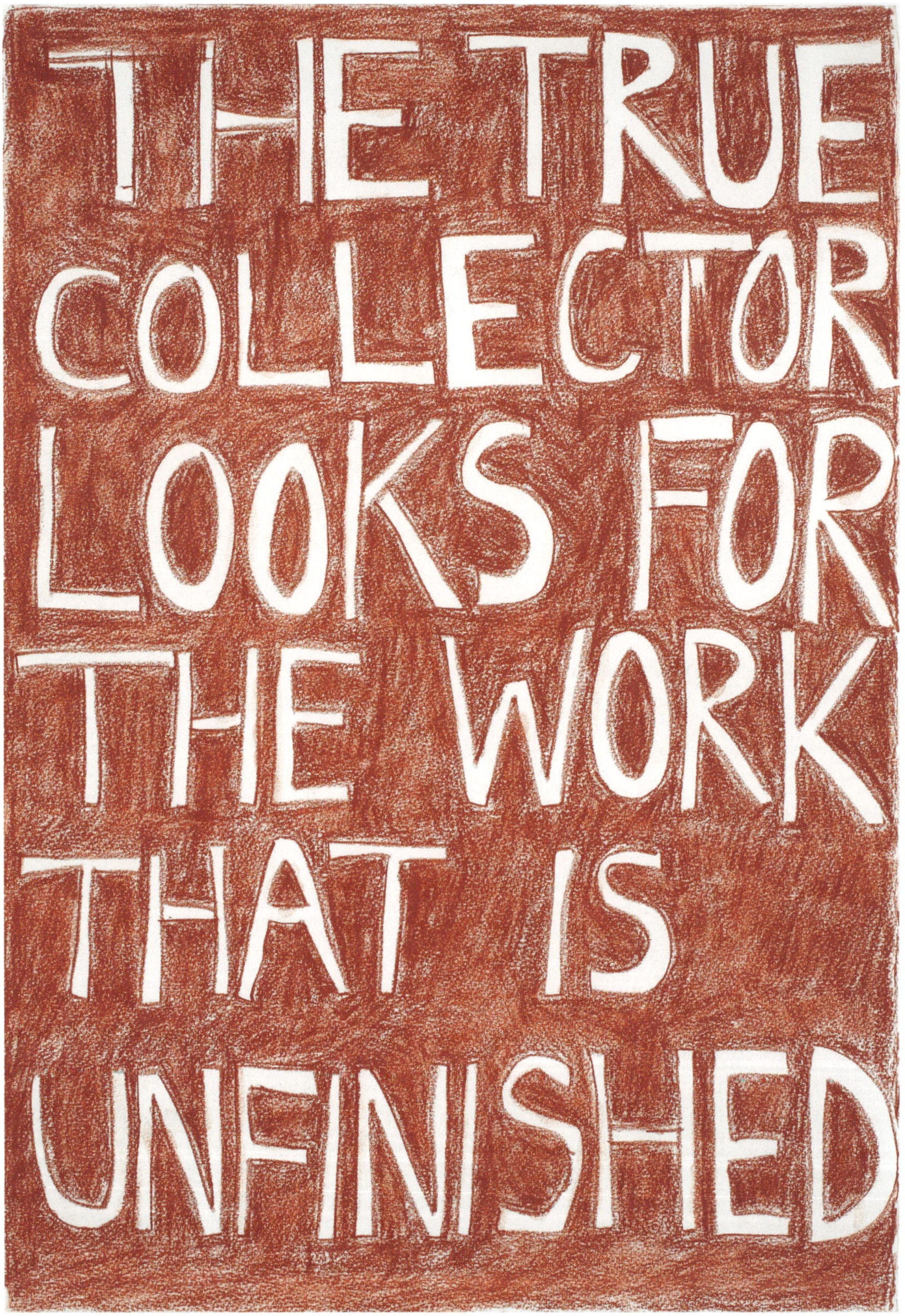

THE TRUE
COLLECTOR
LOOKS FOR
THE WORK
THAT IS
UNFINISHED

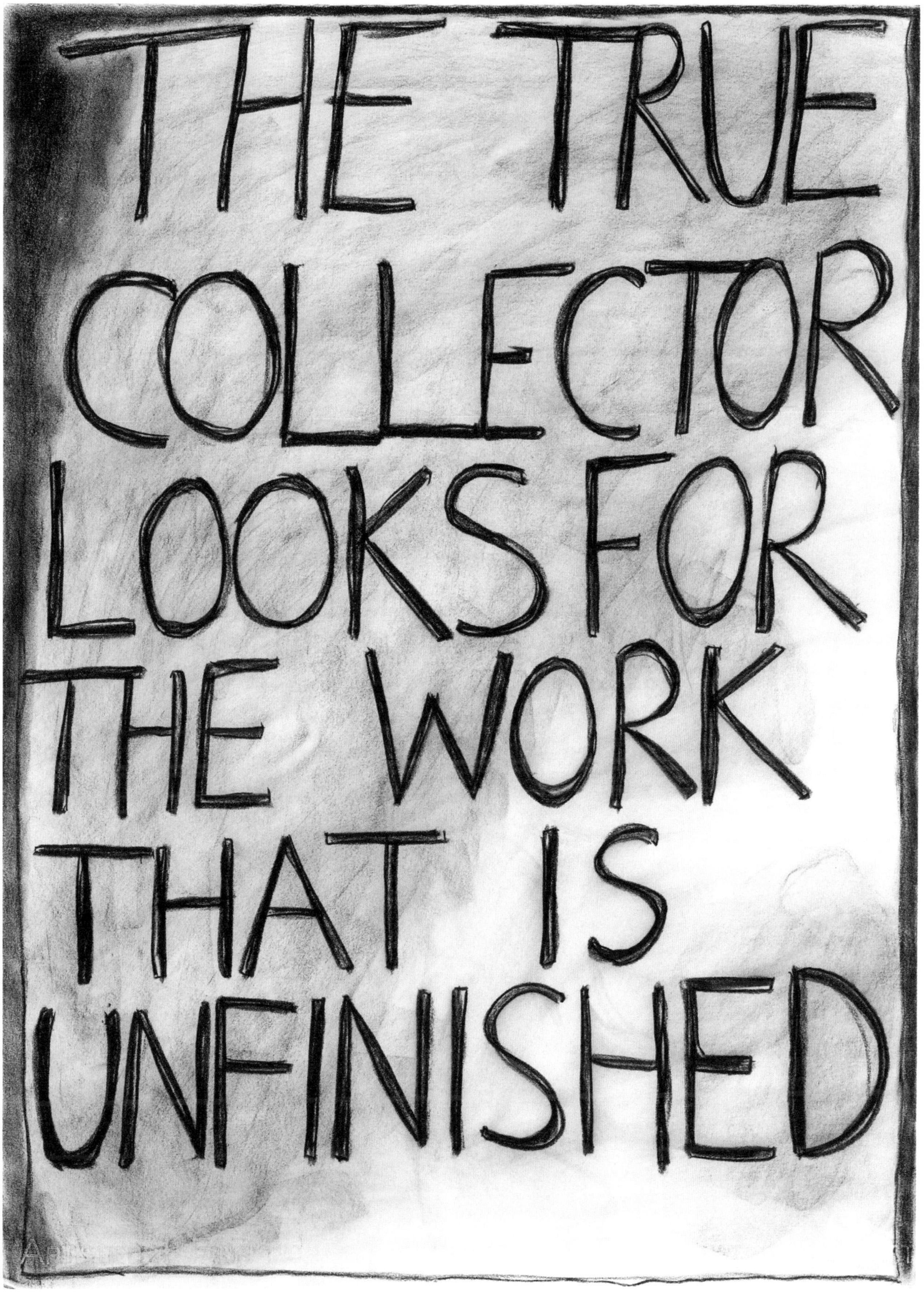

THE TRUE
COLLECTOR
LOOKS FOR
THE WORK
THAT IS
UNFINISHED

... and the world flew off its axis

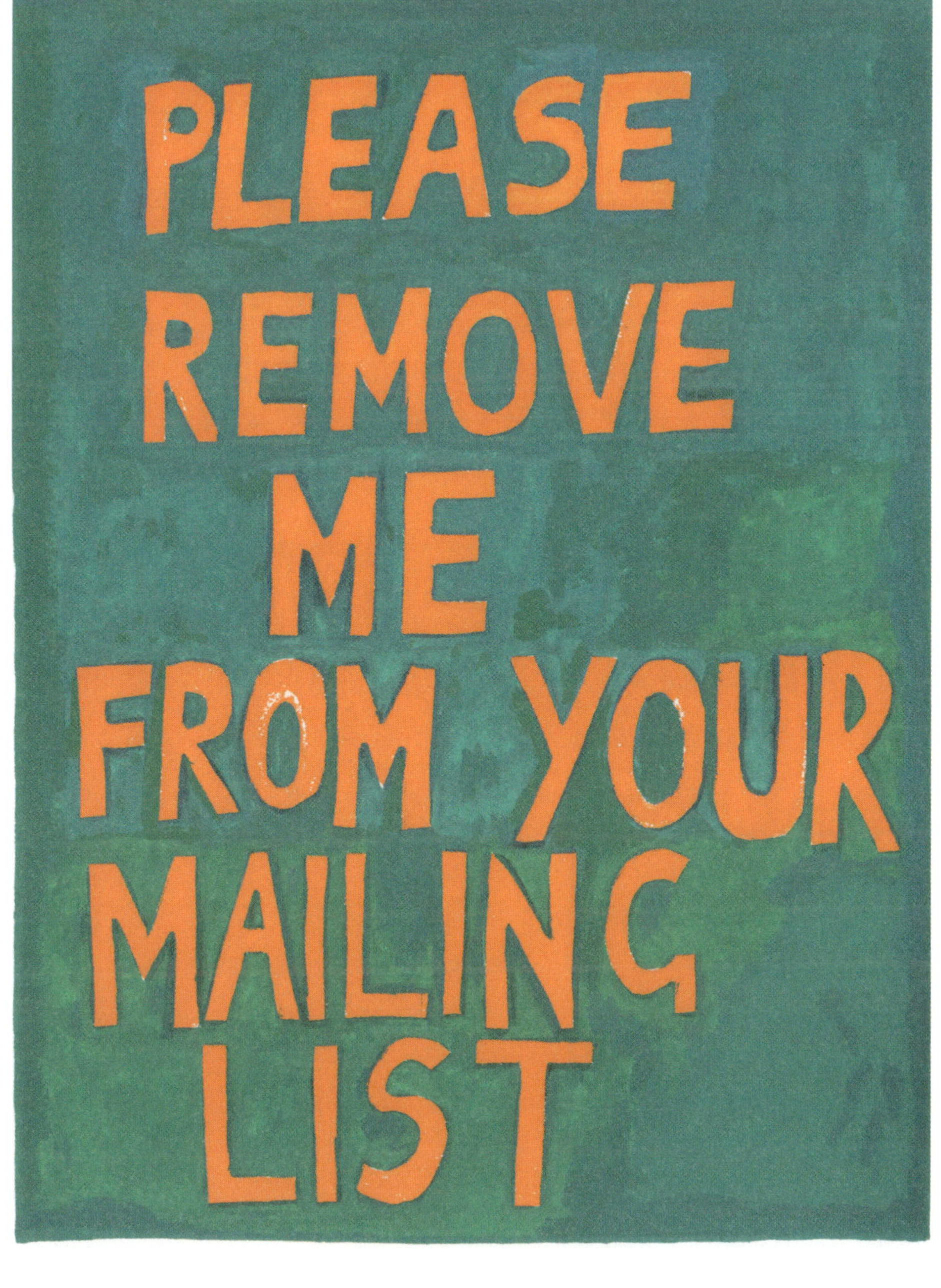
PLEASE
REMOVE
ME
FROM YOUR
MAILING
LIST

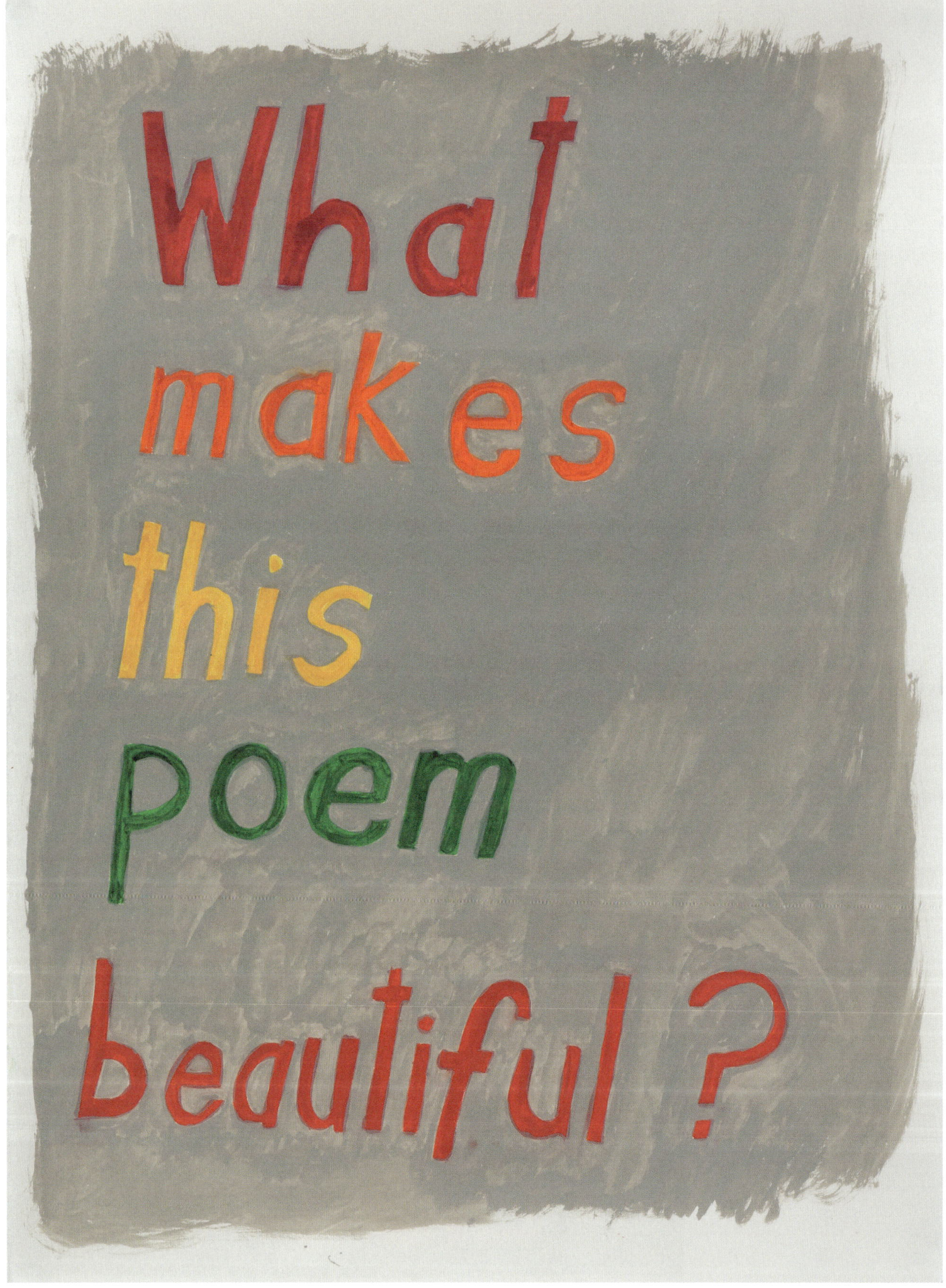
What
makes
this
poem
beautiful ?

What
makes
this
poem
beautiful?

What ?
makes
this * *
poem
beautiful ?

0.3% OF

THE WORLD'S

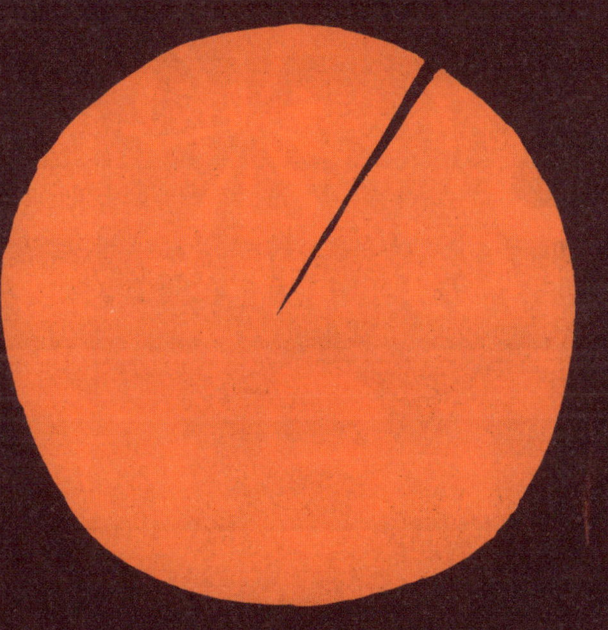

REFUGEES

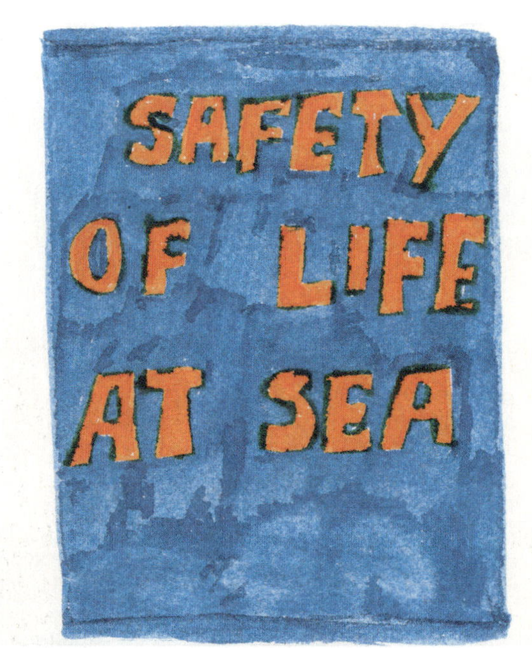
SAFETY
OF LIFE
AT SEA

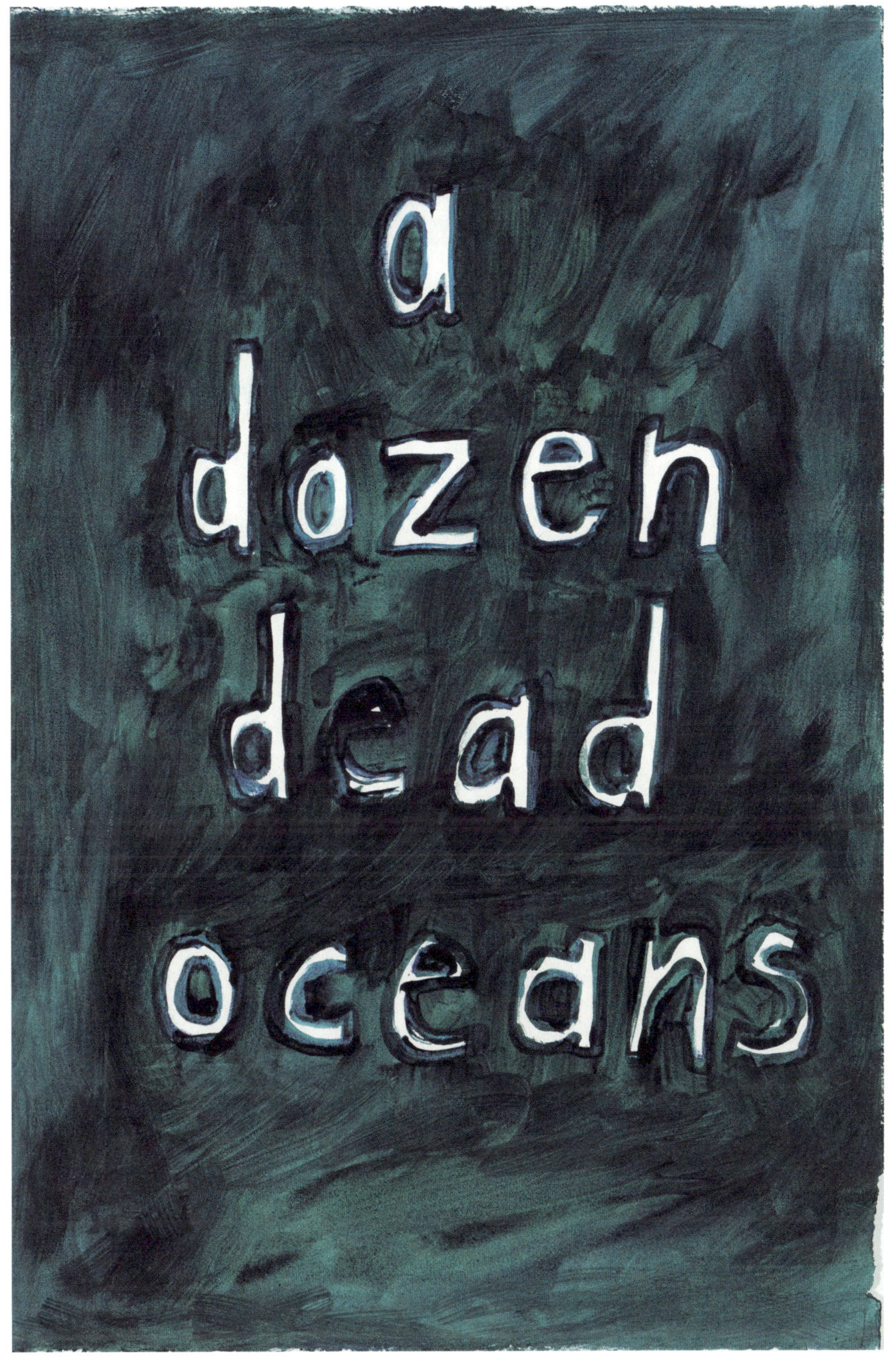
a
dozen
dead
oceans

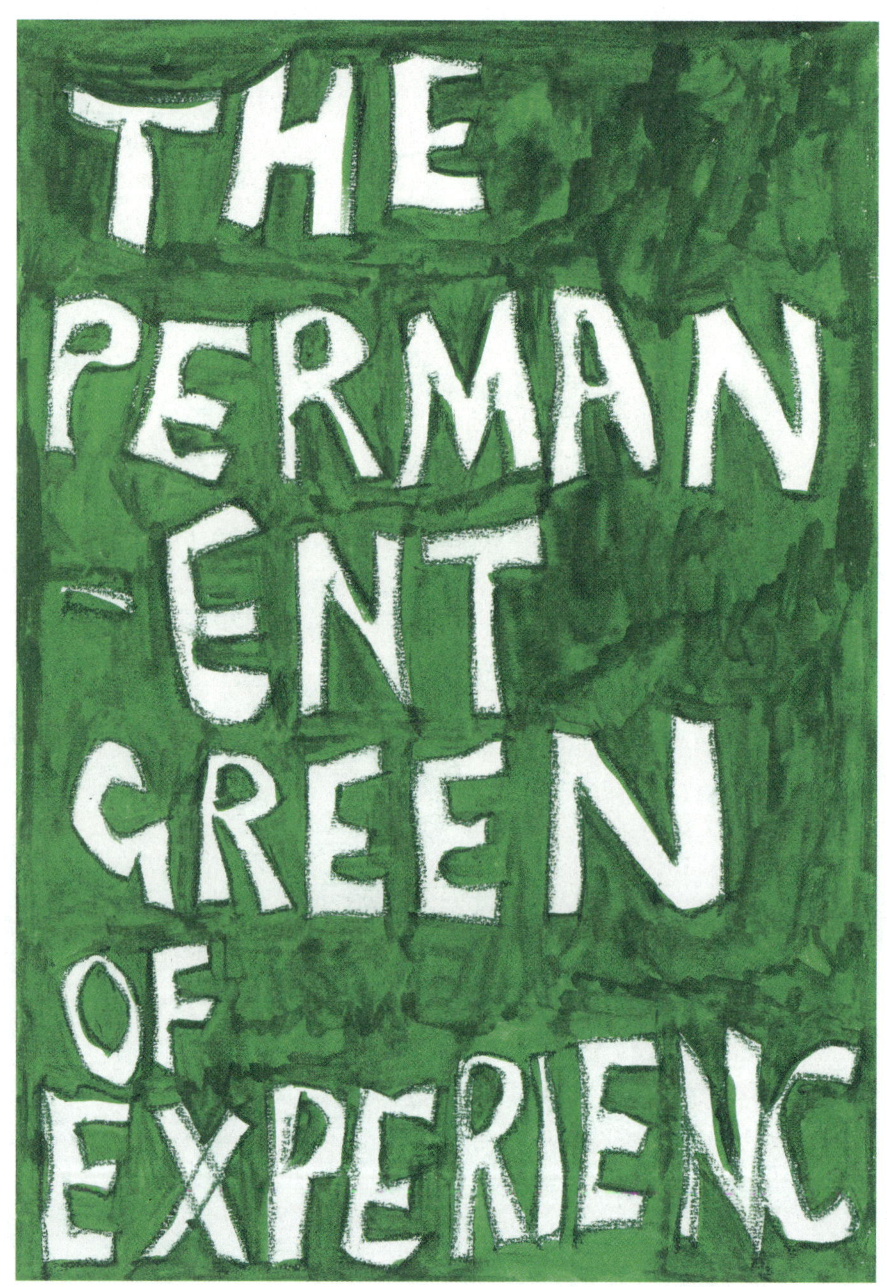
THE
PERMAN
-ENT
GREEN
OF
EXPERIENC

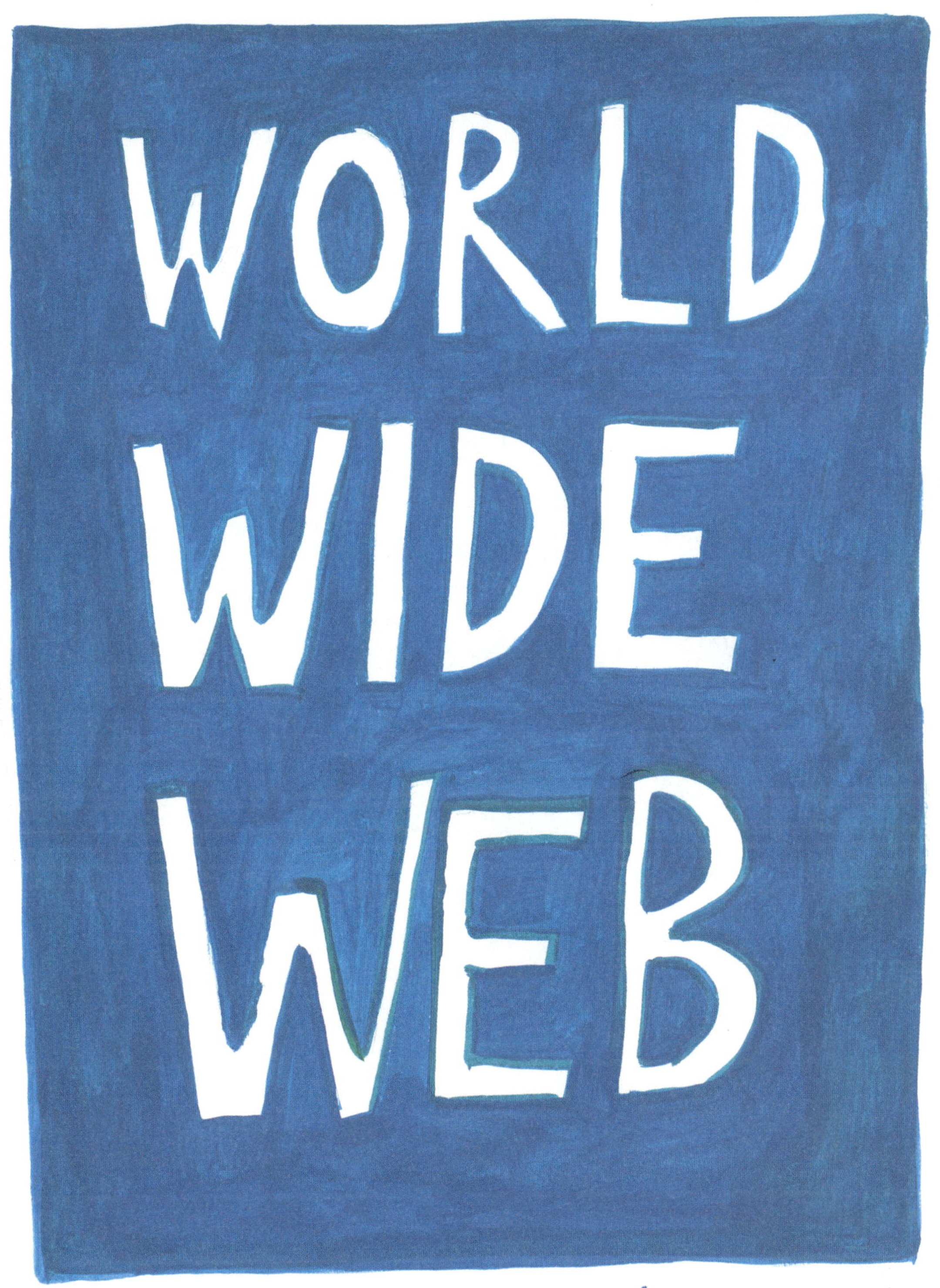
WORLD
WIDE
WEB

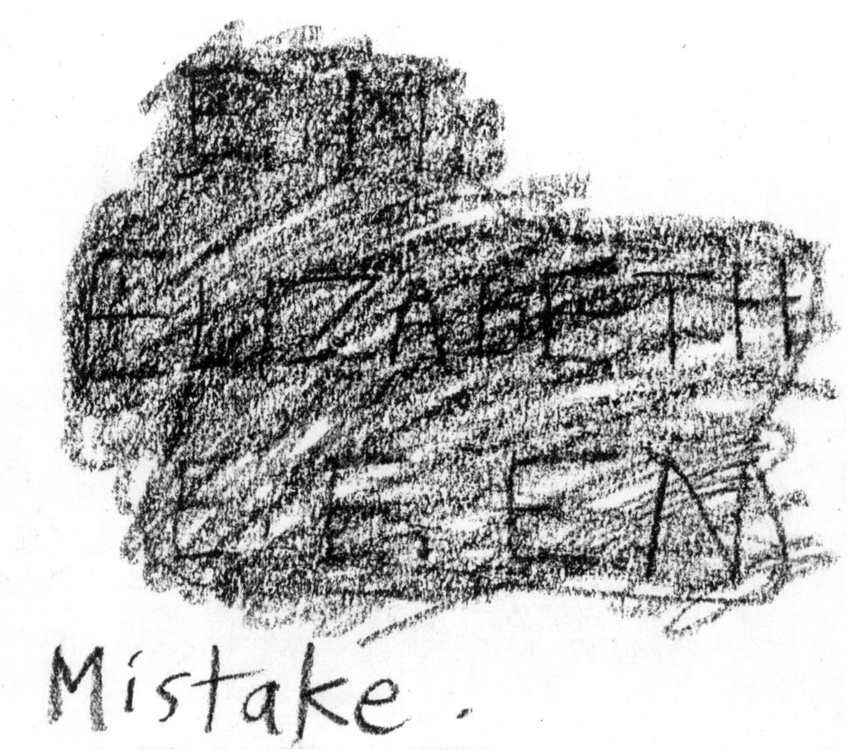
Mistake.

THE TRUE COLLECTOR LOOKS FOR THE WORK THAT IS UNFINISHED

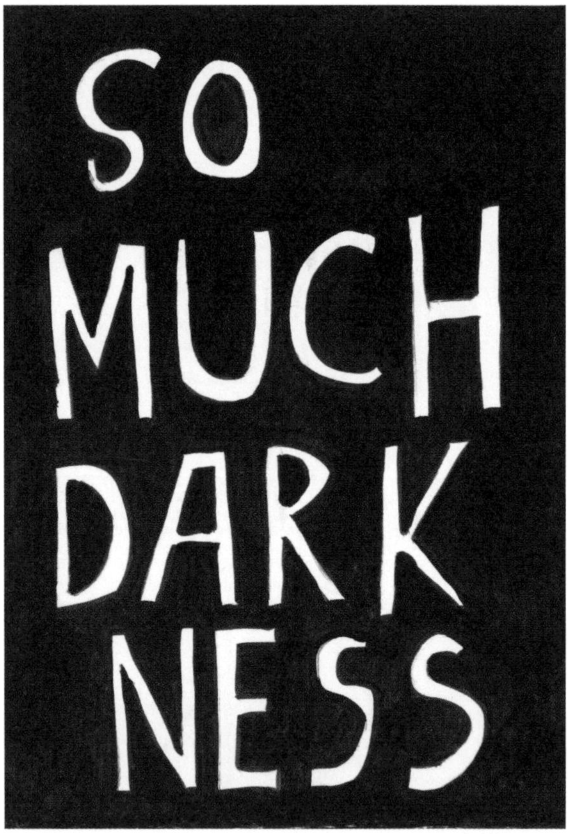

SO
MUCH
DARK
NESS

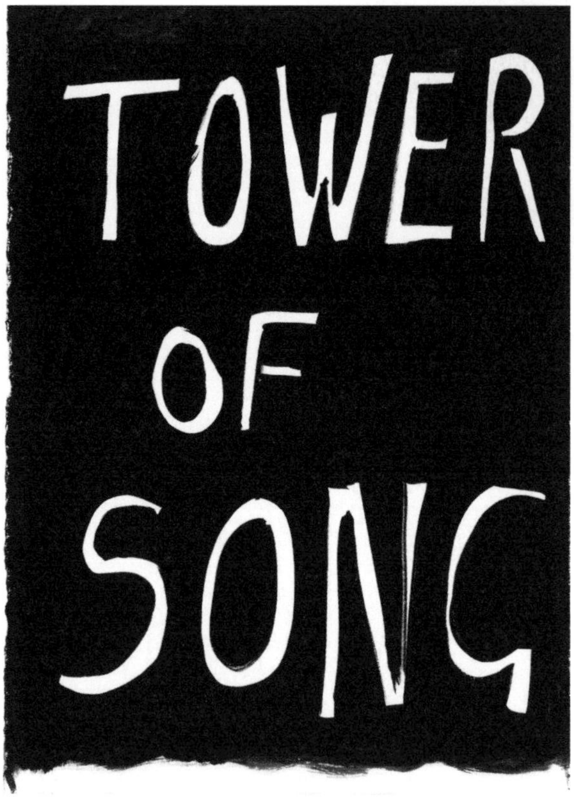

TOWER
OF
SONG

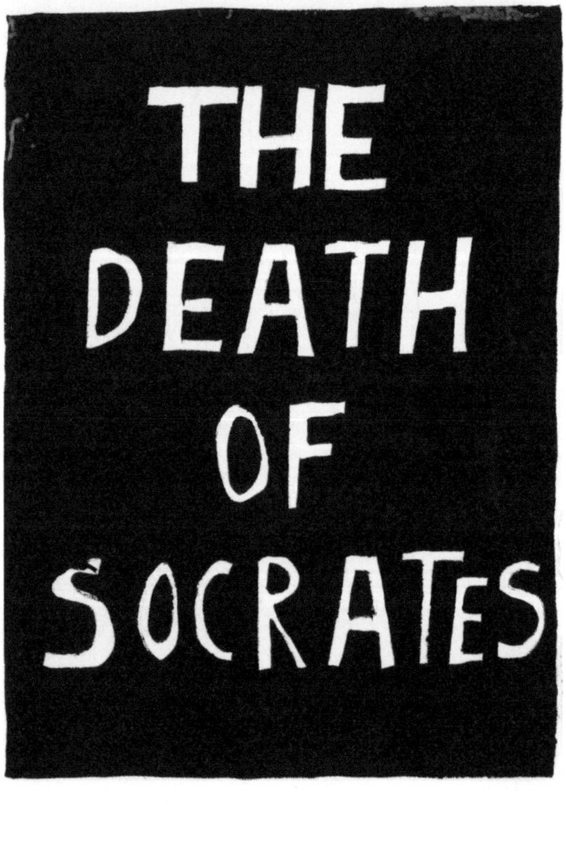

THE
DEATH
OF
SOCRATES

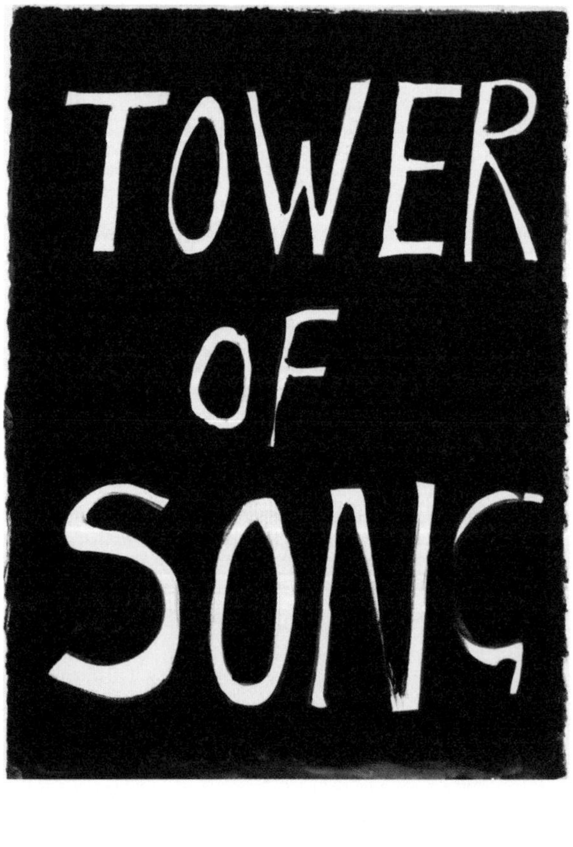

TOWER
OF
SONG

SO MANY
LIGHTS
AND
SO MUCH
DARKNESS

SO
MUCH
DARKNESS!

LAS PINTURAS NEGRAS

SO
MUCH
DARKNESS

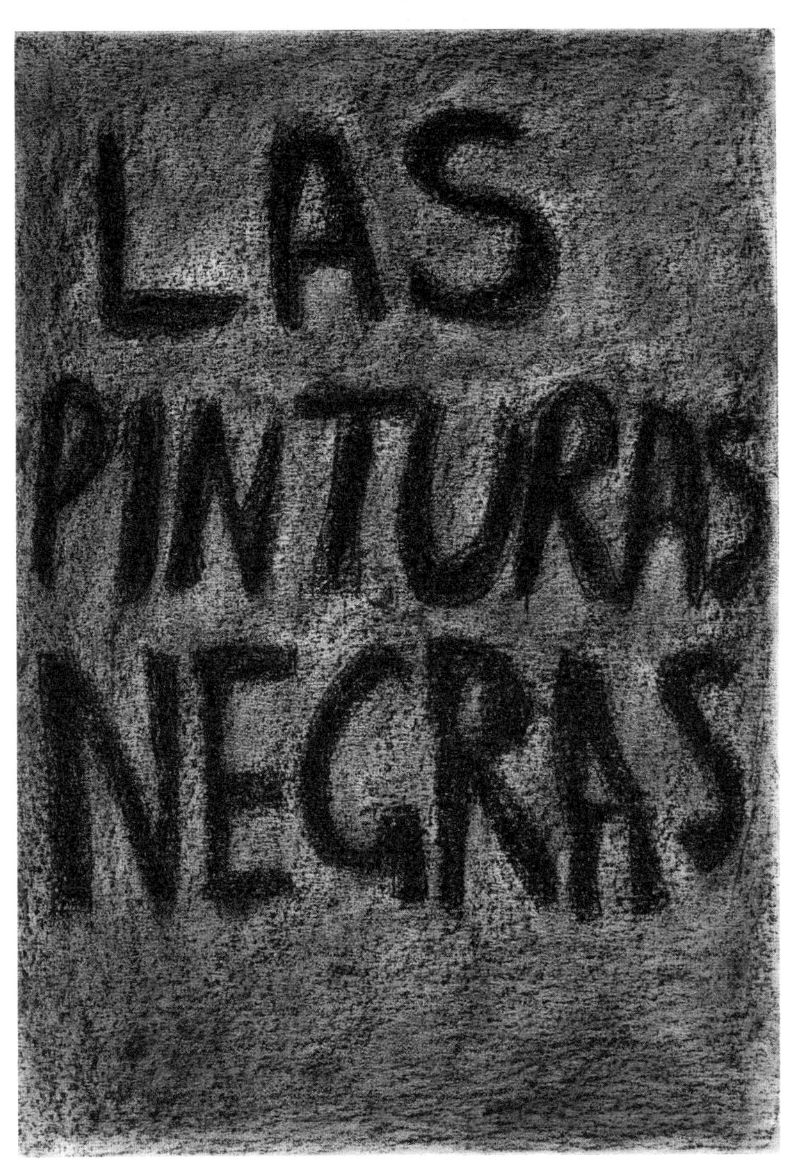

LIGHTS
ON

LIGHTS
OFF

THE 10,000 THINGS

Read
what you
write
in Artfan

You
no longer
realise
even though
you
achieve

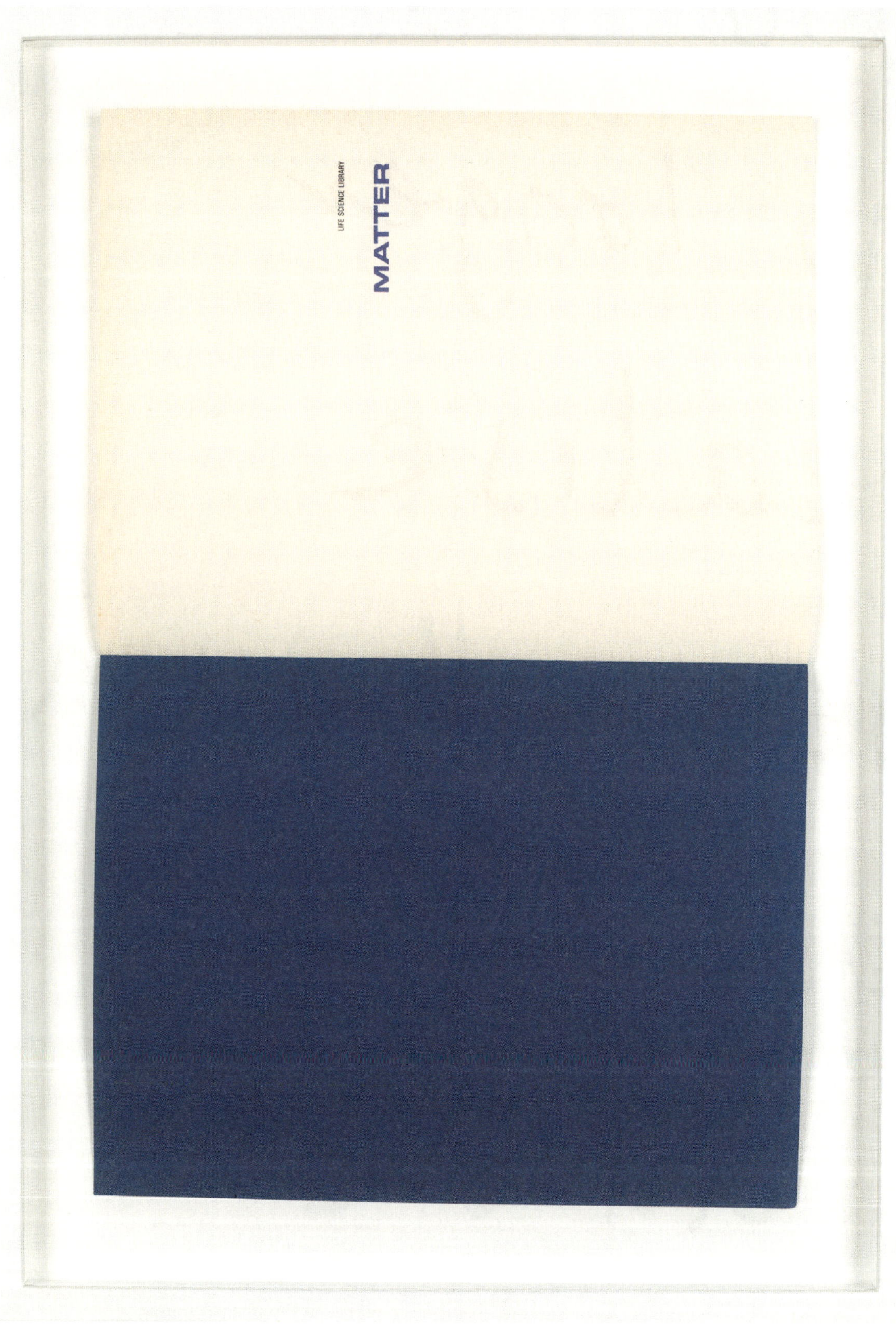
LIFE SCIENCE LIBRARY
MATTER

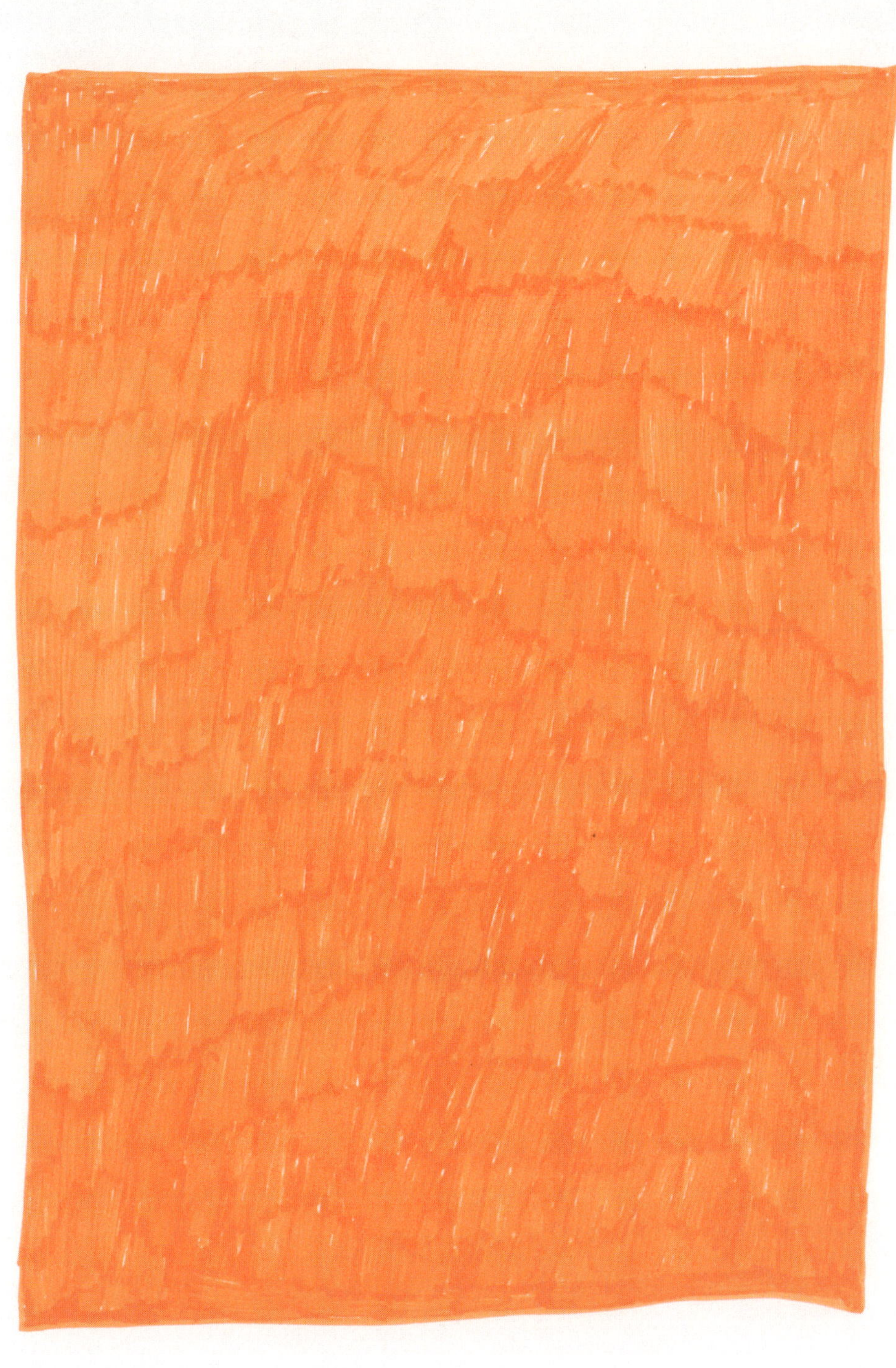

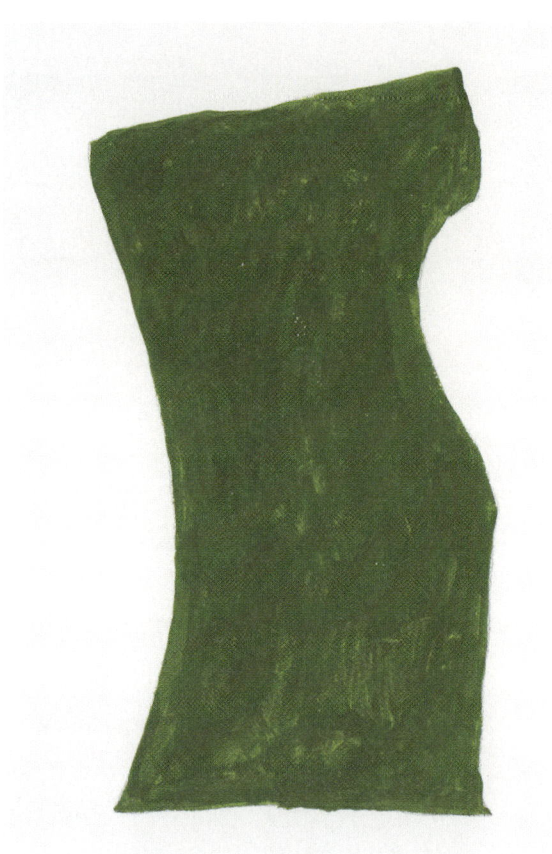

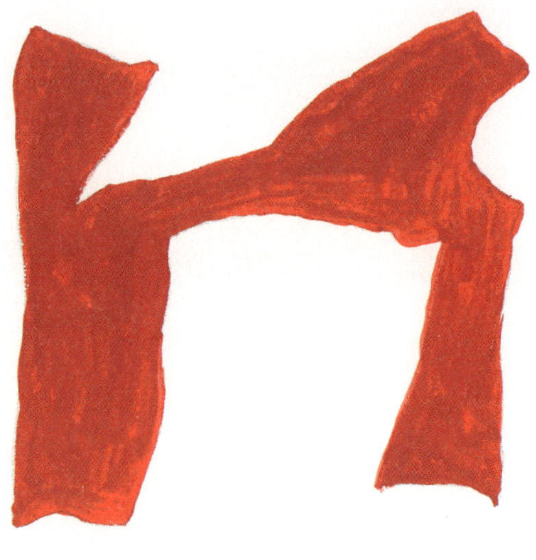

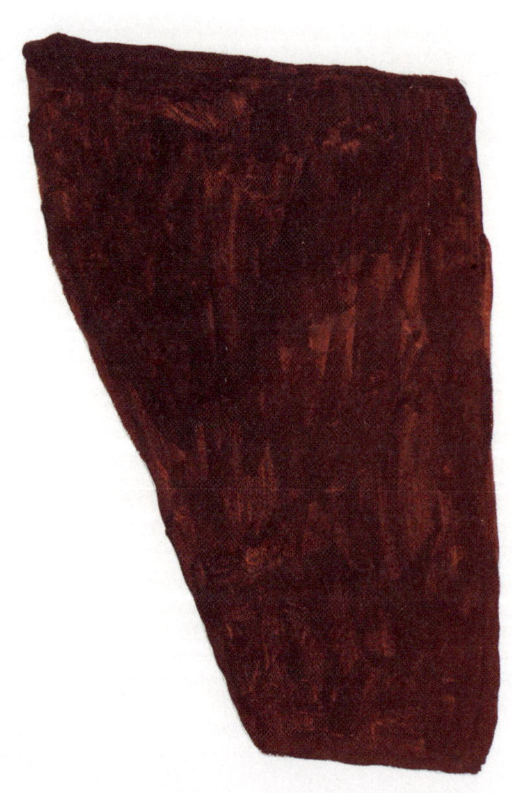

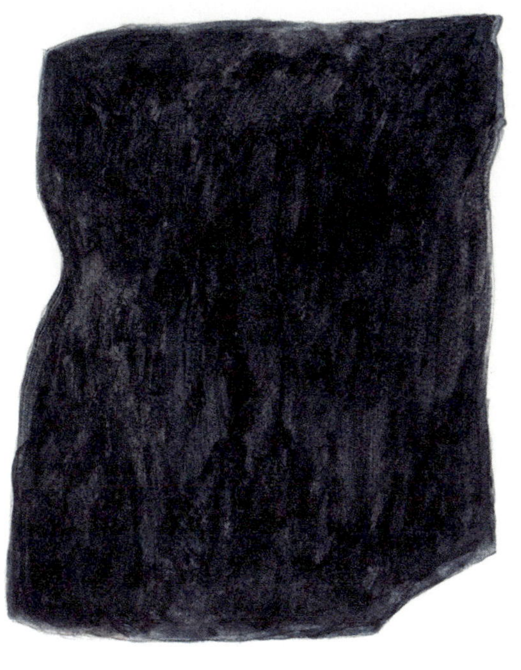

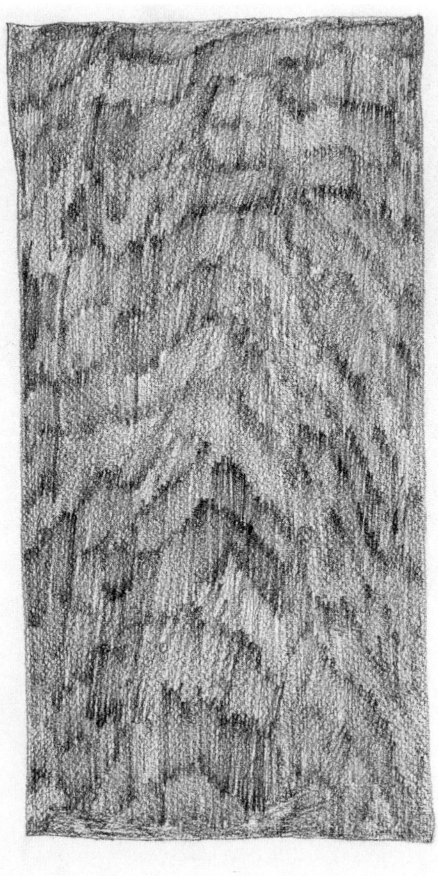

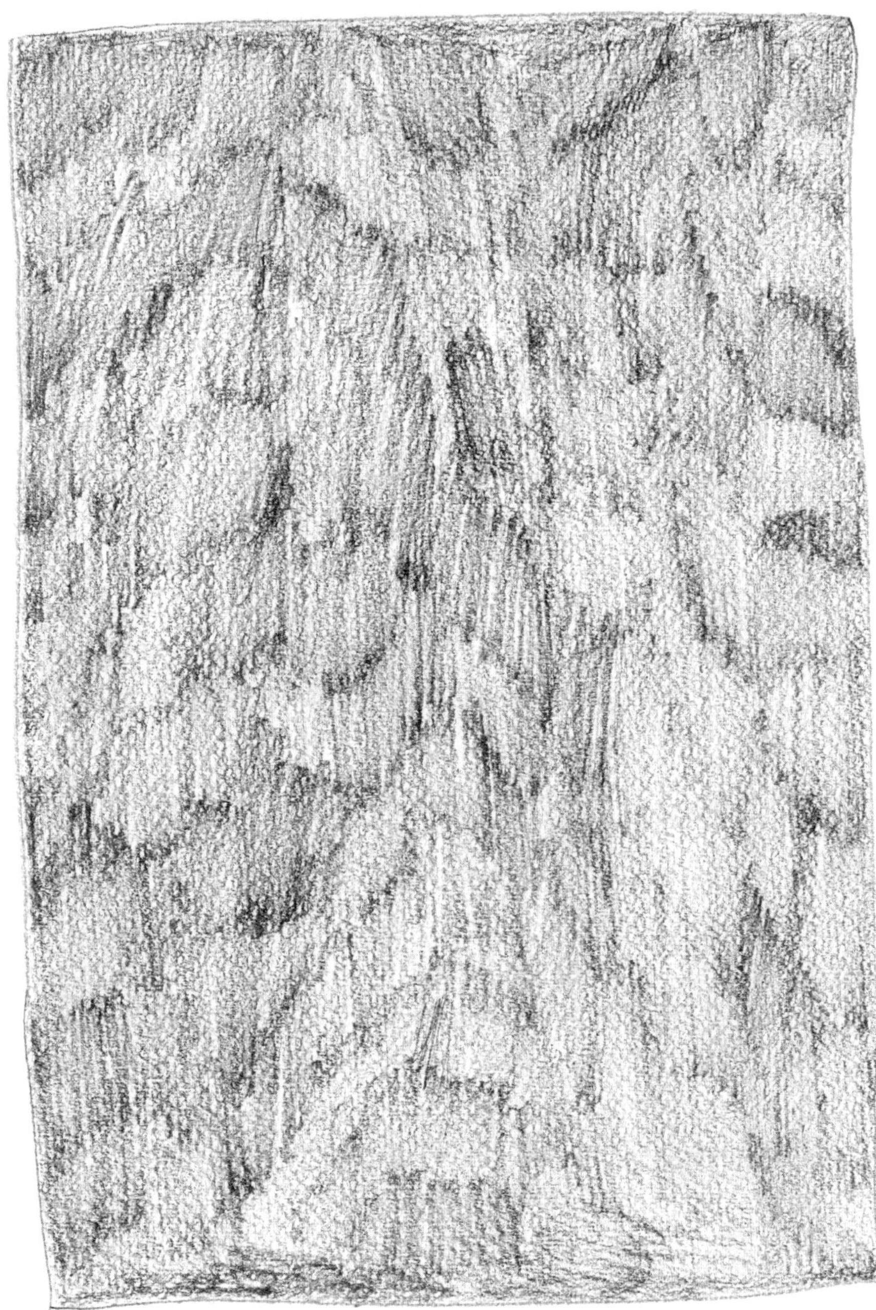

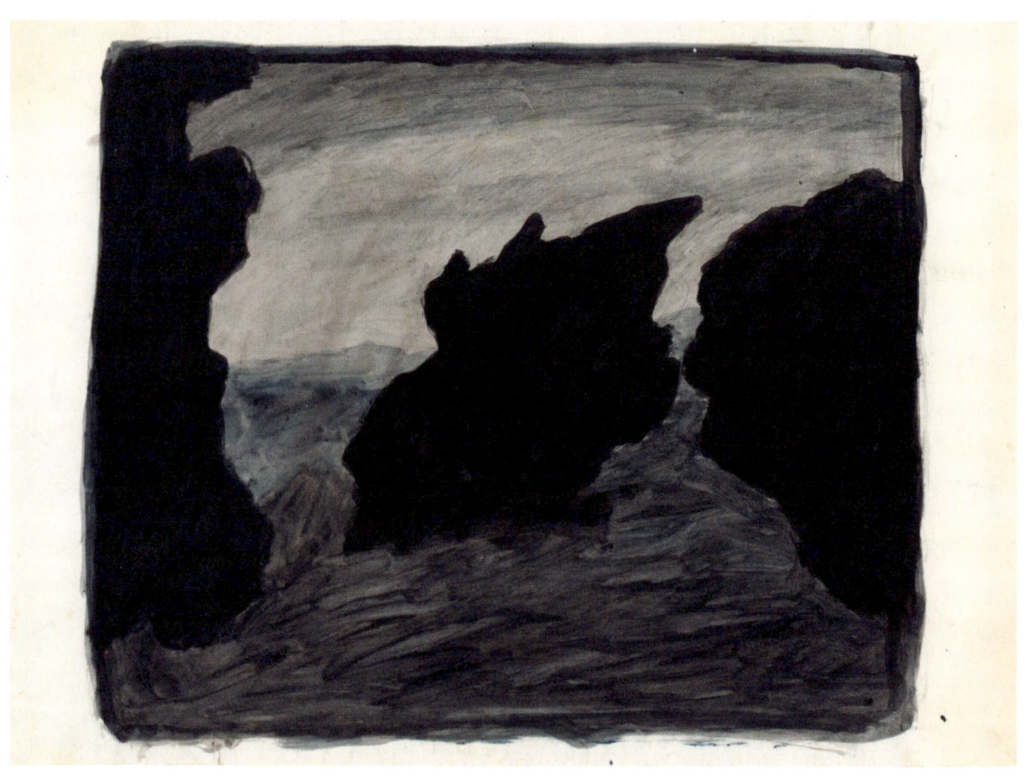

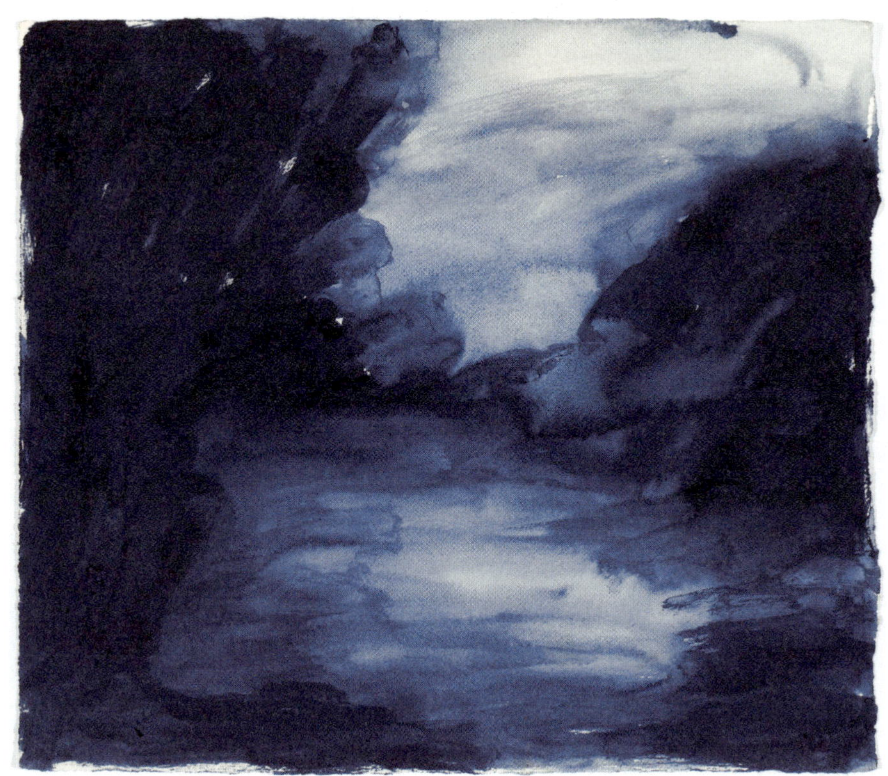

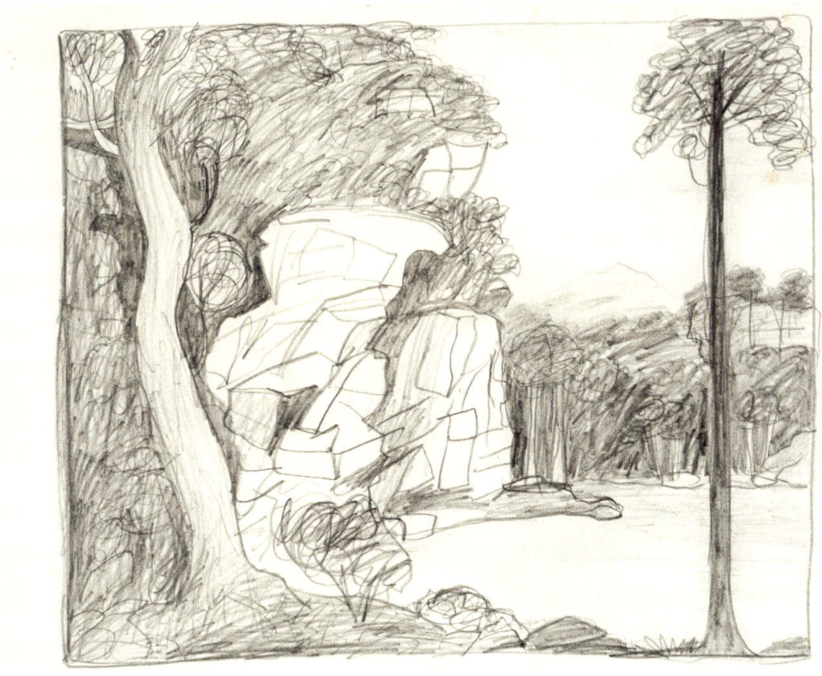

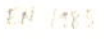

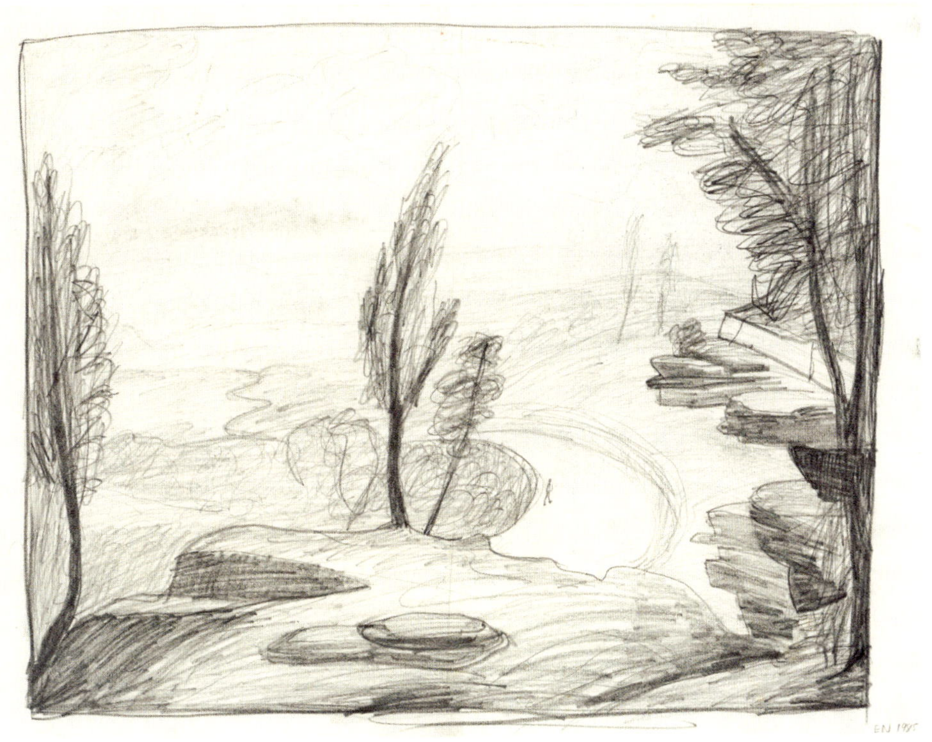

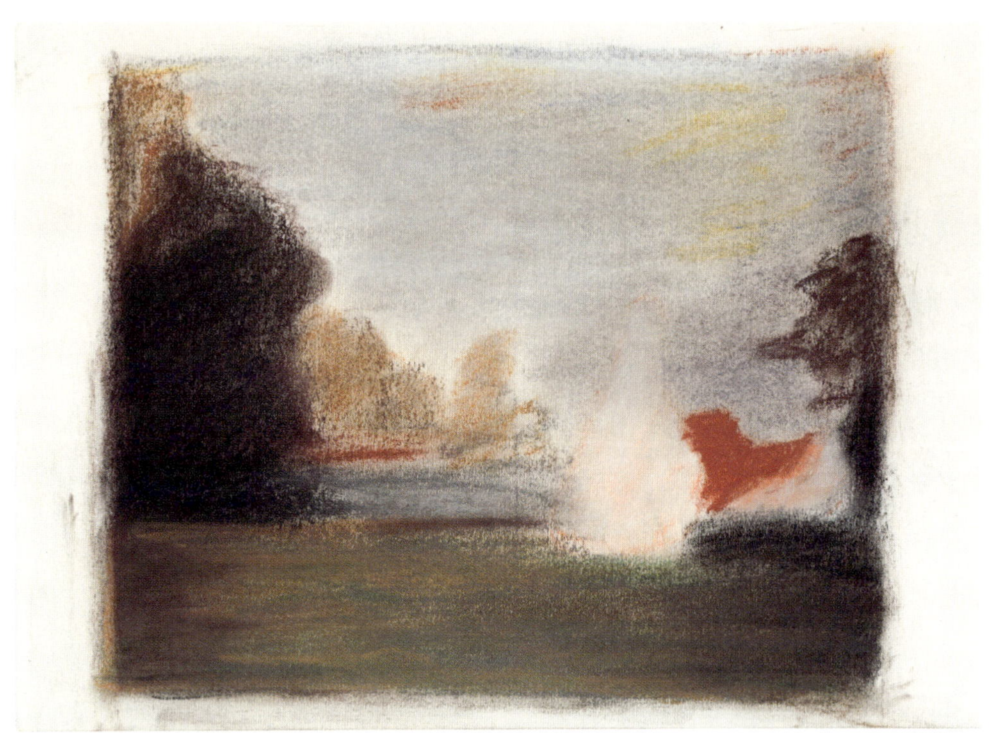

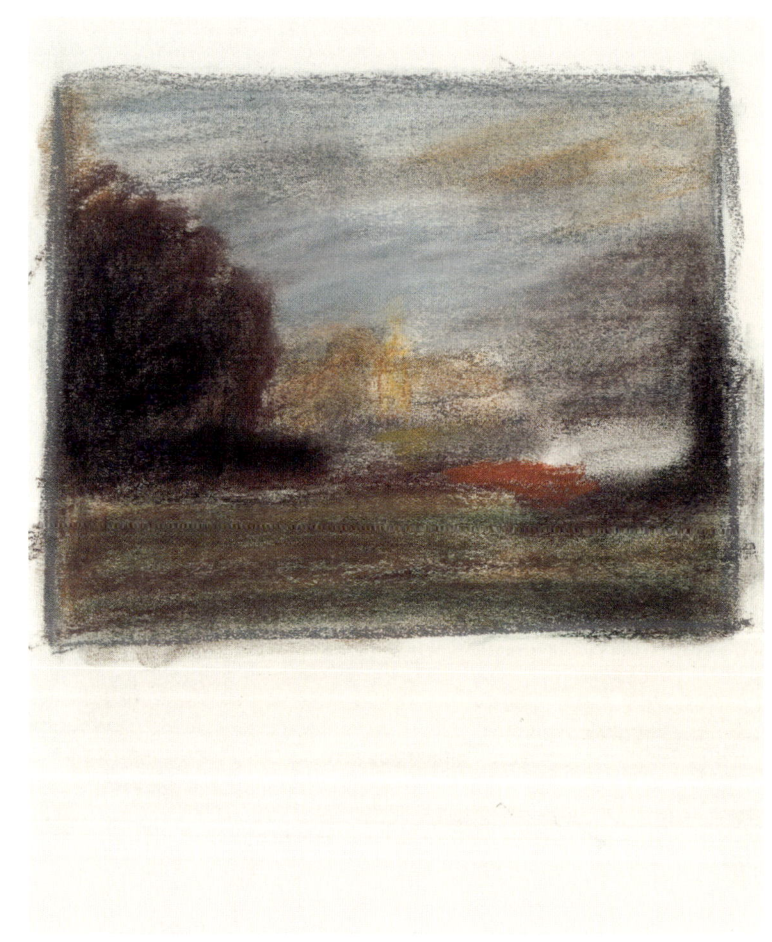

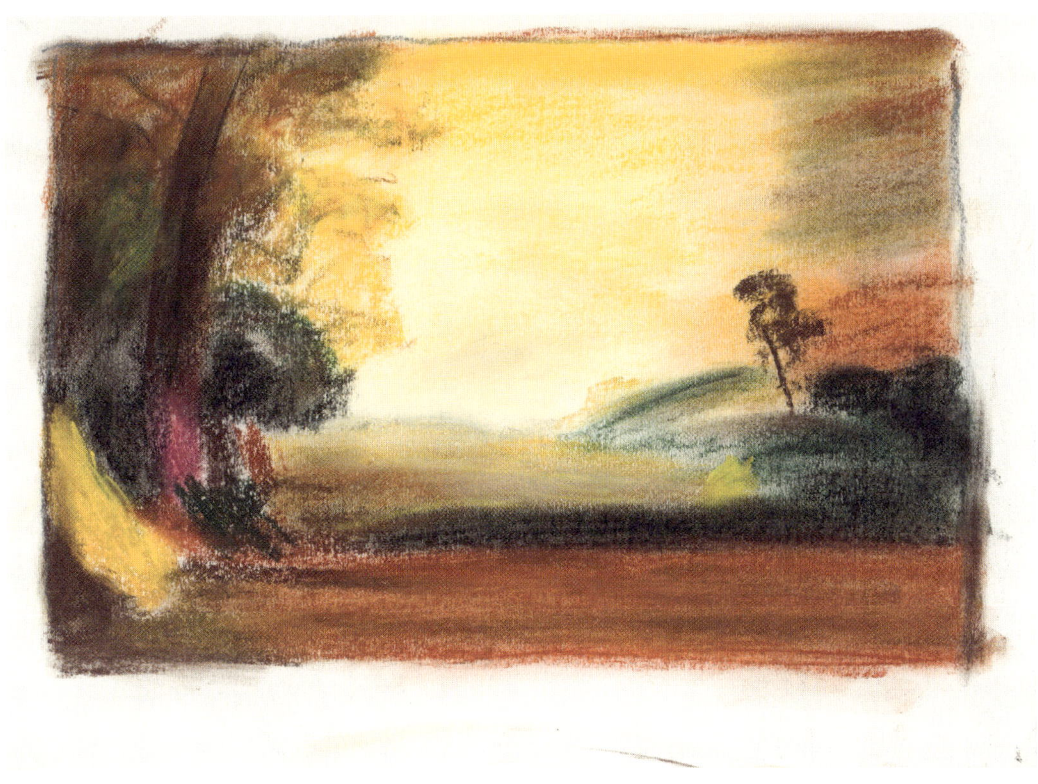

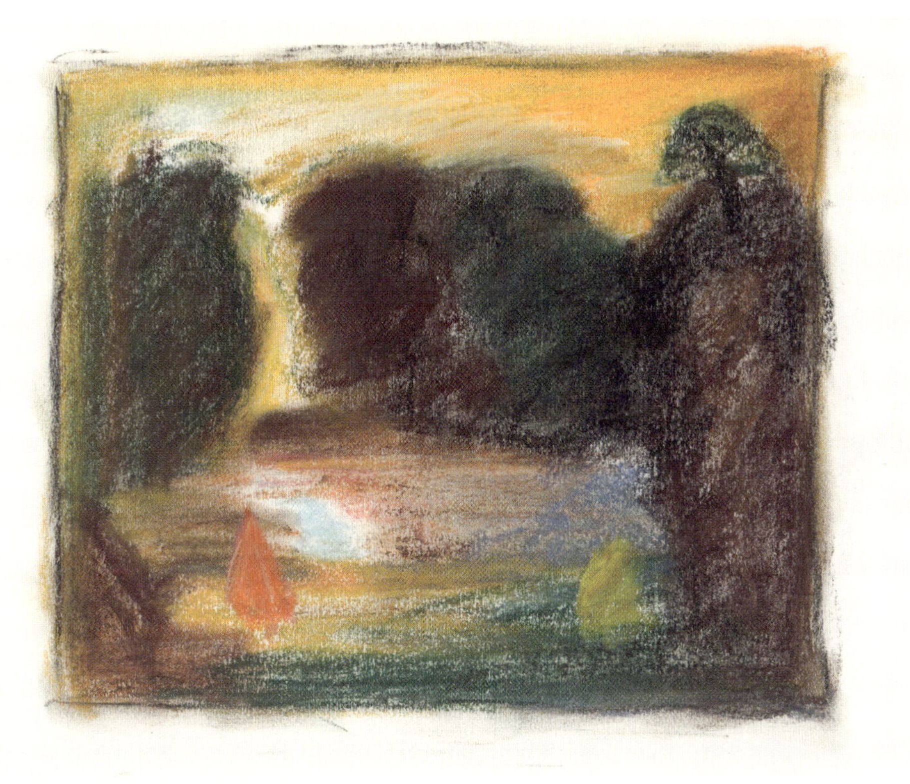

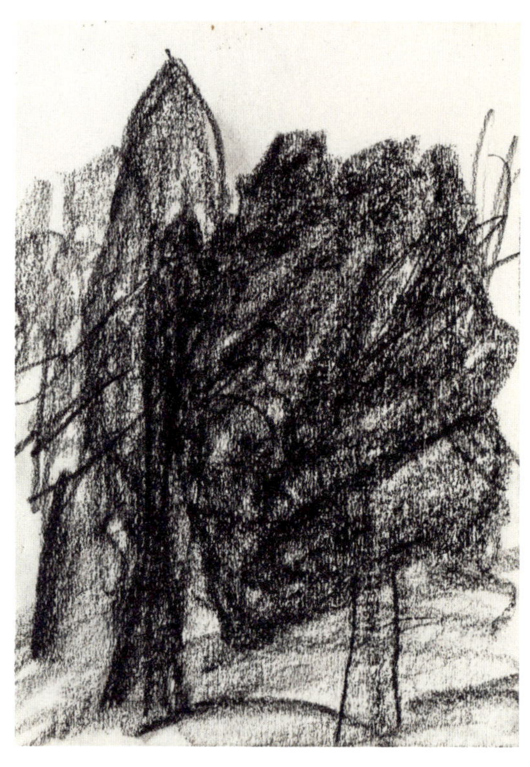

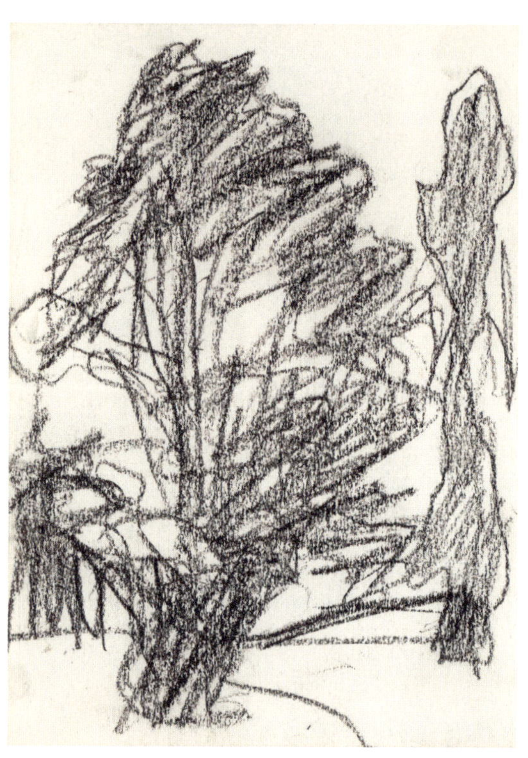

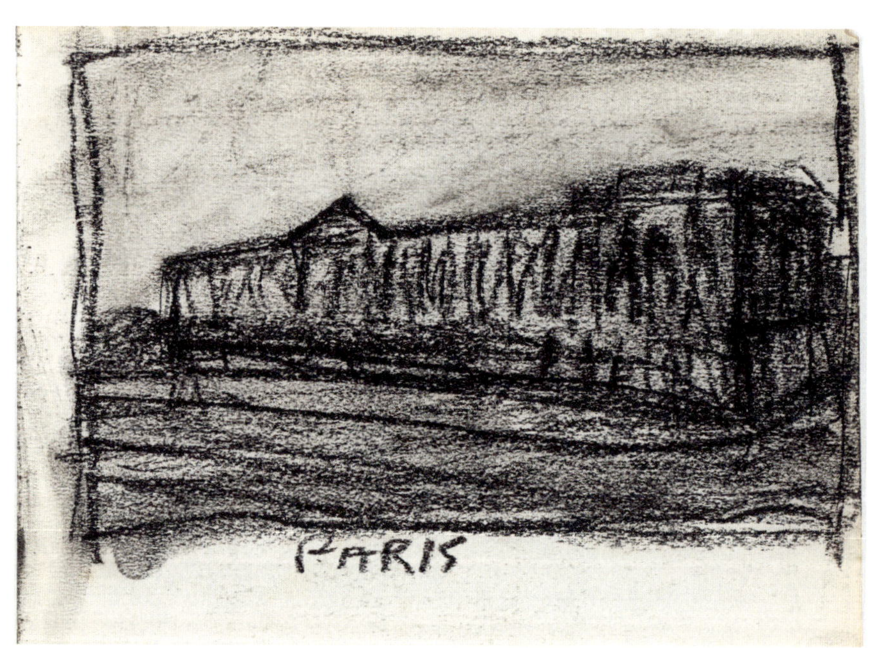
PARIS

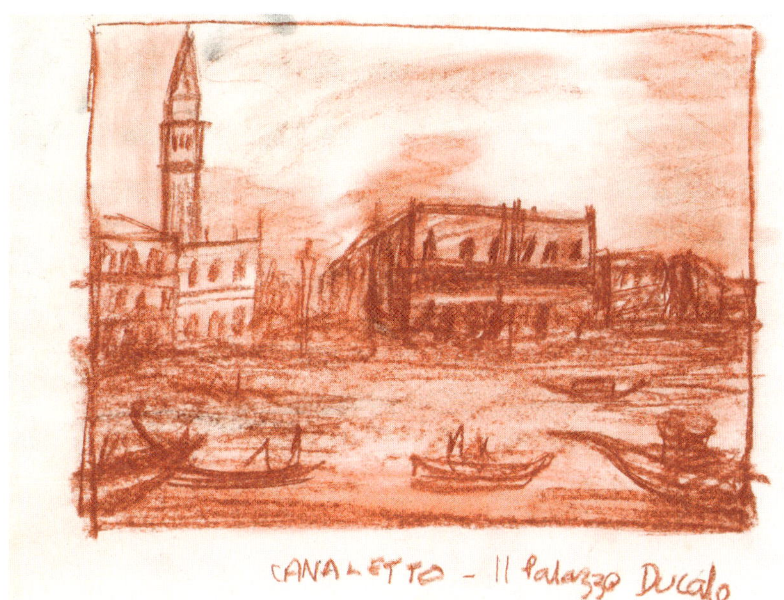
CANALETTO - Il Palazzo Ducale.

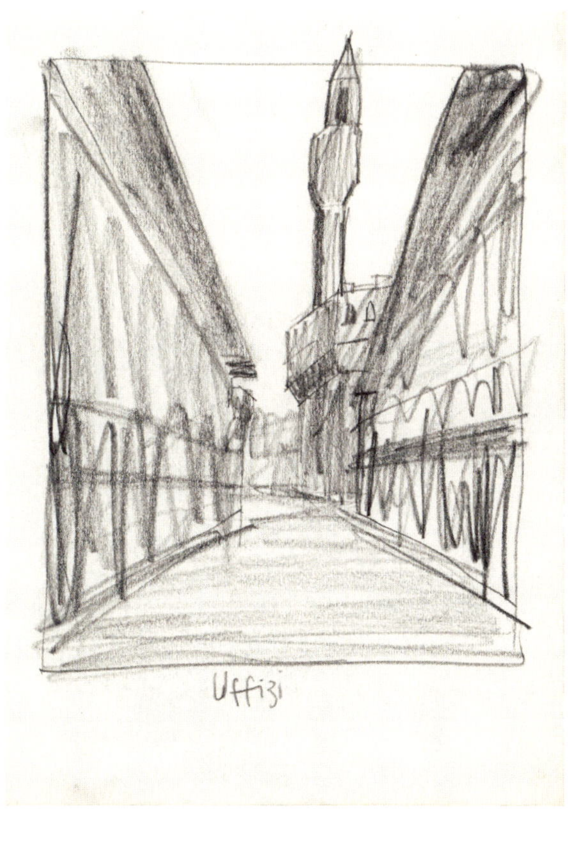
Uffizi

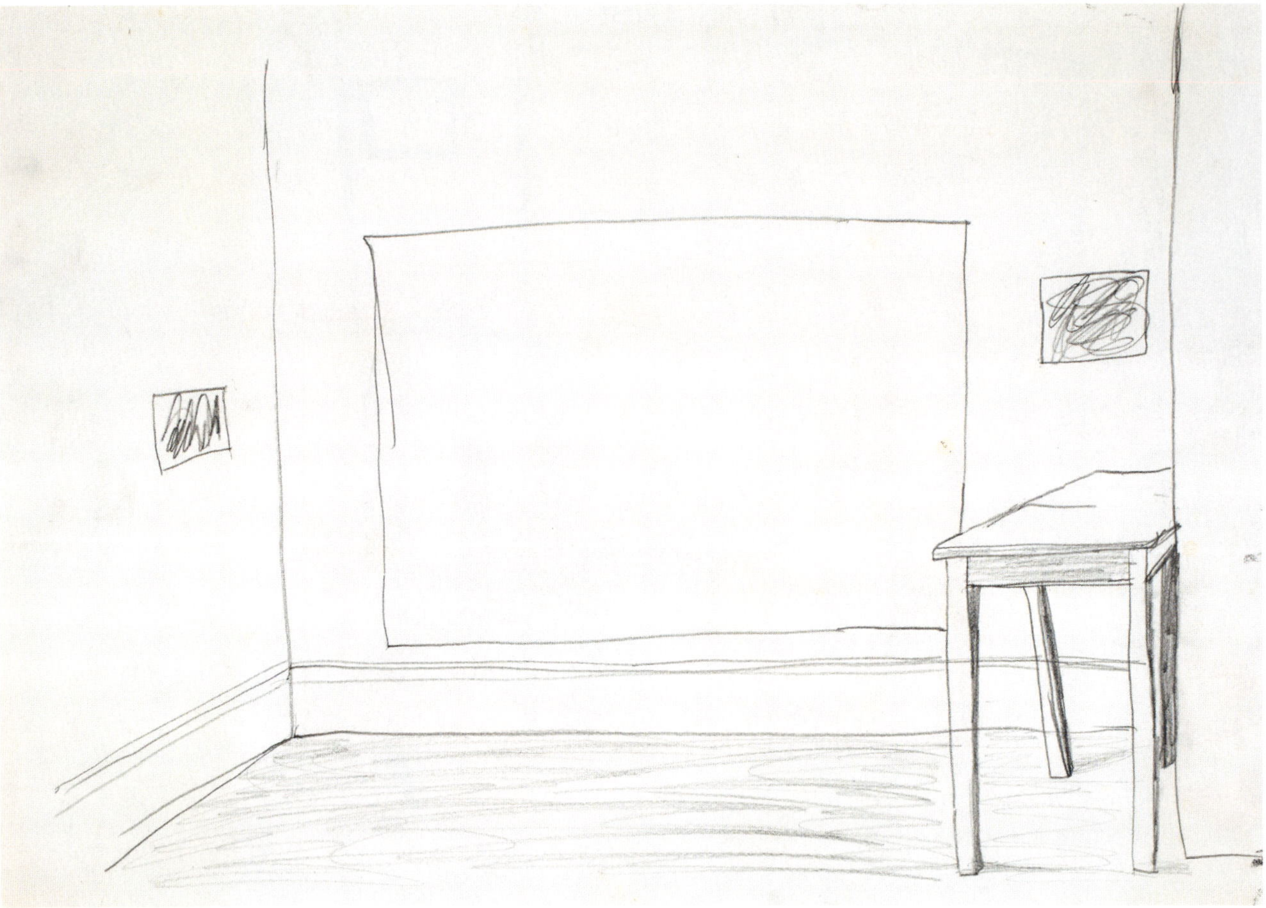

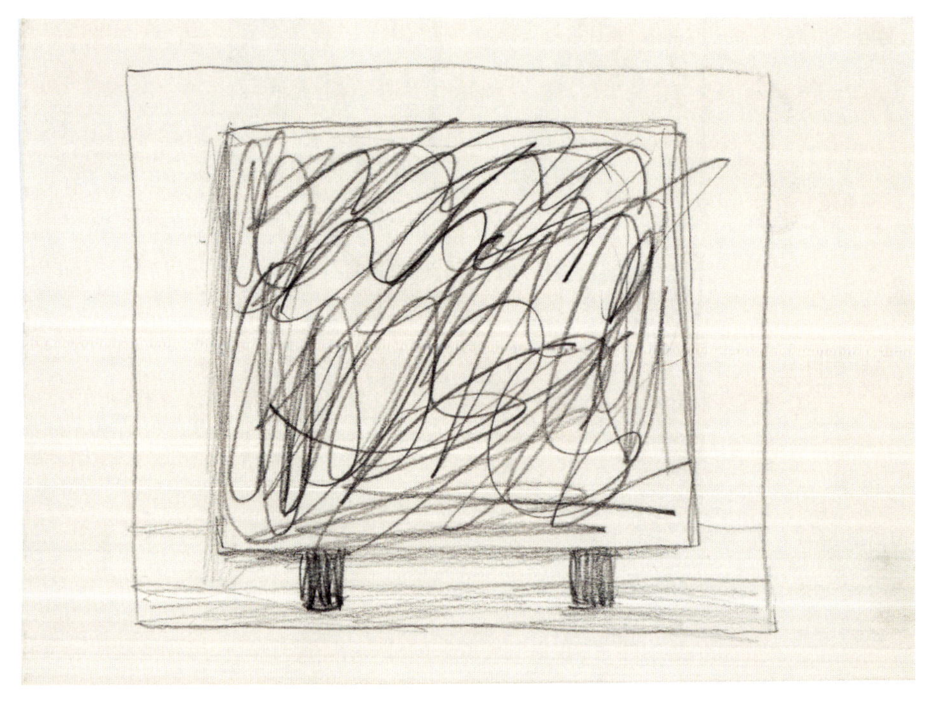

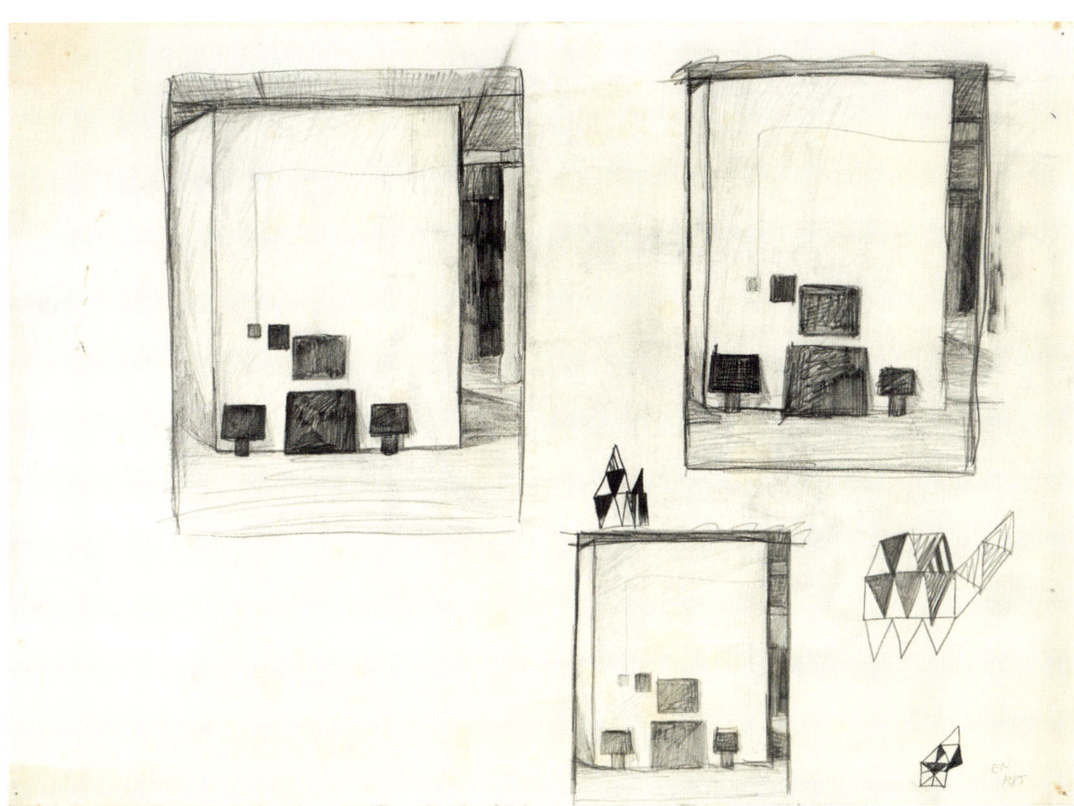

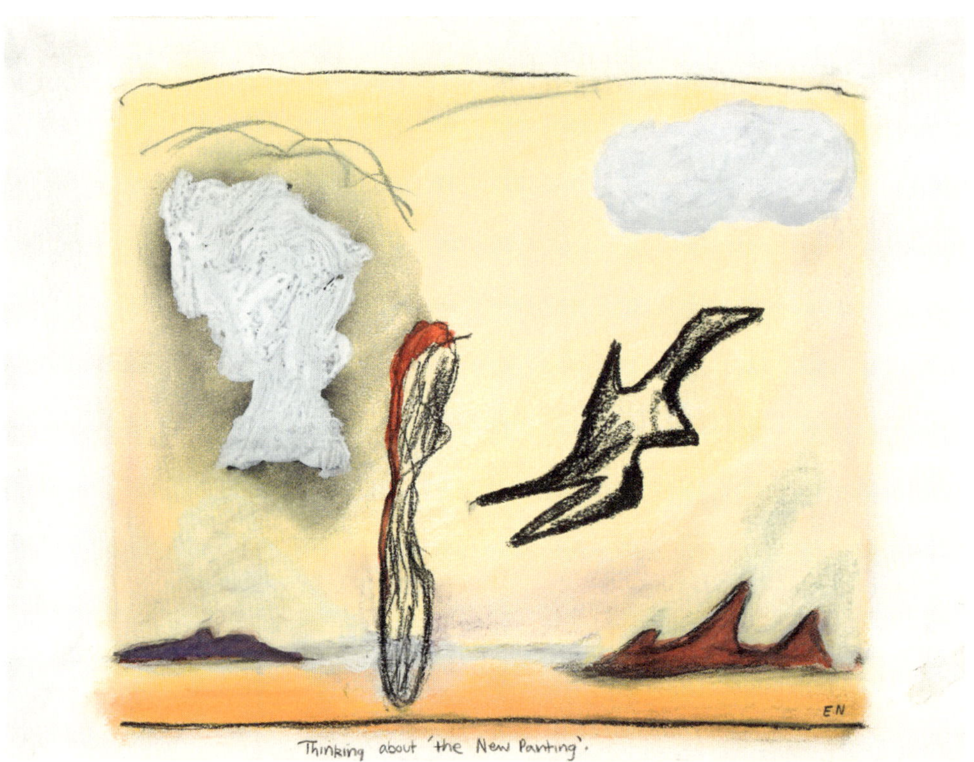
EN
Thinking about 'the New Panting'.

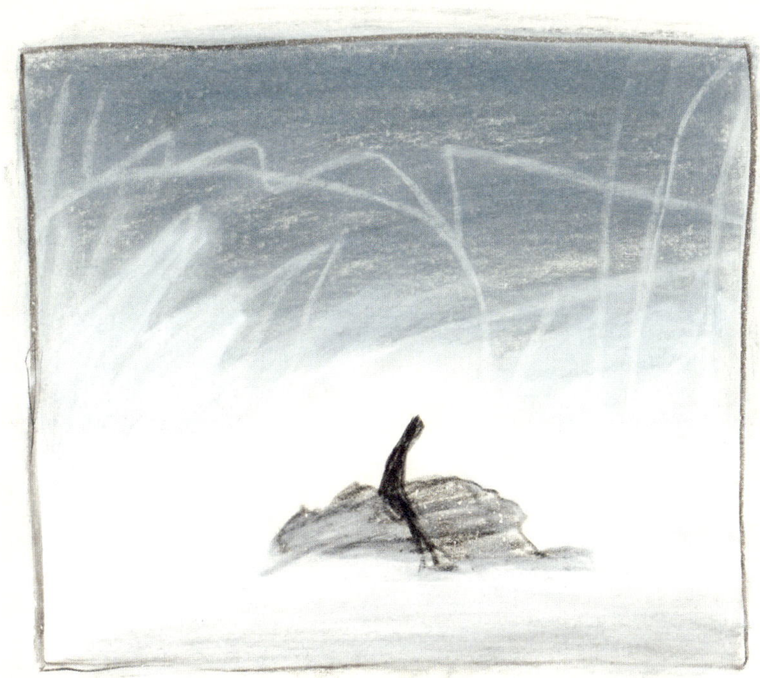

"I'm cold" the lover says.

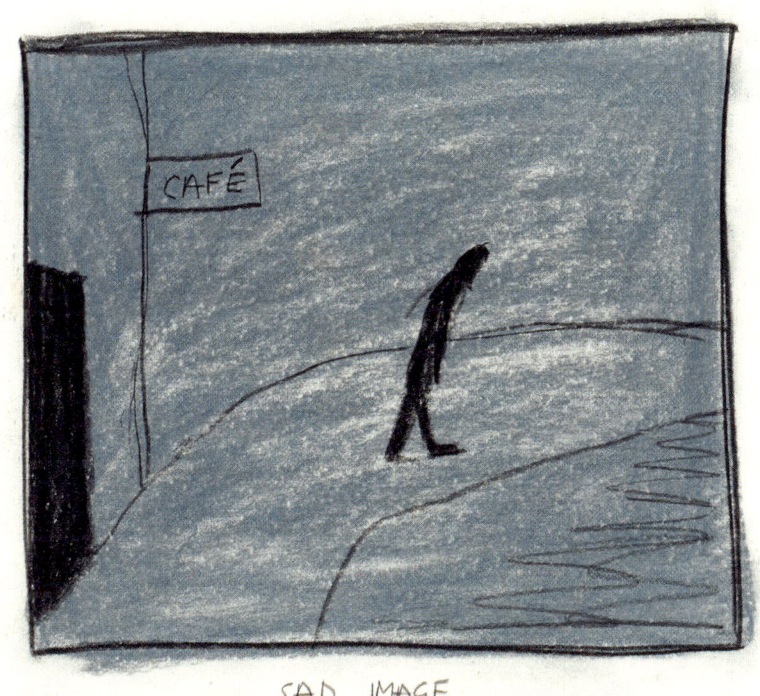

SAD IMAGE

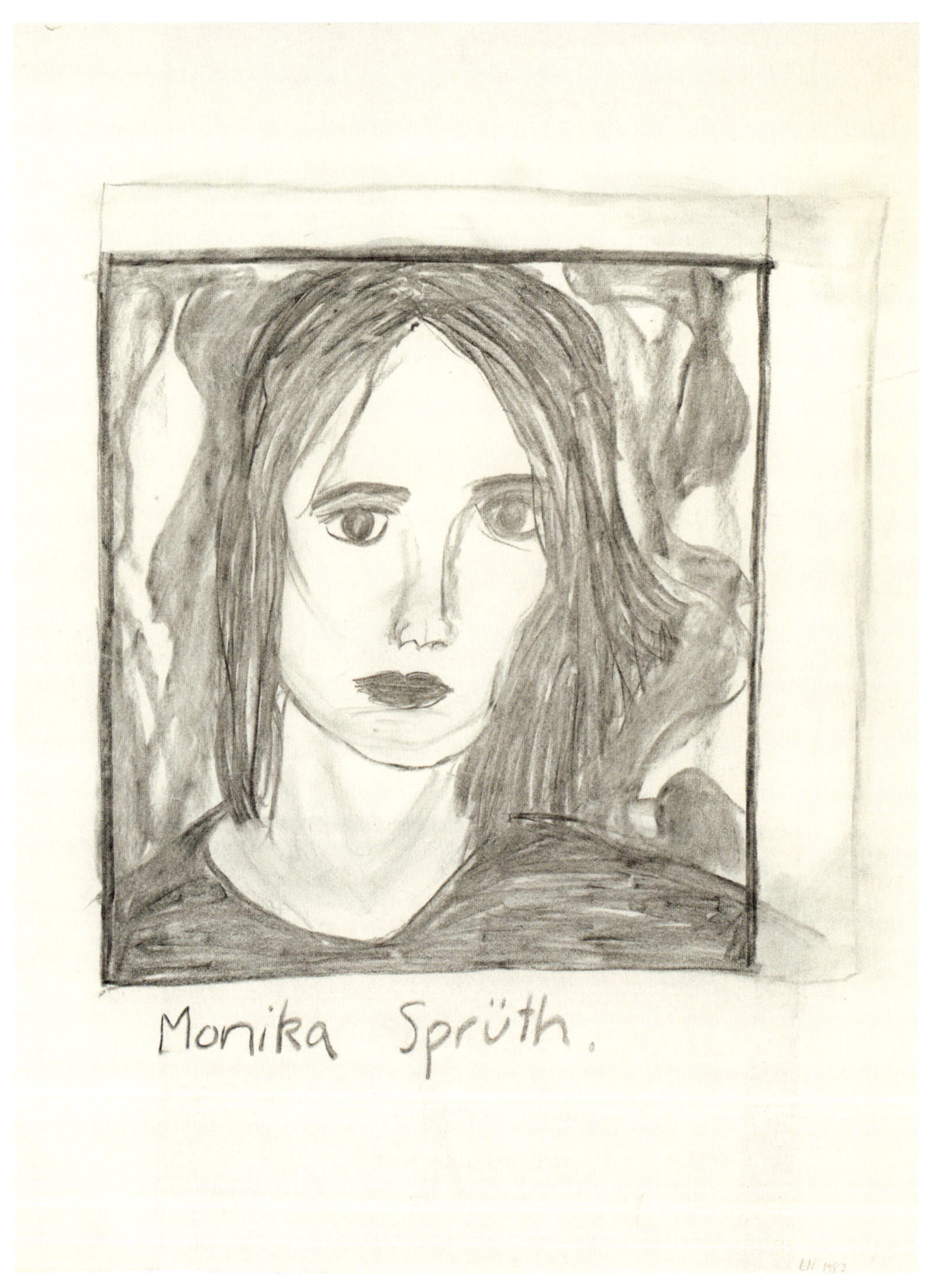
Monika Sprüth.

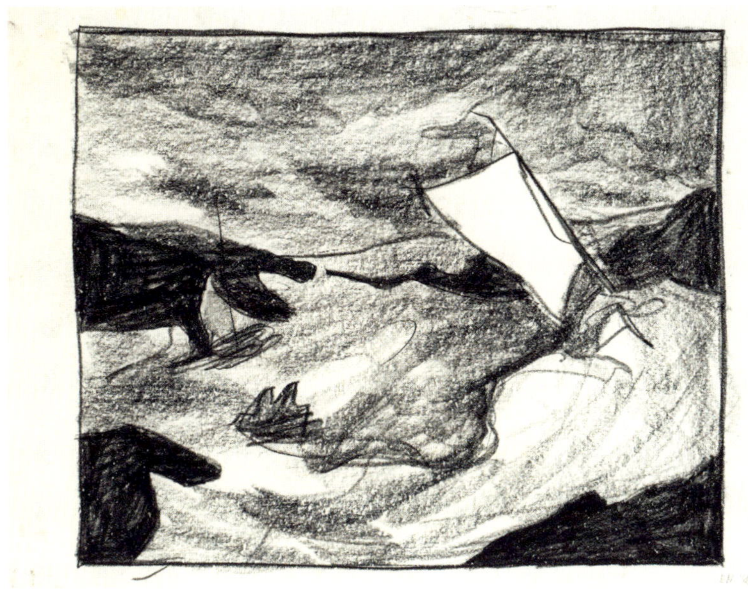

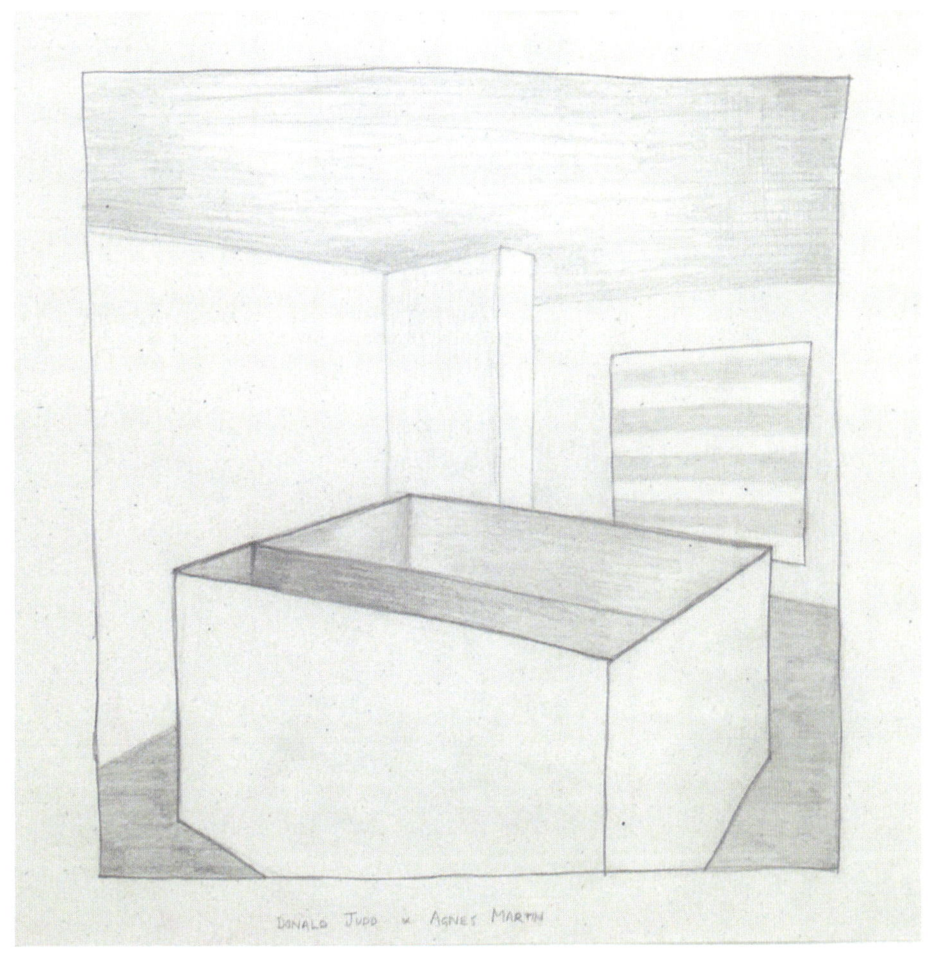
DONALD JUDD + AGNES MARTIN

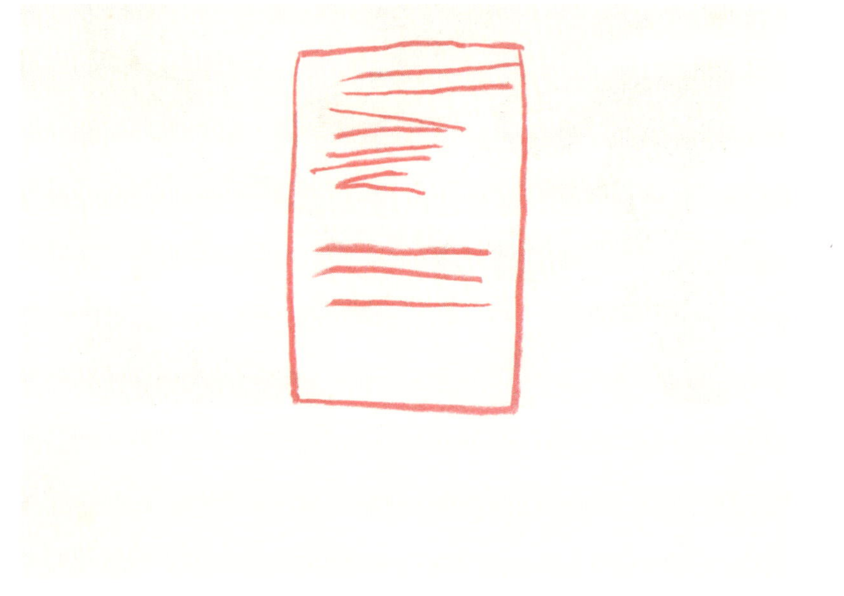

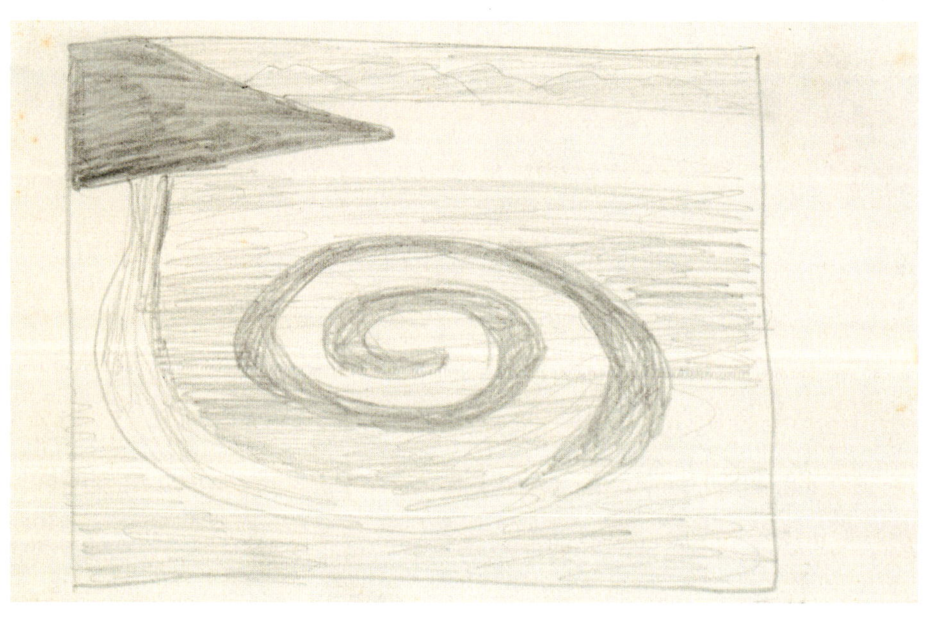

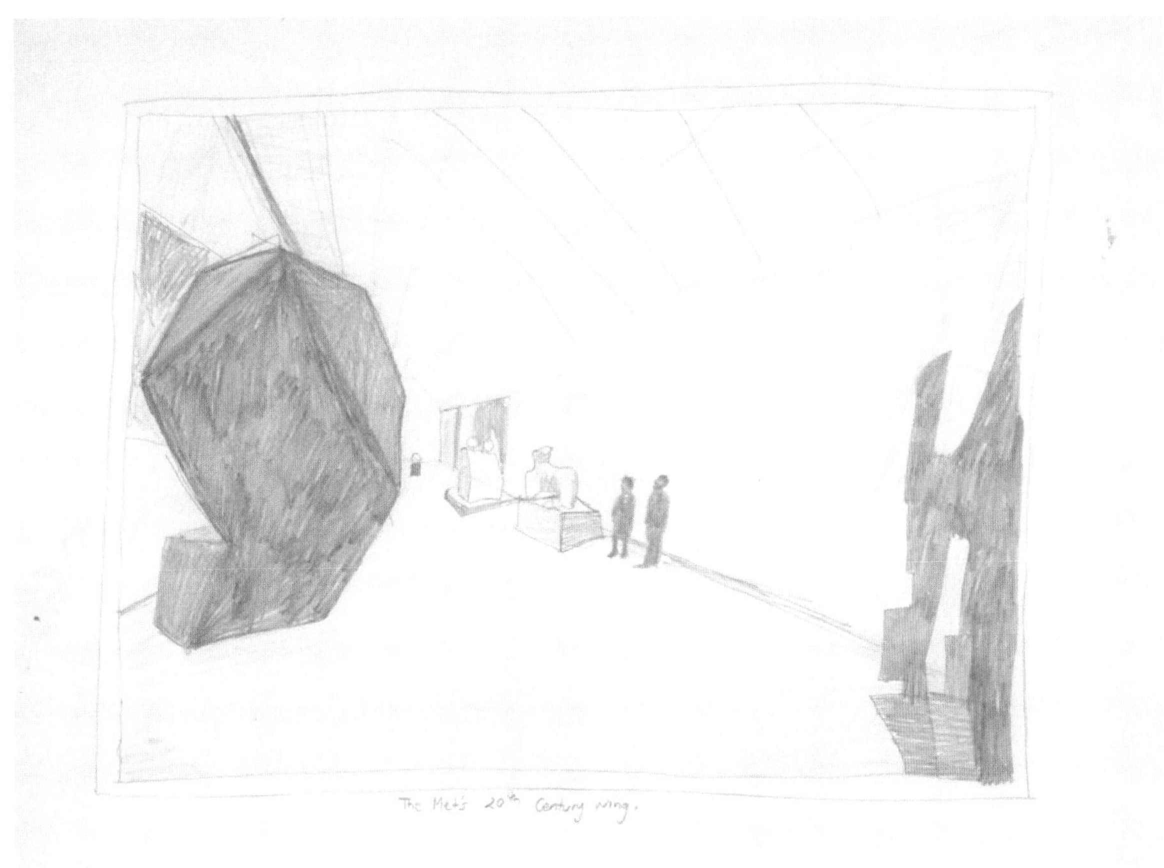
The Met's 20th Century Wing.

A gallery of works by living artists.
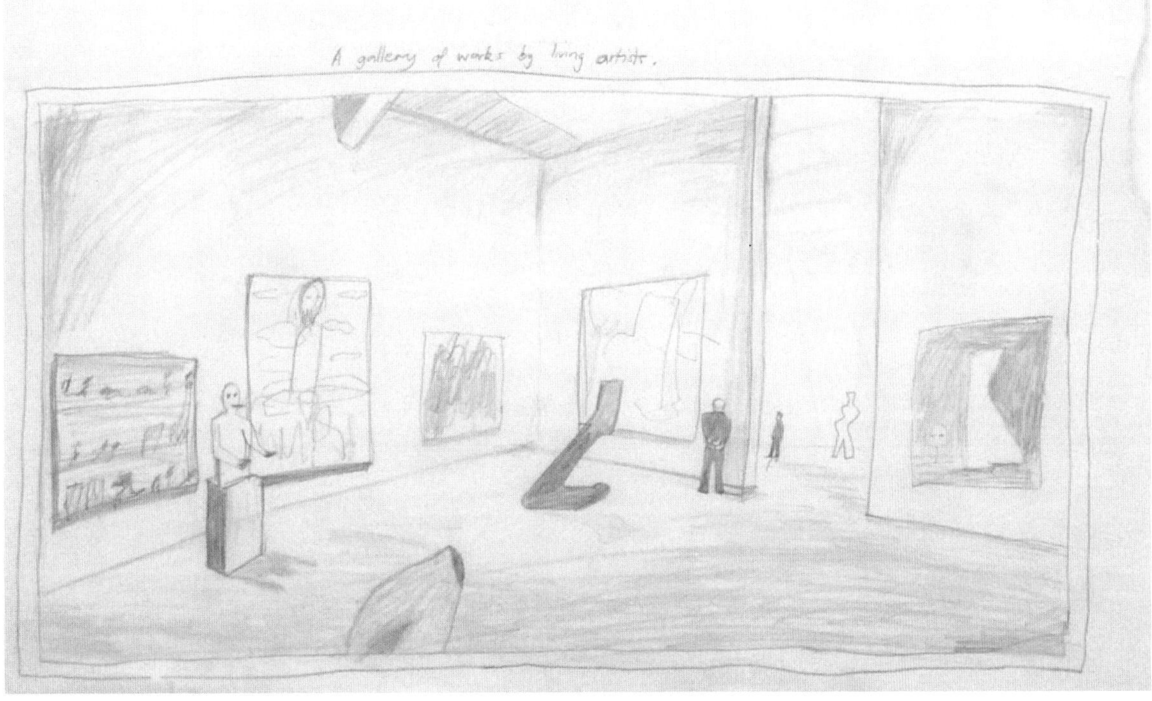

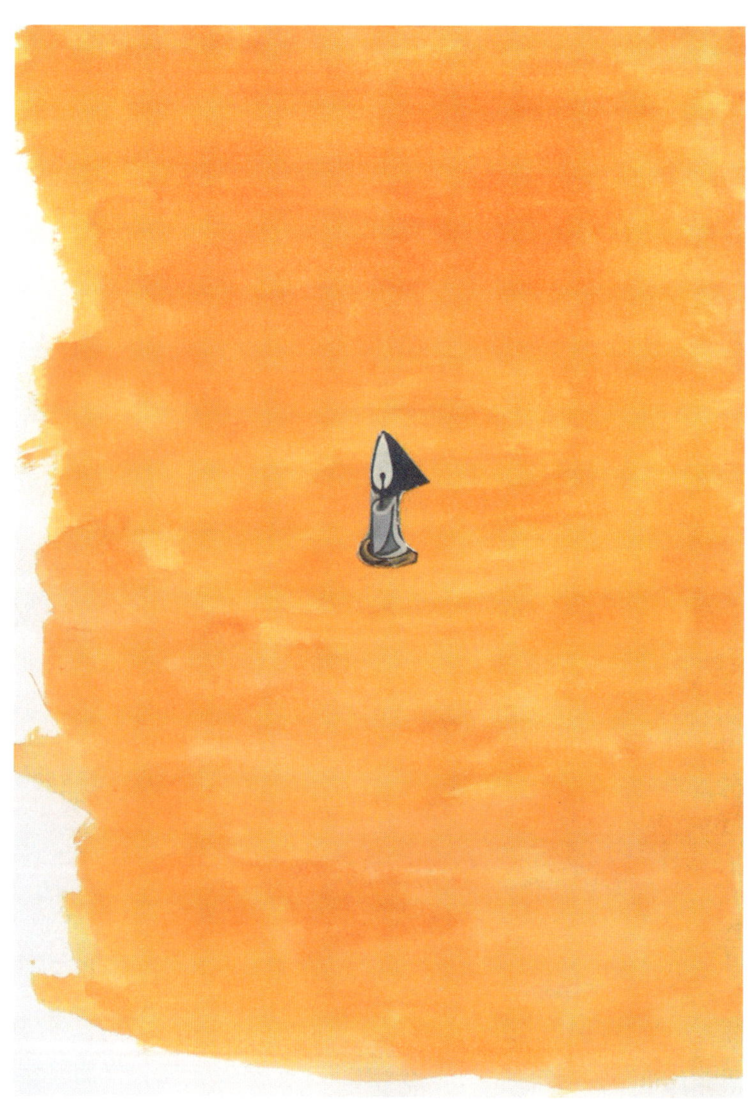

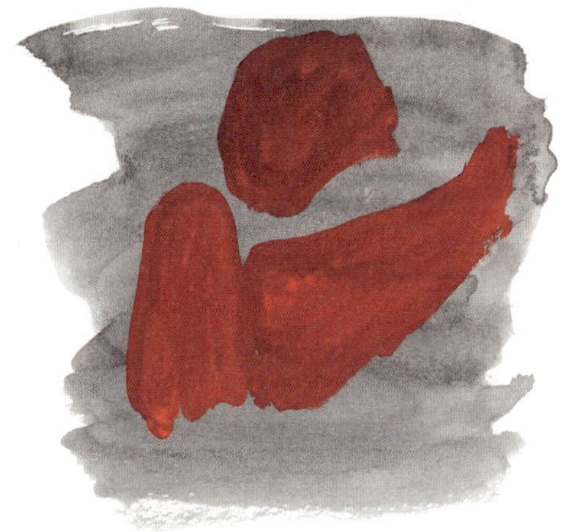

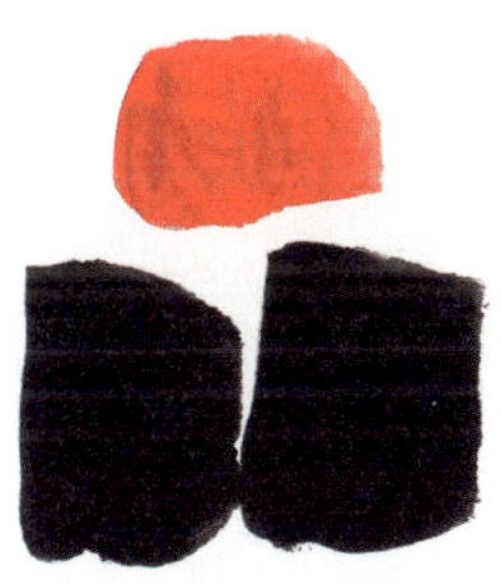

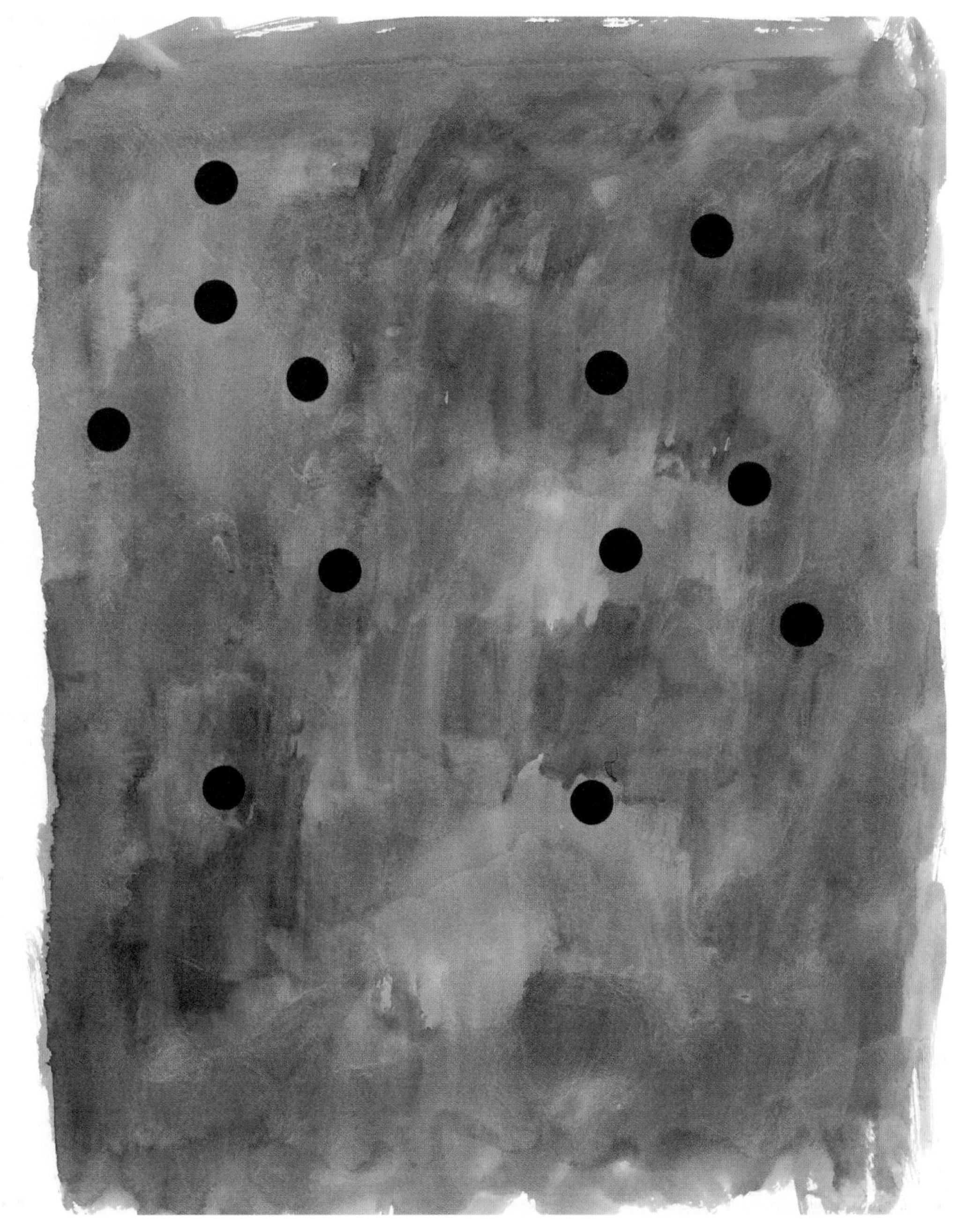

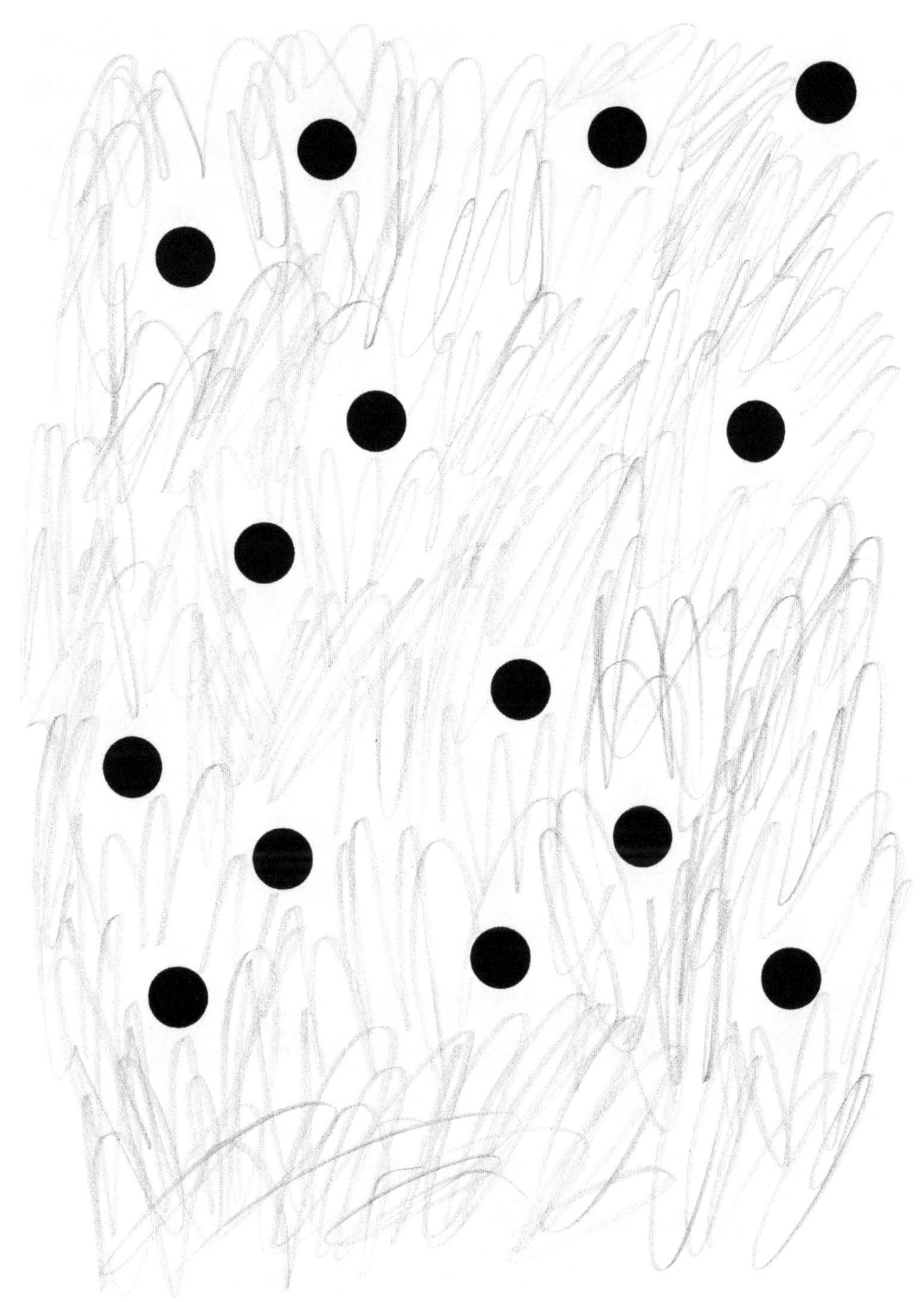

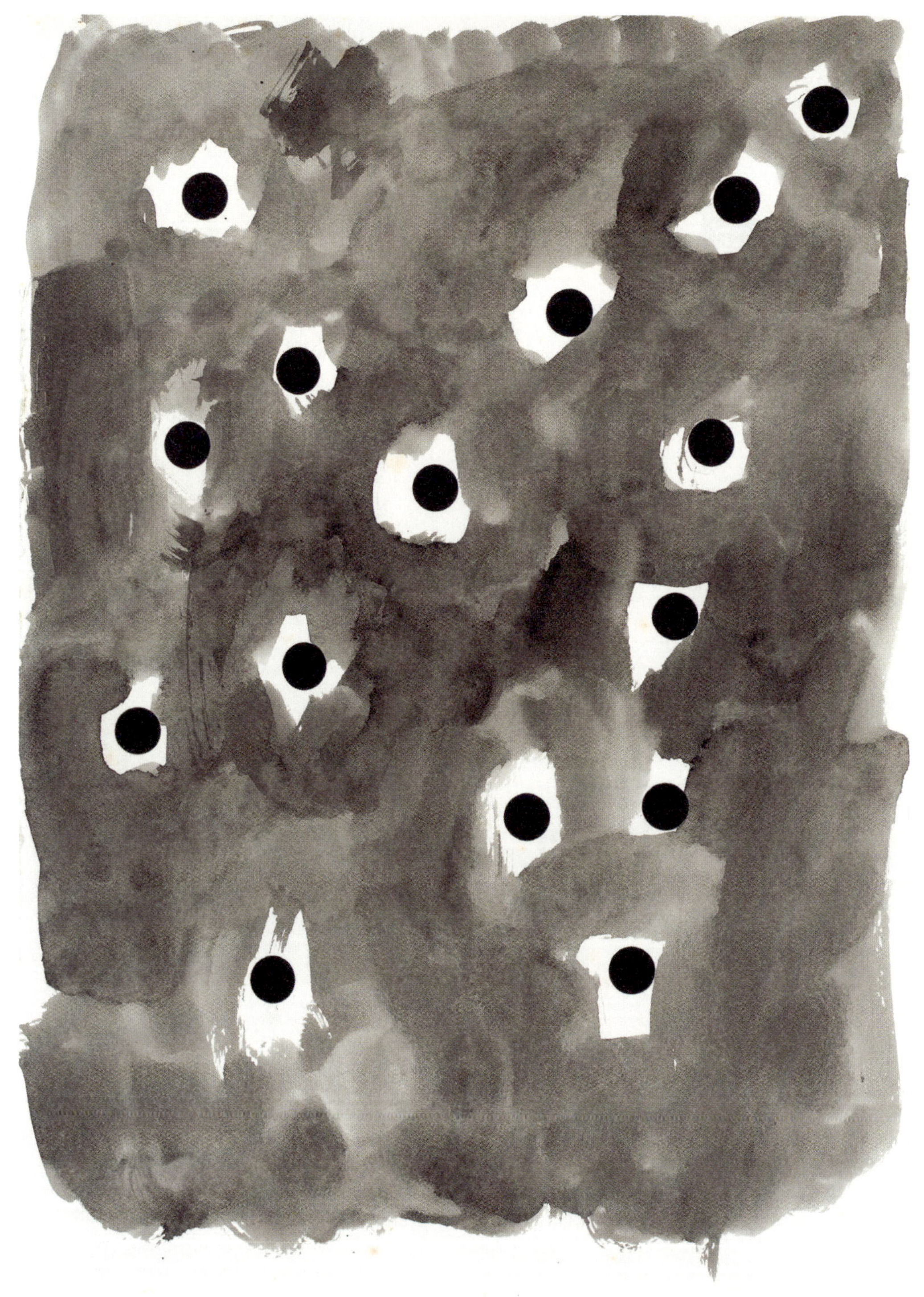

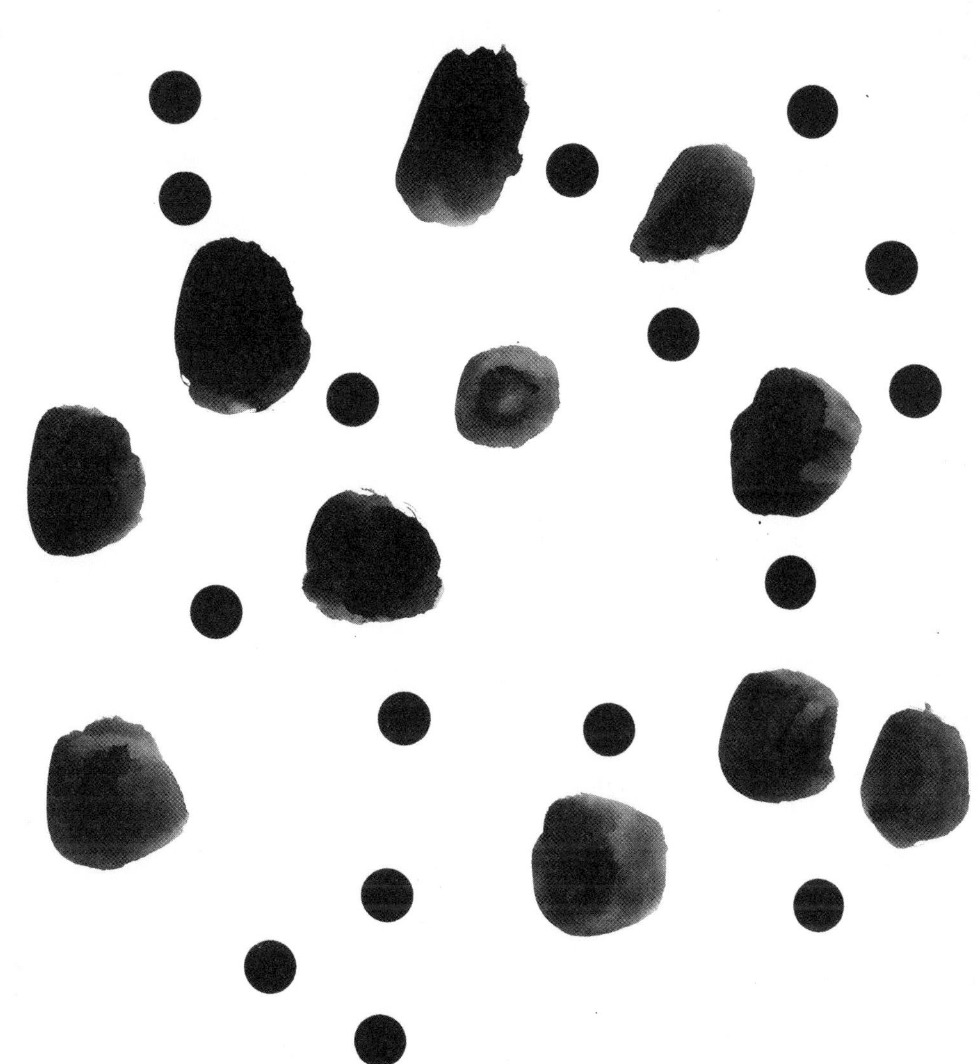

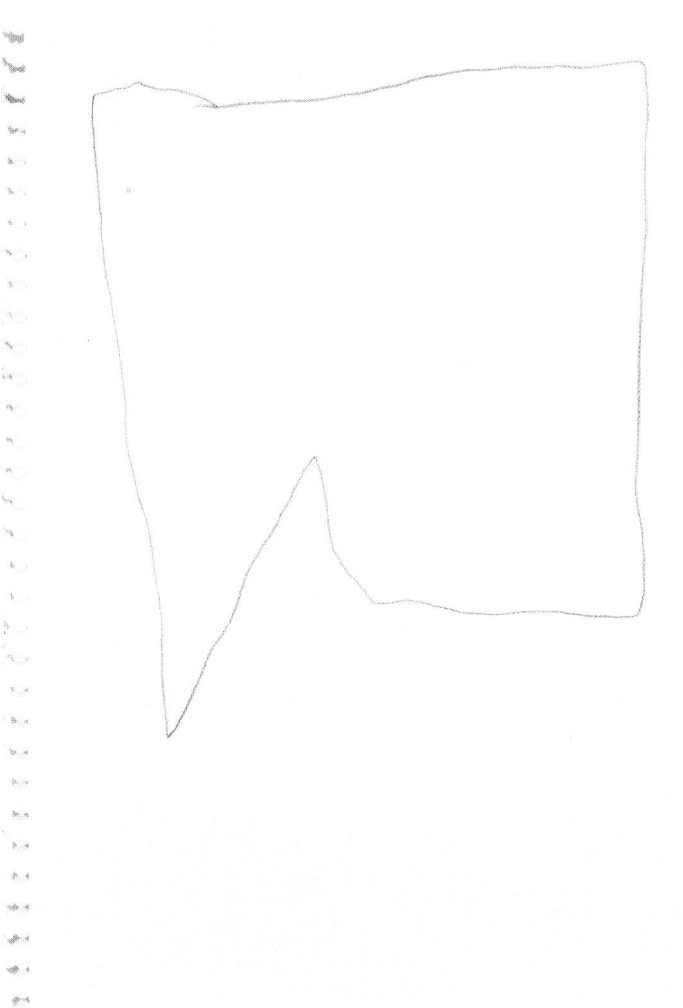

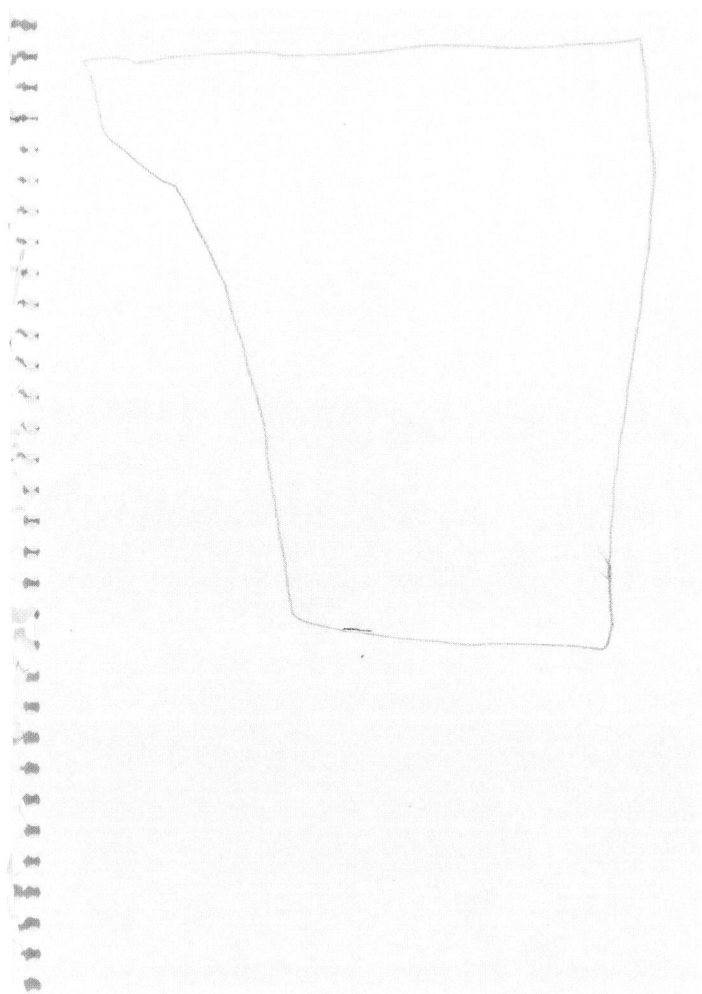

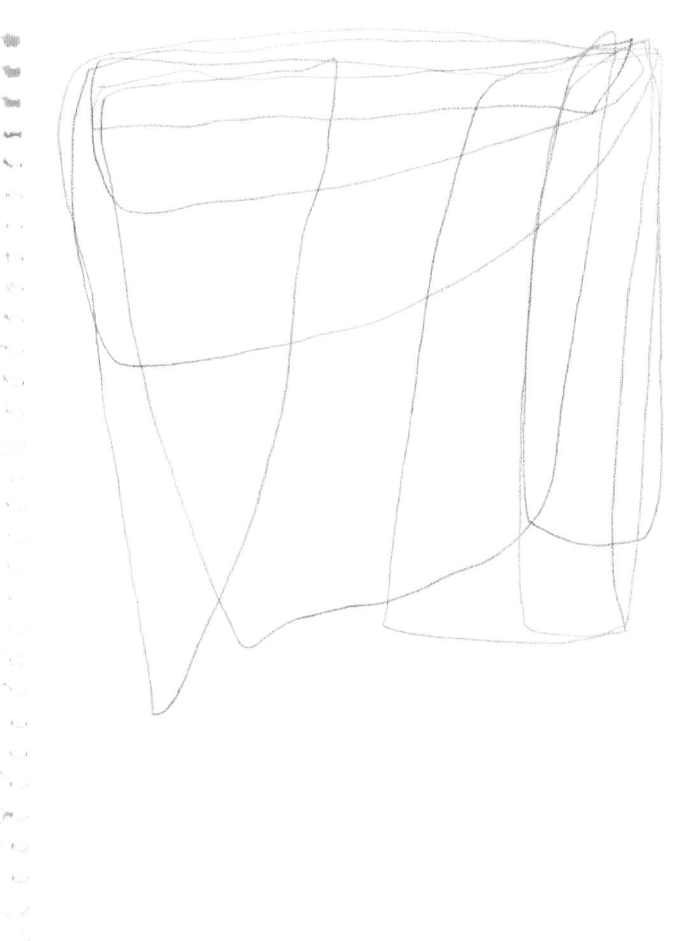

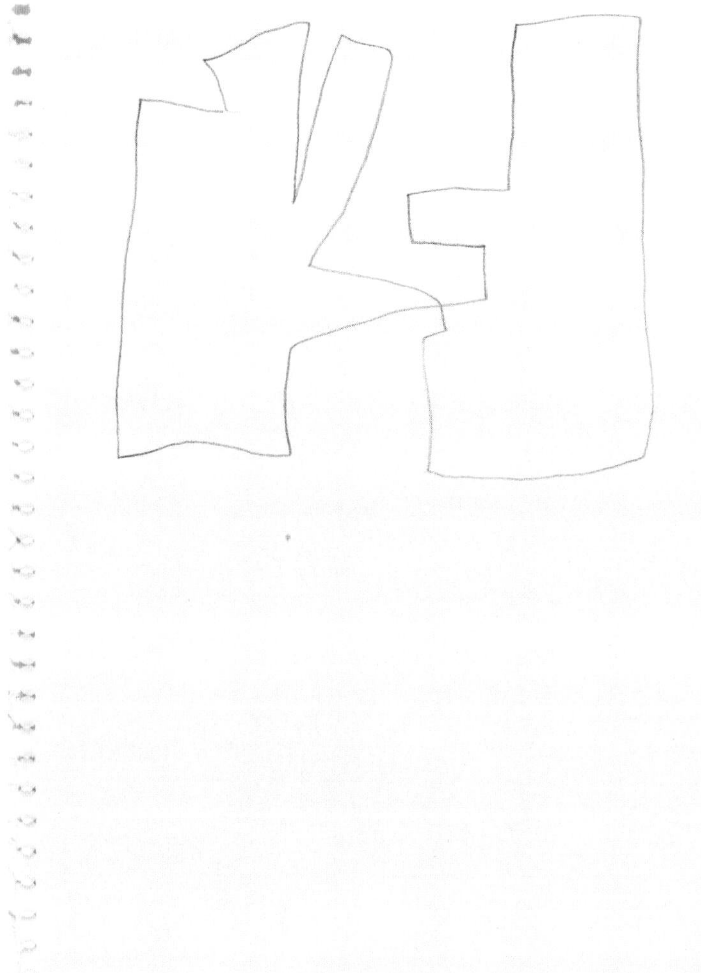

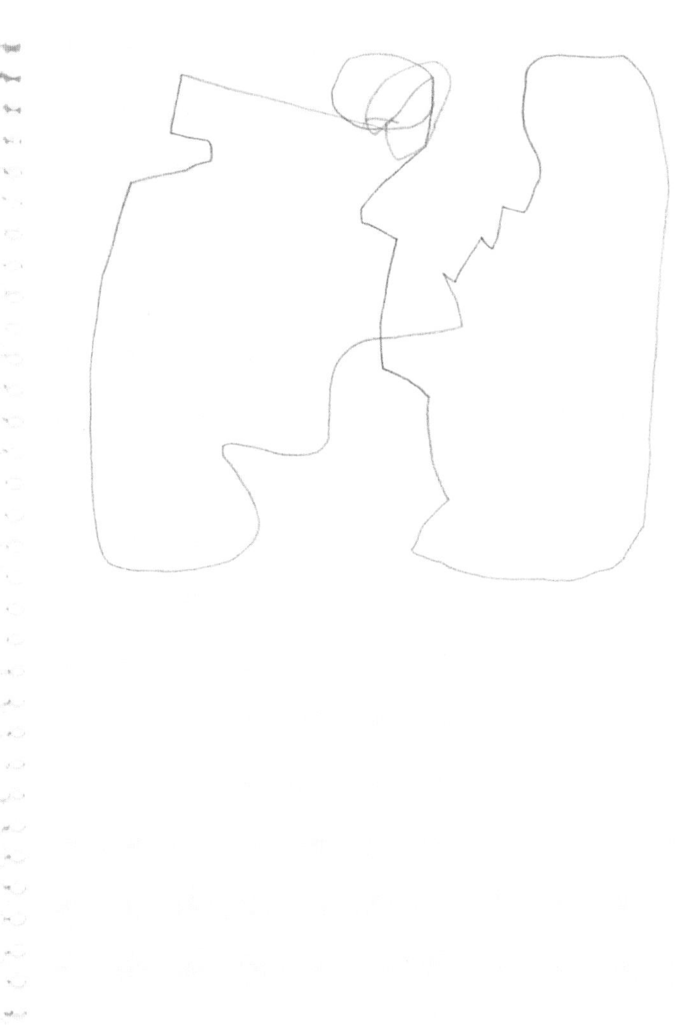

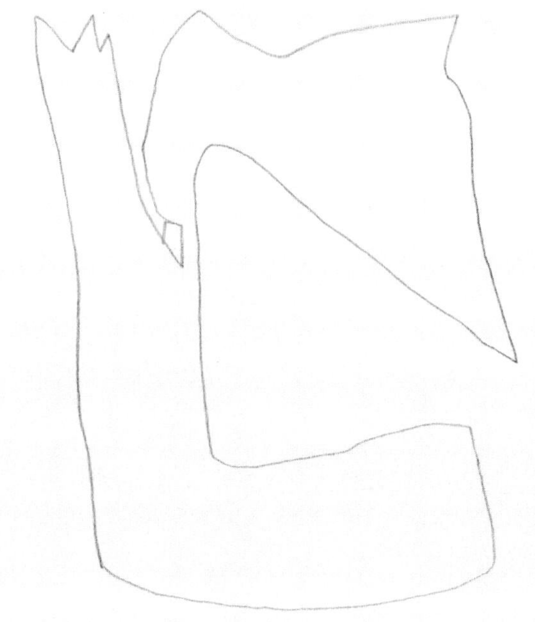

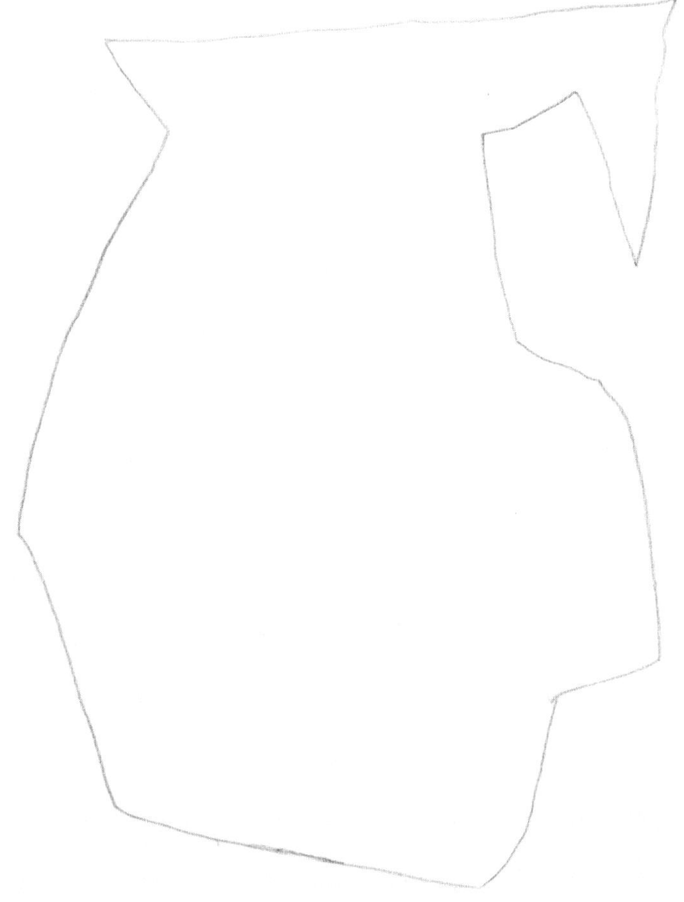

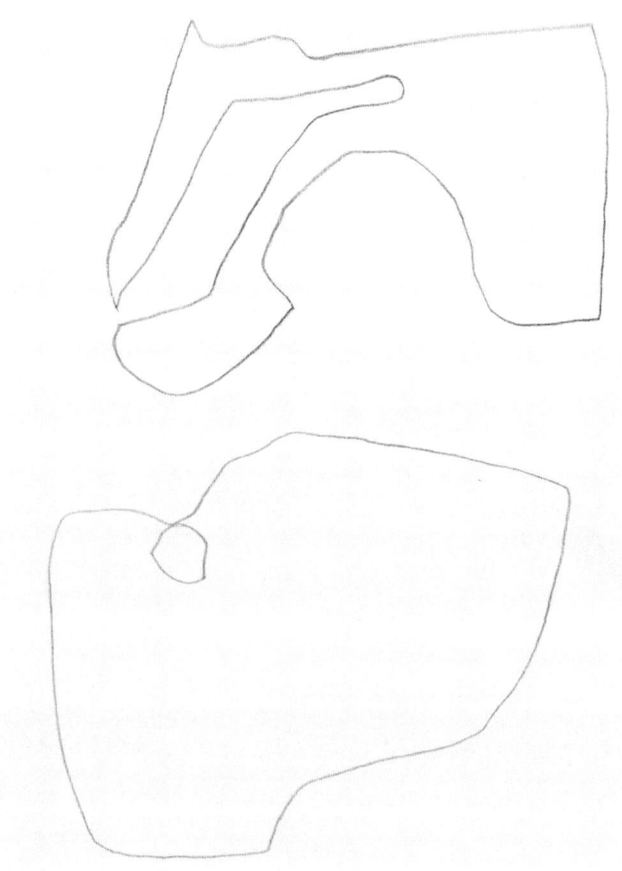

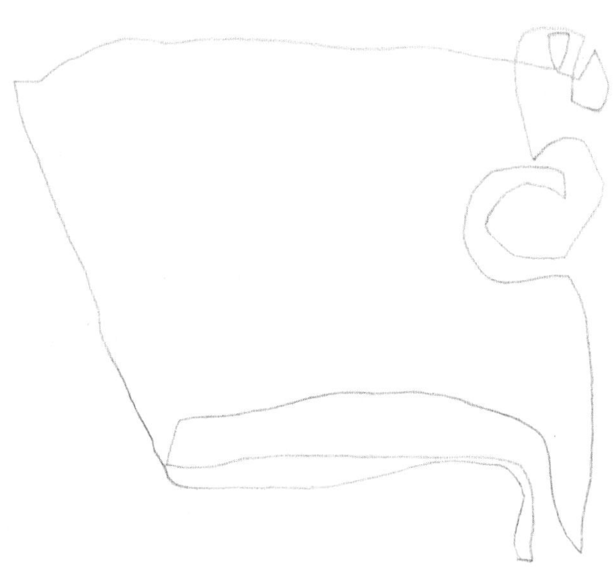

Elizabeth Newman
Drawings

Published by Neon Parc and Discipline.
neonparc.com.au
discipline.net.au

Edited by Helen Hughes and Francis Plagne
Text by Elizabeth Newman, Francis Plagne, Helen Hughes, and Erik Jensen
Designed by Alexandra Margetic
Artwork photography by Christian Capurro and Simon Hewson
Photograph editing by Aden Miller
Printed by Printon, Tallinn, Estonia
Edition of 500
Distributed in Australia by Manic Books

ISBN: 978-0-9945388-8-8

Acknowledgements
The publishers acknowledge the Wurundjeri people of the Kulin Nation as sovereign custodians of the land on which they live and work. Always was, always will be Aboriginal land.

The artist thanks Neon Parc and Darren Knight Gallery.

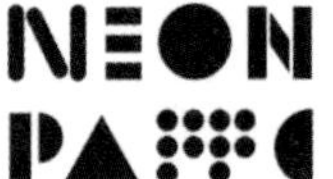